Amelia Cole and the ENEMY UNLEASHED

WRITERS
ADAM P. KNAVE & D.J. KIRKBRIDE

ARTIST & COLORIST
NICK BROKENSHIRE

LETTERER
RACHEL DEERING

COLOR FLATTER • ISSUES 13-15
RUIZ MORENO

TRADE DESIGNER
DYLAN TODD

GET ALL THE ADVENTURES OF AMELIA COLE

VOLUME 1 *AMELIA COLE AND THE UNKNOWN WORLD*

VOLUME 2 *AMELIA COLE AND THE HIDDEN WAR*

VOLUME 3 *AMELIA COLE AND THE ENEMY UNLEASHED*

VOLUME 4 *AMELIA COLE AND THE IMPOSSIBLE FATE*
(SUMMER 2015)

...AND MORE TO COME!

ISBN: 978-1-63140-055-1

17 16 15 14 1 2 3 4

IDW®
www.IDWPUBLISHING.com
IDW founded by Ted Adams, Alex Garner, Kris Oprisko, and Robbie Robbins

Ted Adams, CEO & Publisher
Greg Goldstein, President & COO
Robbie Robbins, EVP/Sr. Graphic Artist
Chris Ryall, Chief Creative Officer/Editor-in-Chief
Matthew Ruzicka, CPA, Chief Financial Officer
Alan Payne, VP of Sales
Dirk Wood, VP of Marketing
Lorelei Bunjes, VP of Digital Services
Jeff Webber, VP of Digital Publishing & Business Development

Facebook: **facebook.com/idwpublishing**
Twitter: **@idwpublishing**
YouTube: **youtube.com/idwpublishing**
Instagram: **instagram.com/idwpublishing**
deviantART: **idwpublishing.deviantart.com**
Pinterest: **pinterest.com/idwpublishing/idw-staff-faves**

Originally published digitally by Monkeybrain Comics as AMELIA COLE issues #13-18.

INTRODUCTION

Somewhere out there is an alternate reality in which I am not a comics writer but, rather, a stage magician. Other than comics, magic was the only thing I was passionate about as a young man, and while I was never disciplined enough to get really good at performing ("Is this your card? Wait. Are you sure? What about this one? Okay, is it the four of – hey, I was close!" "No, kid, you can't examine the bowl. Just look over here and…no, I said don't touch the…fine, I'll go get a towel."), I still study it. I still have an insider's knowledge of how magicians work…and, whether they realize it or not, so do the creators of the book in your hands.

I know. I know. I've read the series since its start. I realize the magic of *Amelia Cole* isn't torn-and-restored cards; it's actual sorcery. But I'm talking about the magicians' tricks that Adam P. Knave and D.J. Kirkbride use in telling Amelia's story. The keynote of any good magic performance is, "things are not always what they seem," and that seems particularly applicable to Amelia's world. There are buses and manholes and light switches – to all outward appearances, it looks like the view outside your window – but here, there's also sorcery in the air.

In the previous volumes in this series, Amelia's been working as the Protector, enforcer of the magical laws, under the orders of a powerful mage called the Magistrate… but (as our story here opens), Amelia has just learned that the Magistrate is about as genuine a wizard as was that man behind the curtain in Oz. Magic's also about reversals. Leading the audience down one path, then turning a hard, sudden left that will leave them amazed but enthralled, and *The Enemy Unleashed* never misses a chance to do that, and well. From the reveals about the Magistrate to the mystery of the Council to what dark secrets the Omega Company discovers, the story you're about to read is a page-turner in the best high-adventure tradition.

Finally, the real fundament of magic is misdirection, and this is where artist Nick Brokenshire and color assistant Ruiz Moreno come in. The illustration is spot-on – subtle and charming and inviting at every step – and along with the excellent coloring, it leads the reader's eye exactly where the storytellers want it to go, every time, unerringly. And by doing so, by controlling the pacing of the visuals, they show tremendous skill in keeping us focused on what we're supposed to be paying attention to and not, in fact, noticing (in retrospect) how suspiciously nervous the Magistrate looks to be, or how Amelia's more worried than she lets on. There's a deceptive subtlety to the art in this series that warrants a close examination.

I really think you'll enjoy *The Enemy Unleashed*. The stakes get much bigger for Amelia and her friends, the perils she faces stand revealed as more dire than she'd originally envisioned, and she really gets the chance to show what she's made of. Comics creators will tell you, rightfully, that this level of storytelling is hard to achieve, but the *Amelia Cole* team has done it. And like all perfectly performed magic, they make something that's very hard to do look very easy.

MARK WAID
Indiana, 2014

A New York Times *bestselling author, Mark has written thousands of comic books and graphic novels in his 28-year career. His award-winning graphic novel with artist Alex Ross,* Kingdom Come, *is one of the best-selling comics collections of all time. Currently, he writes* Daredevil *for Marvel Comics,* Irredeemable *for BOOM! Studios, and* Rocketeer: Cargo Of Doom *for IDW. Mark maintains a process blog at markwaid.com that is full of advice and discussion for experienced print-comics professionals and aspiring digital-comics creators.*

PREVIOUSLY

Amelia Cole grew up living between two worlds: one of magic, and one of science. A while back she became trapped in a blended world she didn't know existed. A young woman of action, she set about trying to make a productive life for herself, using her magic talents to help others whenever she could – which naturally ran her afoul with the law.

Now she's officially The Protector of her city, though she just found out her boss, The Magistrate, carries a battery-operated wand. Why would a mage need to do that...?

Meanwhile, a magic military outfit called Omega Company, which includes Amelia's old enemy, Hector the former Protector, has been fighting magic-draining monsters in the inaccurately-named *Dunes of Forgiveness*.

Through all of this, powerful dark mages known only as The Council are watching both stories unfold very intently...

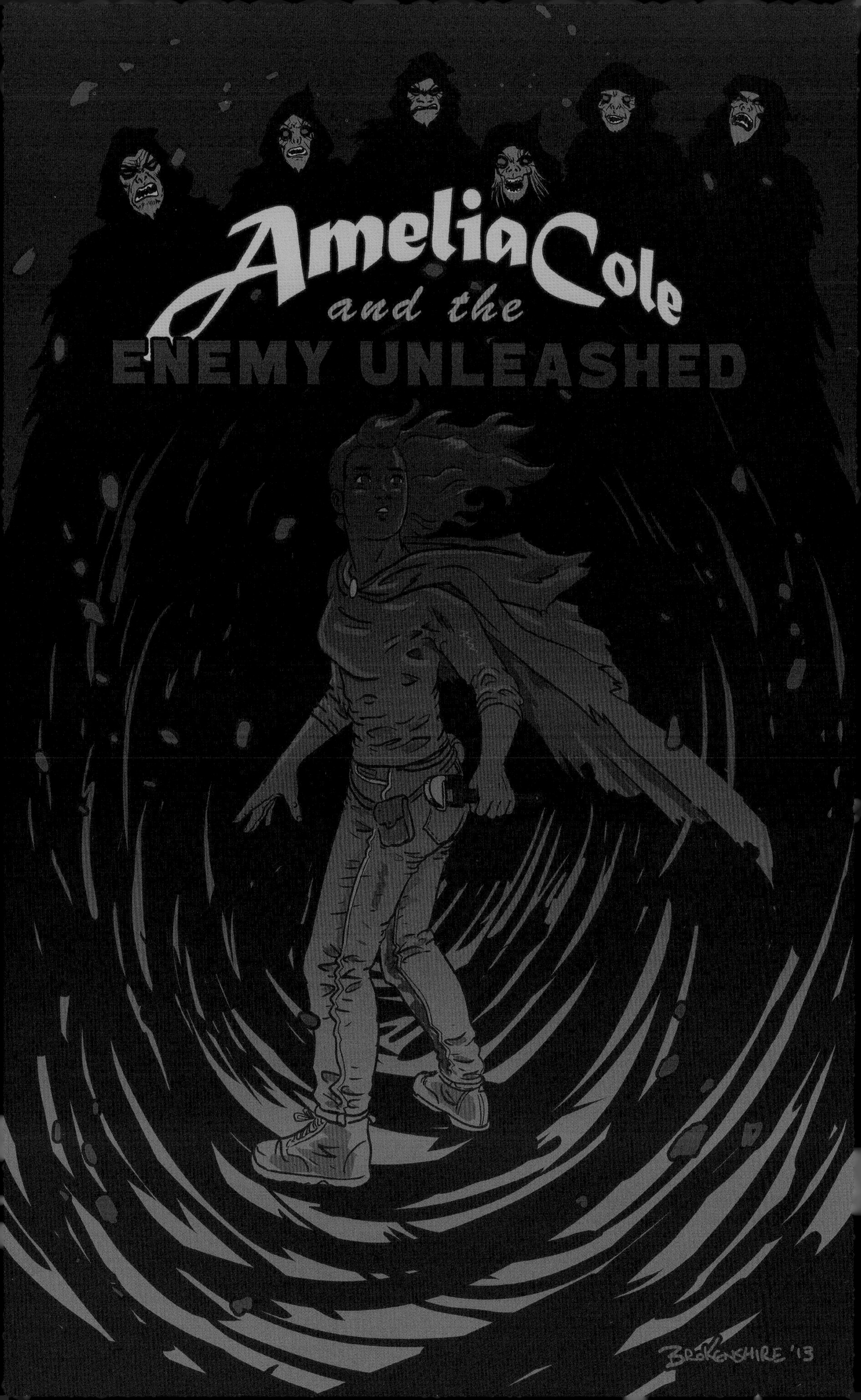
Amelia Cole
and the
ENEMY UNLEASHED
BROKENSHIRE '13

CHAPTER 1

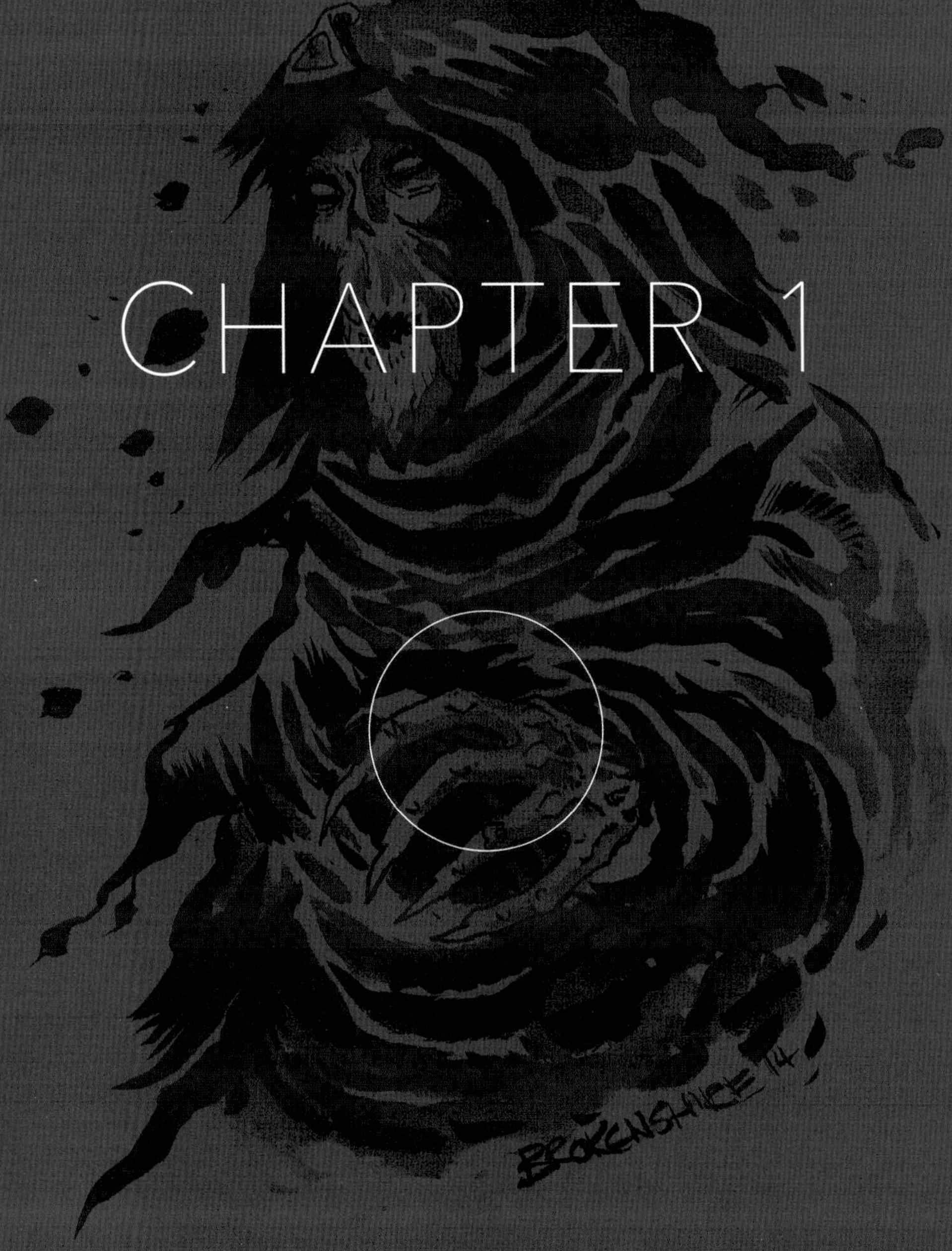
BROKENSHIRE '14

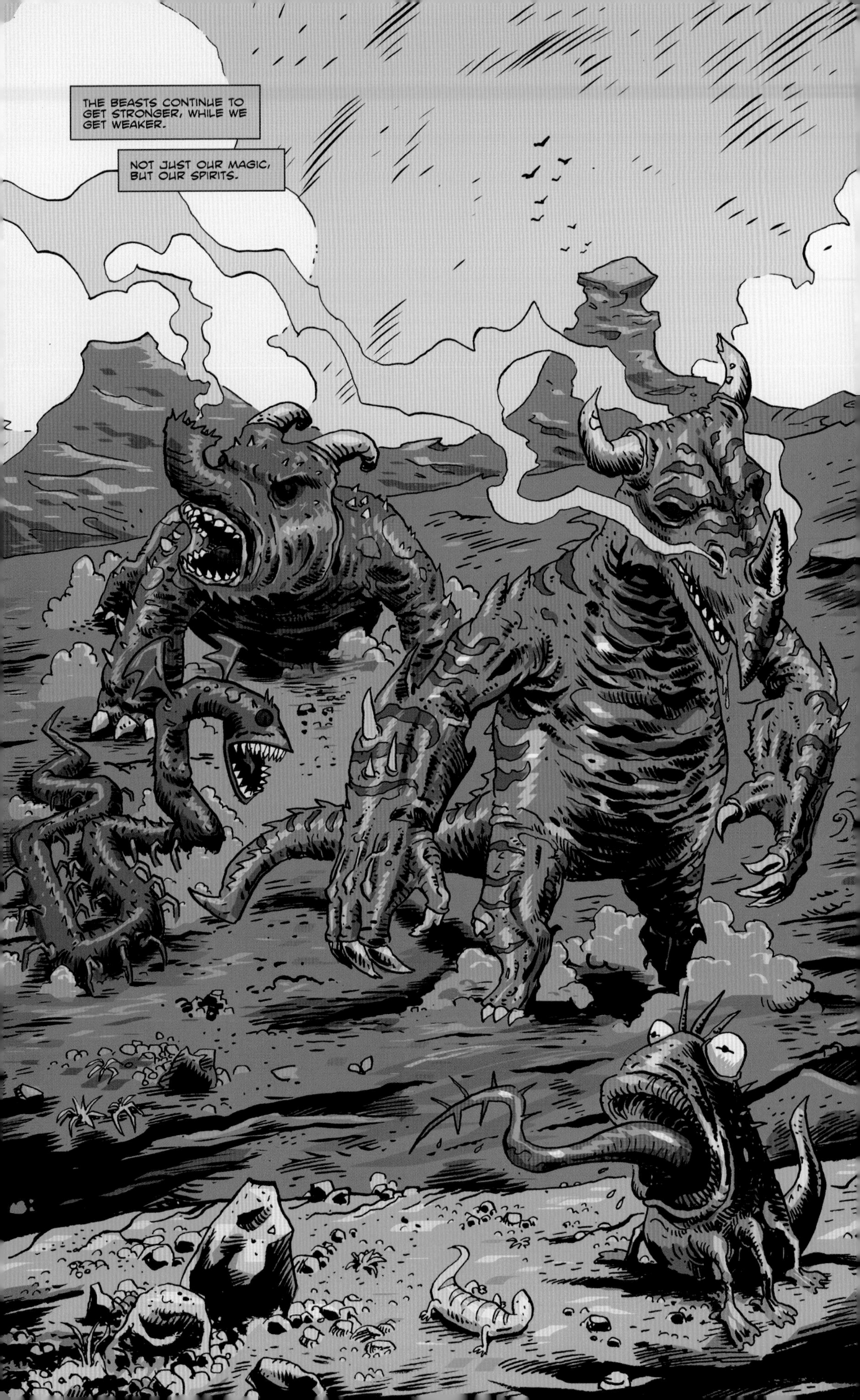
THE BEASTS CONTINUE TO GET STRONGER, WHILE WE GET WEAKER.
NOT JUST OUR MAGIC, BUT OUR SPIRITS.

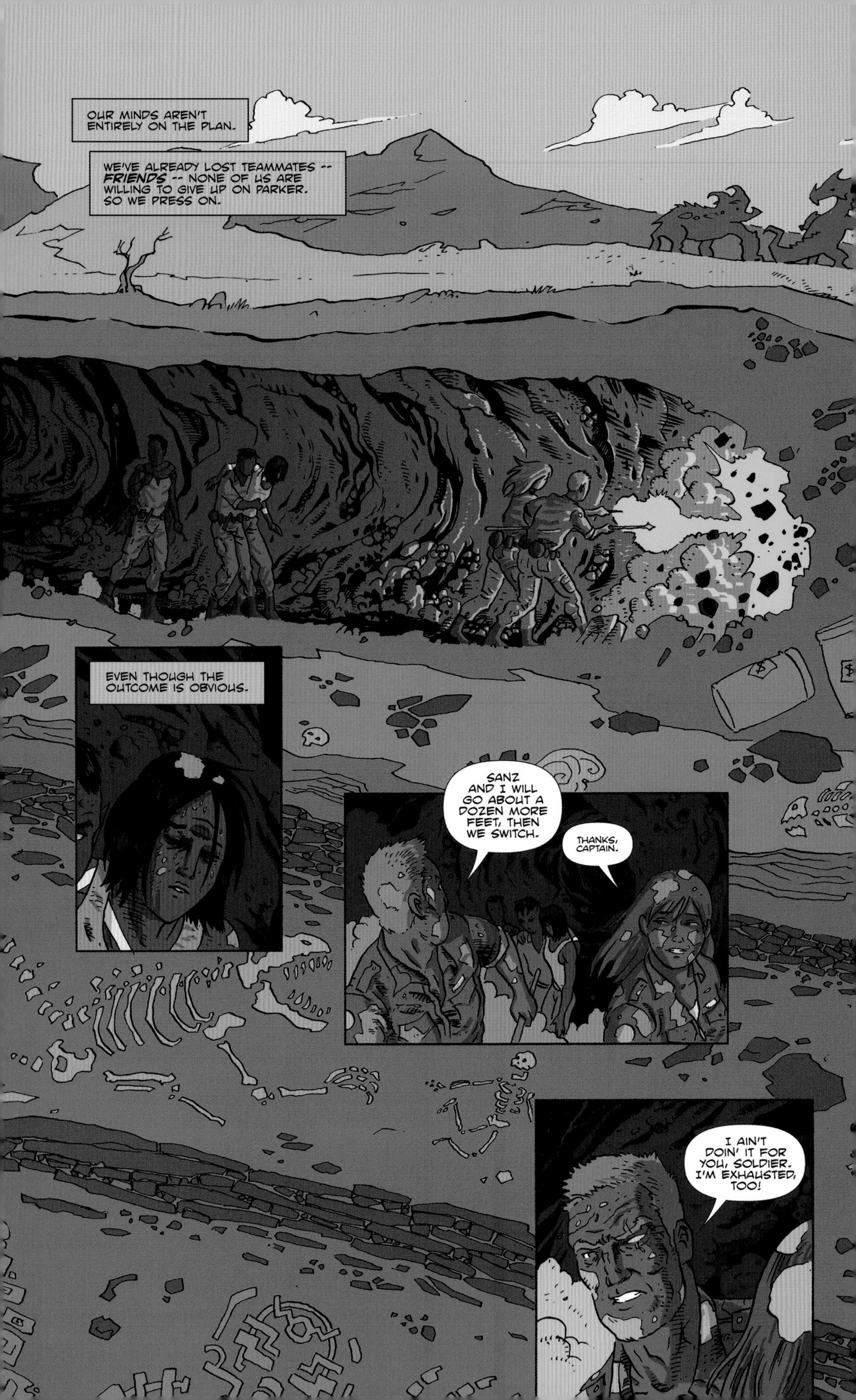
OUR MINDS AREN'T ENTIRELY ON THE PLAN.
WE'VE ALREADY LOST TEAMMATES -- FRIENDS -- NONE OF US ARE WILLING TO GIVE UP ON PARKER. SO WE PRESS ON.
EVEN THOUGH THE OUTCOME IS OBVIOUS.
SANZ AND I WILL GO ABOUT A DOZEN MORE FEET, THEN WE SWITCH.
THANKS, CAPTAIN.
I AIN'T DOIN' IT FOR YOU, SOLDIER. I'M EXHAUSTED, TOO!

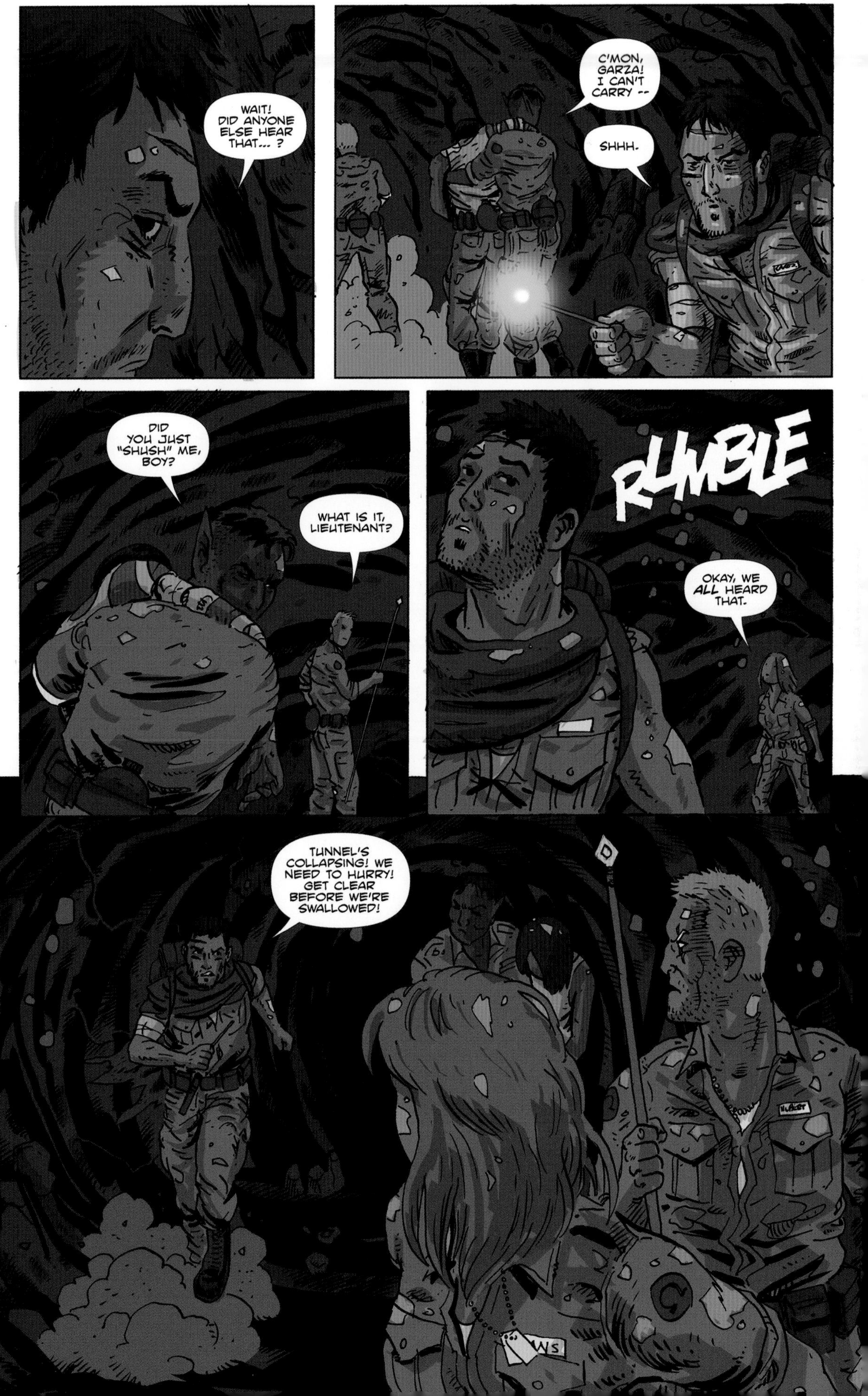
WAIT! DID ANYONE ELSE HEAR THAT... ?
C'MON, GARZA! I CAN'T CARRY --
SHHH.
DID YOU JUST "SHUSH" ME, BOY?
WHAT IS IT, LIEUTENANT?
RUMBLE
OKAY, WE ALL HEARD THAT.
TUNNEL'S COLLAPSING! WE NEED TO HURRY! GET CLEAR BEFORE WE'RE SWALLOWED!

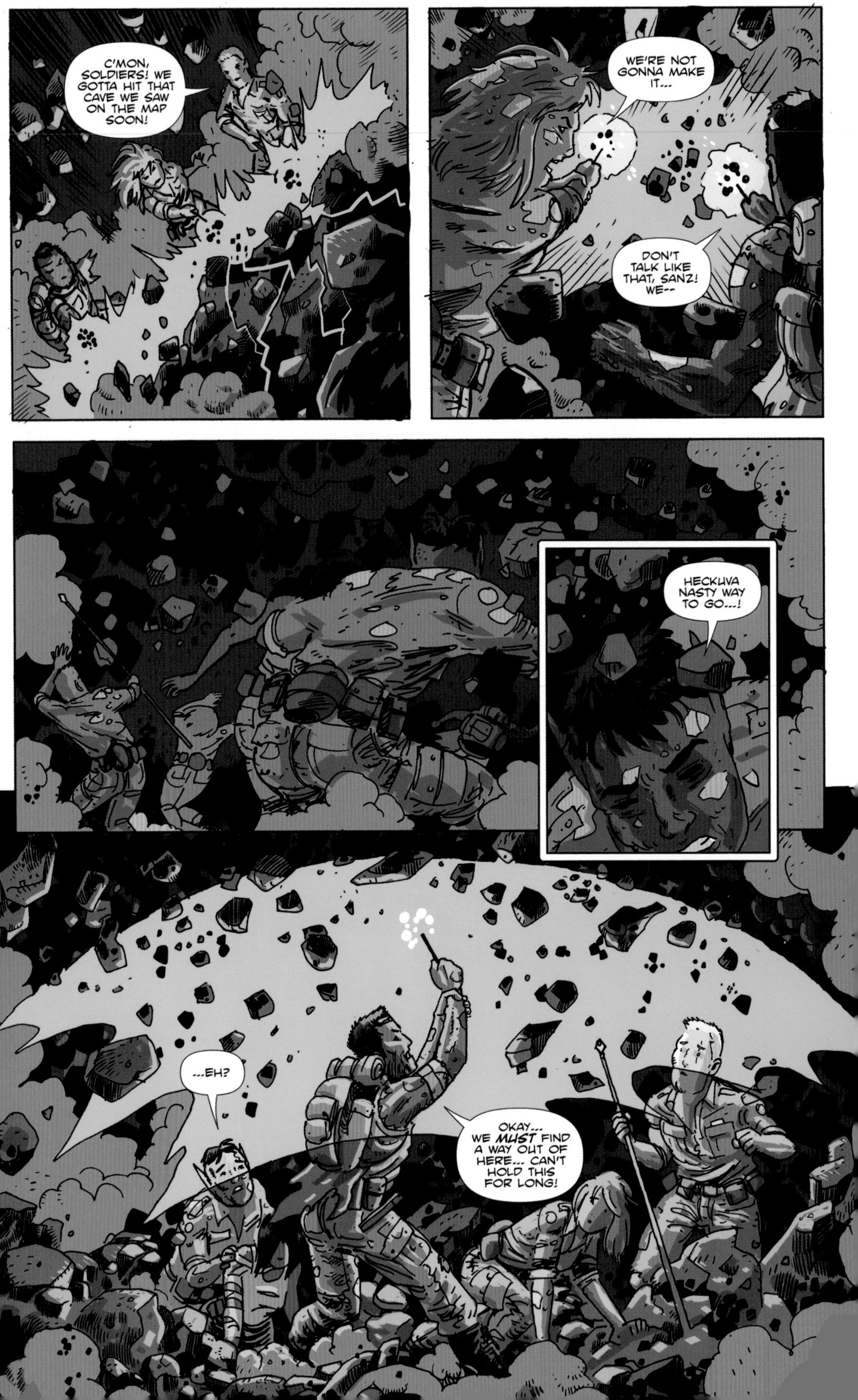
C'MON, SOLDIERS! WE GOTTA HIT THAT CAVE WE SAW ON THE MAP SOON!
WE'RE NOT GONNA MAKE IT...
DON'T TALK LIKE THAT, SANZ! WE--
HECKUVA NASTY WAY TO GO...!
...EH?
OKAY... WE *MUST* FIND A WAY OUT OF HERE... CAN'T HOLD THIS FOR LONG!

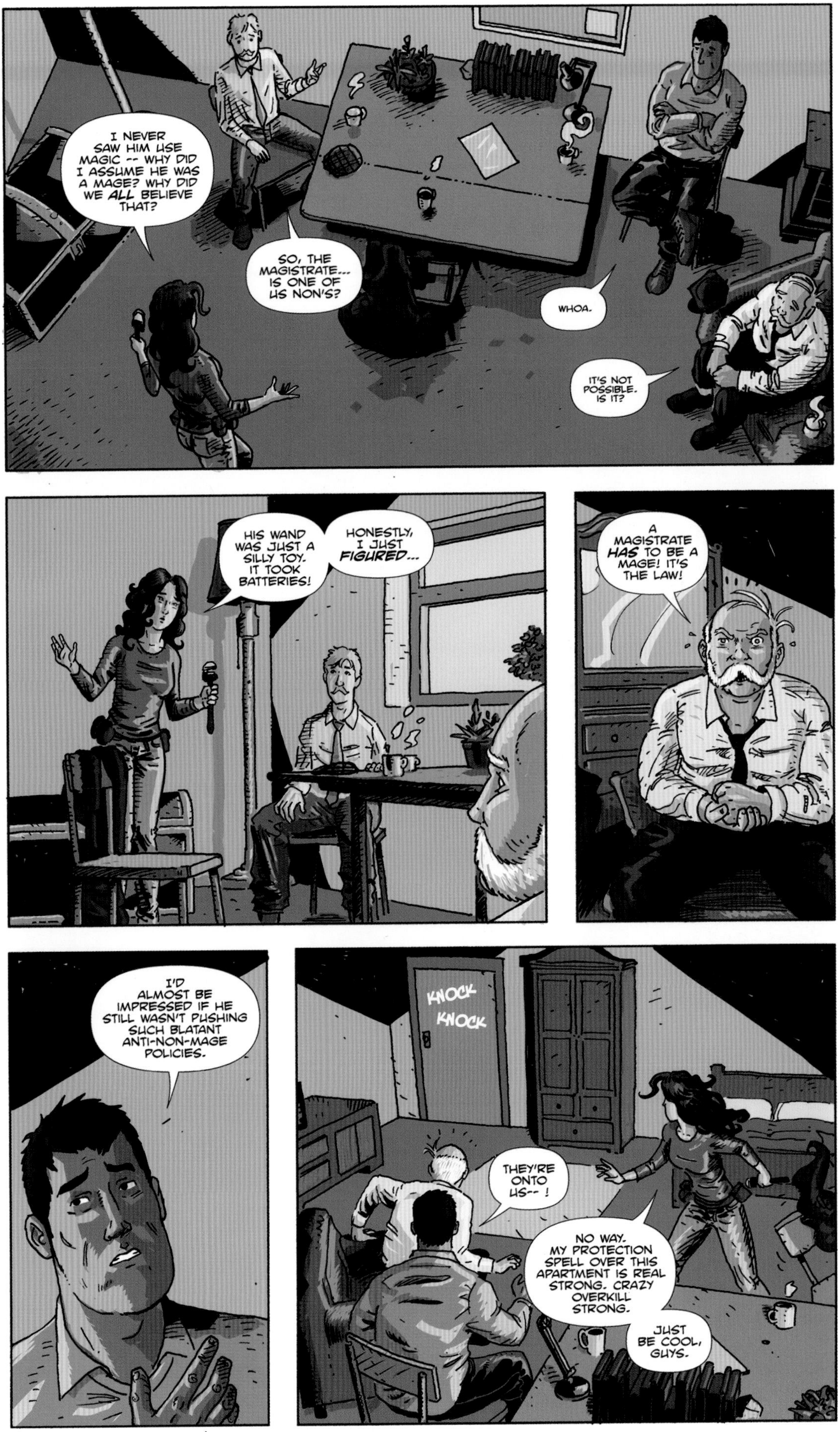
I NEVER SAW HIM USE MAGIC -- WHY DID I ASSUME HE WAS A MAGE? WHY DID WE ALL BELIEVE THAT?
SO, THE MAGISTRATE... IS ONE OF US NON'S?
WHOA.
IT'S NOT POSSIBLE. IS IT?
HIS WAND WAS JUST A SILLY TOY. IT TOOK BATTERIES!
HONESTLY, I JUST FIGURED...
A MAGISTRATE HAS TO BE A MAGE! IT'S THE LAW!
I'D ALMOST BE IMPRESSED IF HE STILL WASN'T PUSHING SUCH BLATANT ANTI-NON-MAGE POLICIES.
KNOCK
KNOCK
THEY'RE ONTO US-- !
NO WAY. MY PROTECTION SPELL OVER THIS APARTMENT IS REAL STRONG. CRAZY OVERKILL STRONG.
JUST BE COOL, GUYS.

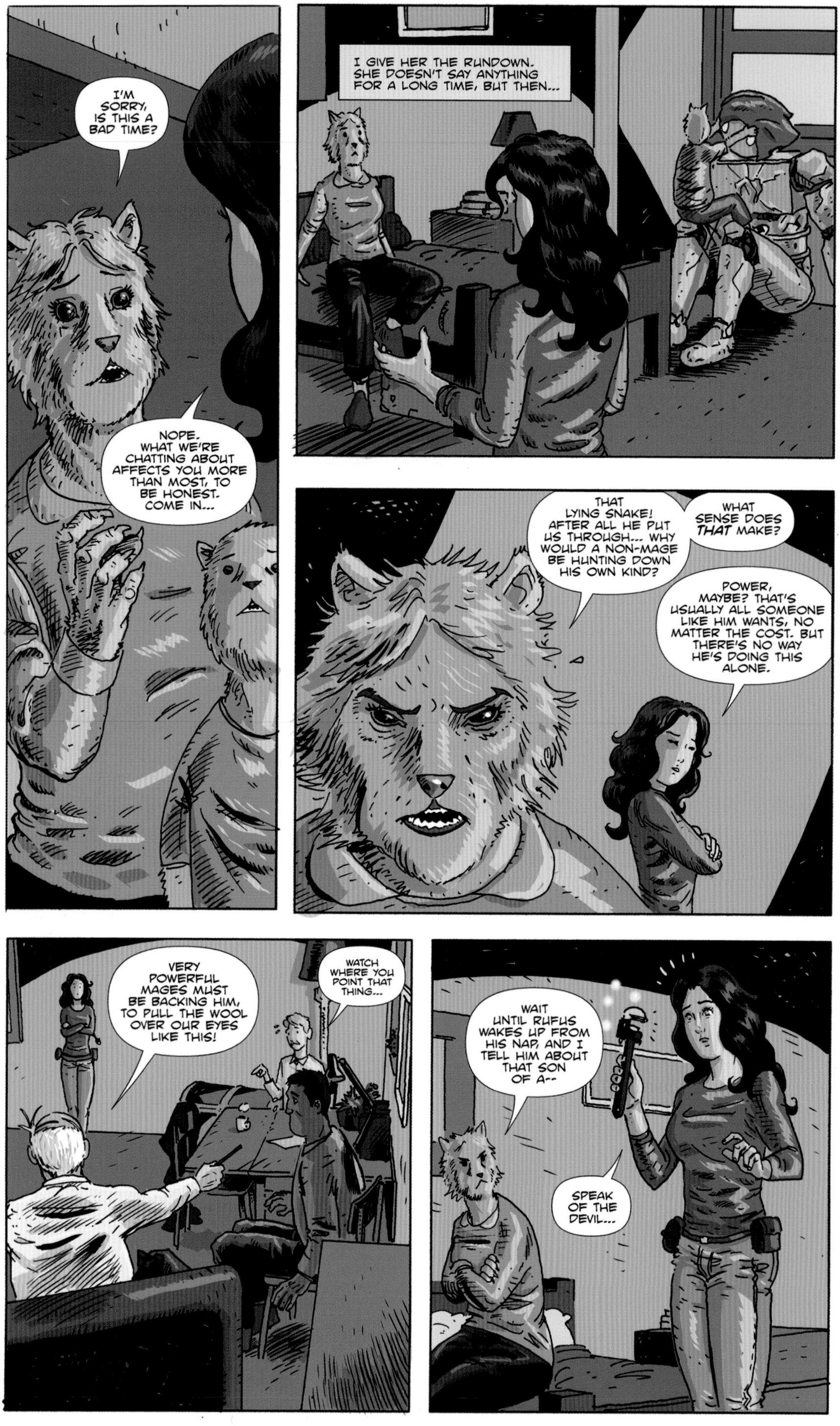
I'M SORRY, IS THIS A BAD TIME?
NOPE. WHAT WE'RE CHATTING ABOUT AFFECTS YOU MORE THAN MOST, TO BE HONEST. COME IN...
I GIVE HER THE RUNDOWN. SHE DOESN'T SAY ANYTHING FOR A LONG TIME, BUT THEN...
THAT LYING SNAKE! AFTER ALL HE PUT US THROUGH... WHY WOULD A NON-MAGE BE HUNTING DOWN HIS OWN KIND?
WHAT SENSE DOES *THAT* MAKE?
POWER, MAYBE? THAT'S USUALLY ALL SOMEONE LIKE HIM WANTS, NO MATTER THE COST. BUT THERE'S NO WAY HE'S DOING THIS ALONE.
VERY POWERFUL MAGES MUST BE BACKING HIM, TO PULL THE WOOL OVER OUR EYES LIKE THIS!
WATCH WHERE YOU POINT THAT THING...
WAIT UNTIL RUFUS WAKES UP FROM HIS NAP, AND I TELL HIM ABOUT THAT SON OF A--
SPEAK OF THE DEVIL...

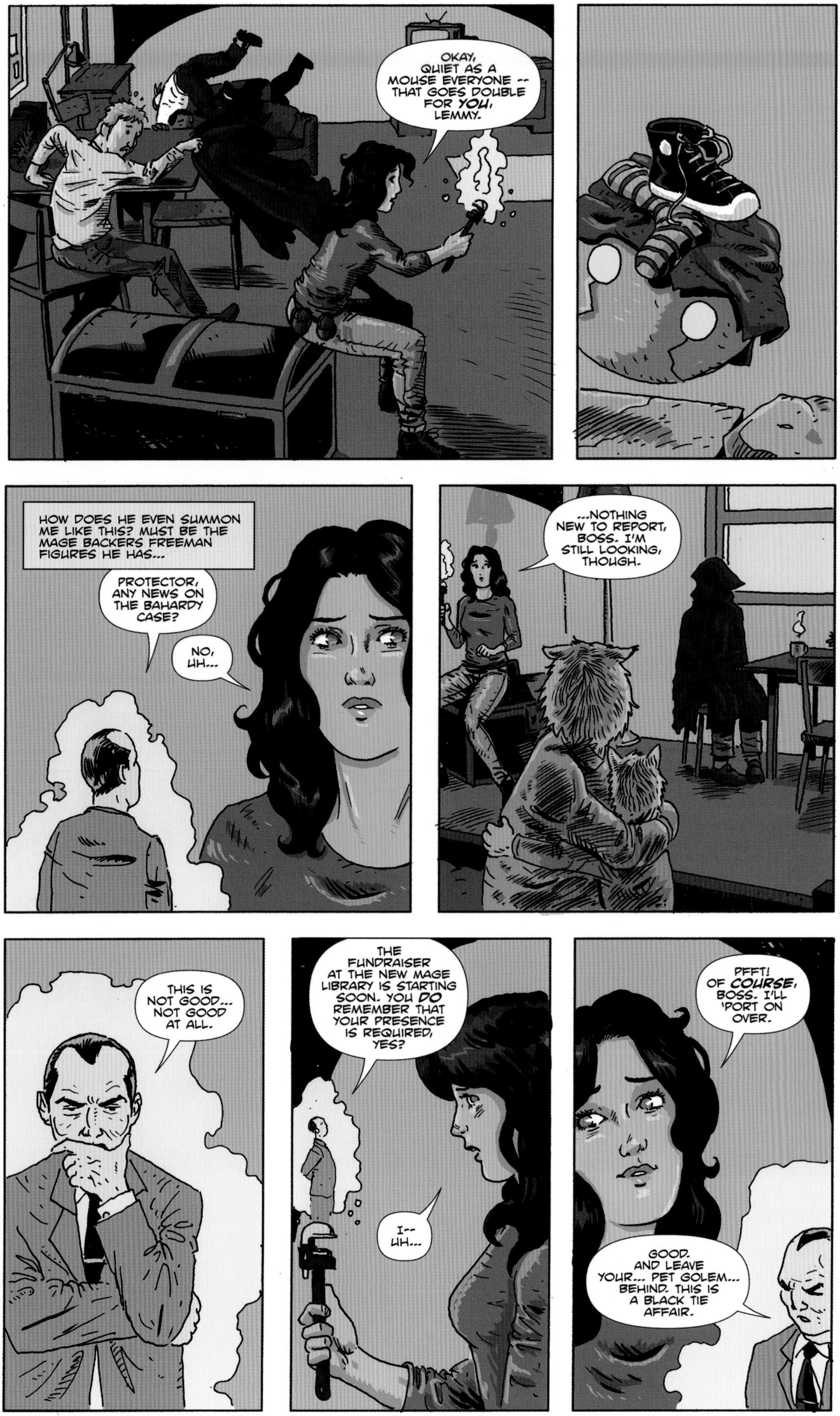
OKAY, QUIET AS A MOUSE EVERYONE -- THAT GOES DOUBLE FOR YOU, LEMMY.
HOW DOES HE EVEN SUMMON ME LIKE THIS? MUST BE THE MAGE BACKERS FREEMAN FIGURES HE HAS...
PROTECTOR, ANY NEWS ON THE BAHARDY CASE?
NO, UH...
...NOTHING NEW TO REPORT, BOSS. I'M STILL LOOKING, THOUGH.
THIS IS NOT GOOD... NOT GOOD AT ALL.
THE FUNDRAISER AT THE NEW MAGE LIBRARY IS STARTING SOON. YOU DO REMEMBER THAT YOUR PRESENCE IS REQUIRED, YES?
I-- UH...
PFFT! OF COURSE, BOSS. I'LL 'PORT ON OVER.
GOOD. AND LEAVE YOUR... PET GOLEM... BEHIND. THIS IS A BLACK TIE AFFAIR.

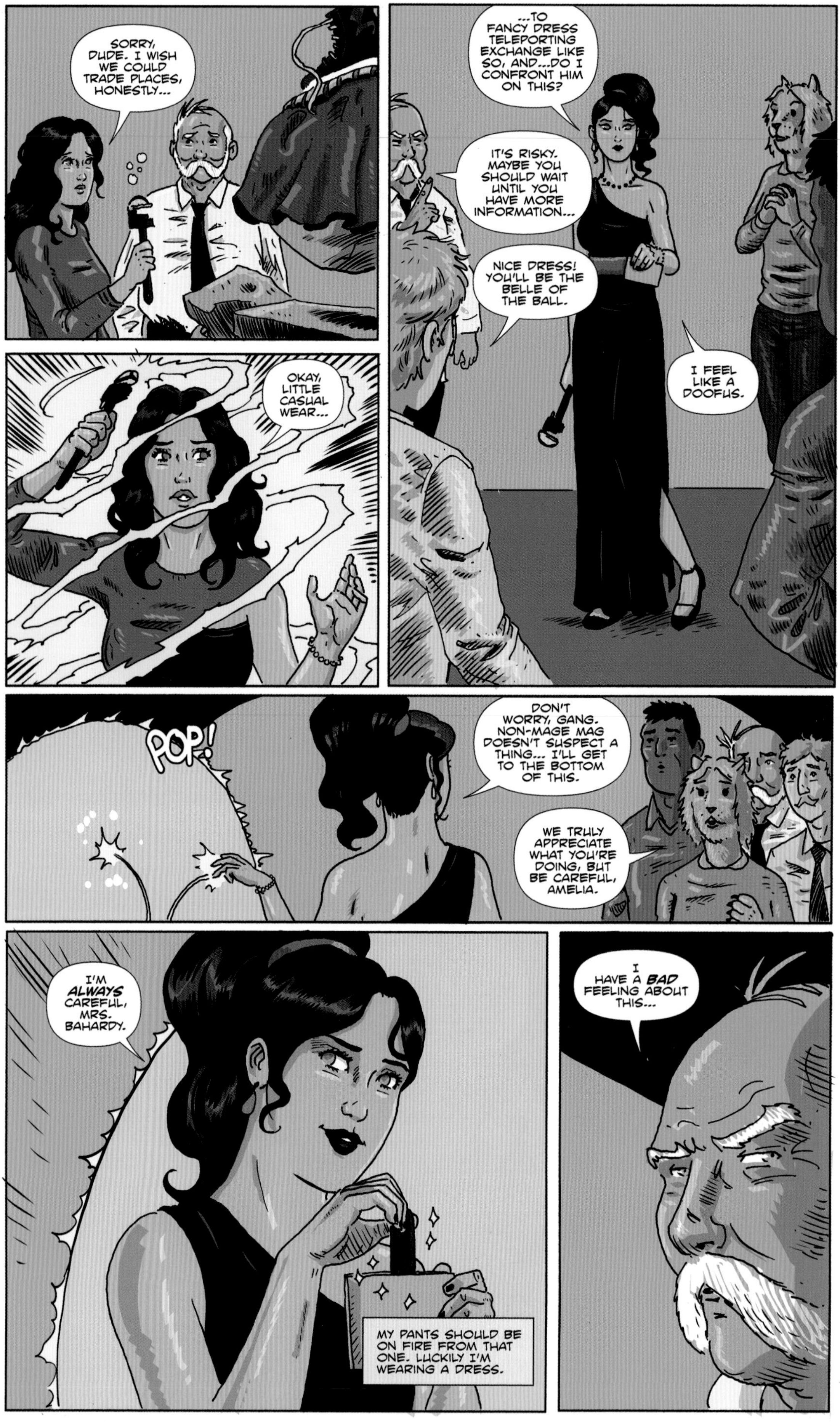
SORRY, DUDE. I WISH WE COULD TRADE PLACES, HONESTLY...
OKAY, LITTLE CASUAL WEAR...
...TO FANCY DRESS TELEPORTING EXCHANGE LIKE SO, AND...DO I CONFRONT HIM ON THIS?
IT'S RISKY. MAYBE YOU SHOULD WAIT UNTIL YOU HAVE MORE INFORMATION...
NICE DRESS! YOU'LL BE THE BELLE OF THE BALL.
I FEEL LIKE A DOOFUS.
POP!
DON'T WORRY, GANG. NON-MAGE MAG DOESN'T SUSPECT A THING... I'LL GET TO THE BOTTOM OF THIS.
WE TRULY APPRECIATE WHAT YOU'RE DOING, BUT BE CAREFUL, AMELIA.
I'M *ALWAYS* CAREFUL, MRS. BAHARDY.
MY PANTS SHOULD BE ON FIRE FROM THAT ONE. LUCKILY I'M WEARING A DRESS.
I HAVE A *BAD* FEELING ABOUT THIS...

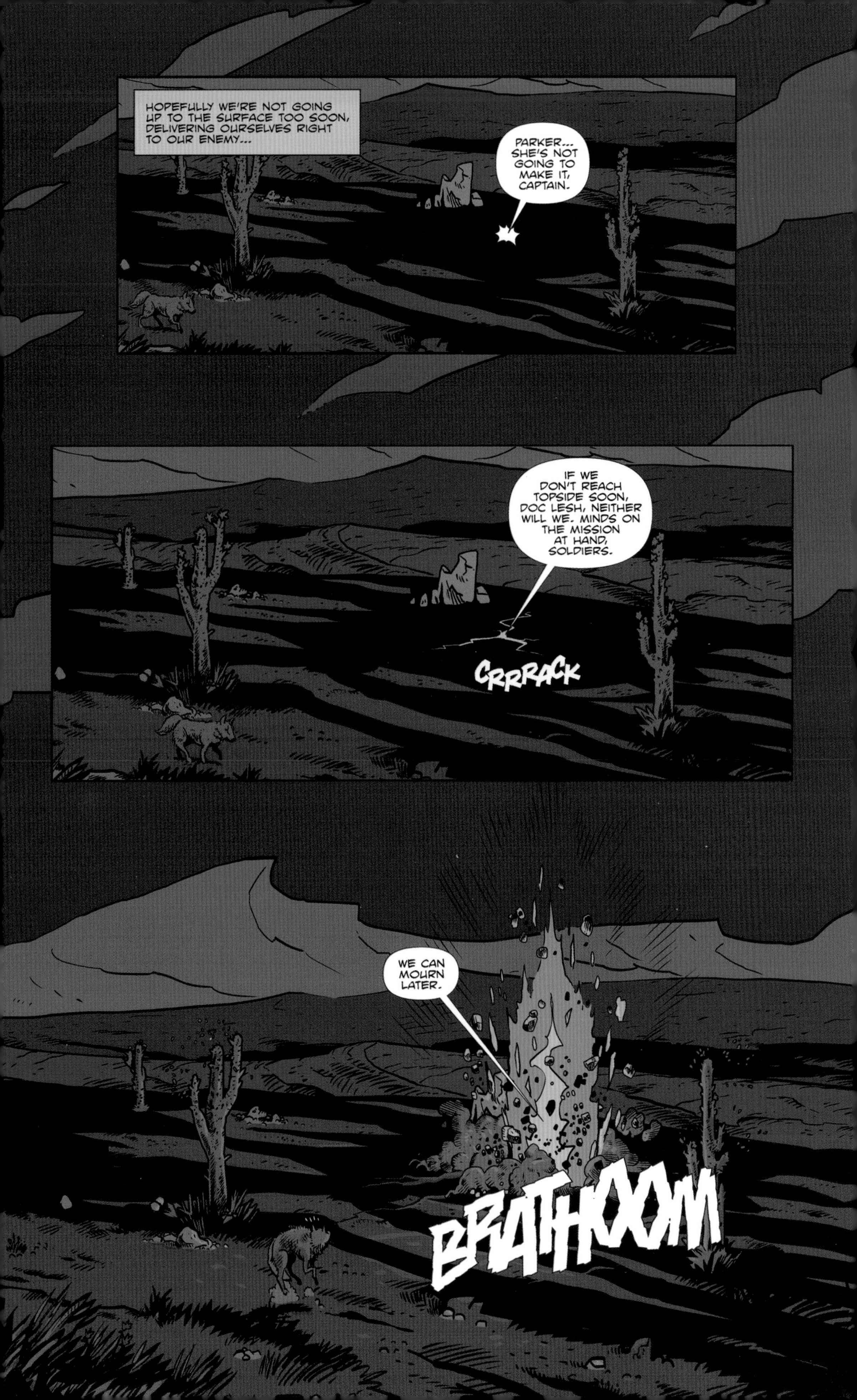
HOPEFULLY WE'RE NOT GOING UP TO THE SURFACE TOO SOON, DELIVERING OURSELVES RIGHT TO OUR ENEMY...
PARKER... SHE'S NOT GOING TO MAKE IT, CAPTAIN.
IF WE DON'T REACH TOPSIDE SOON, DOC LESH, NEITHER WILL WE. MINDS ON THE MISSION AT HAND, SOLDIERS.
CRRRACK
WE CAN MOURN LATER.
BRATHOOM

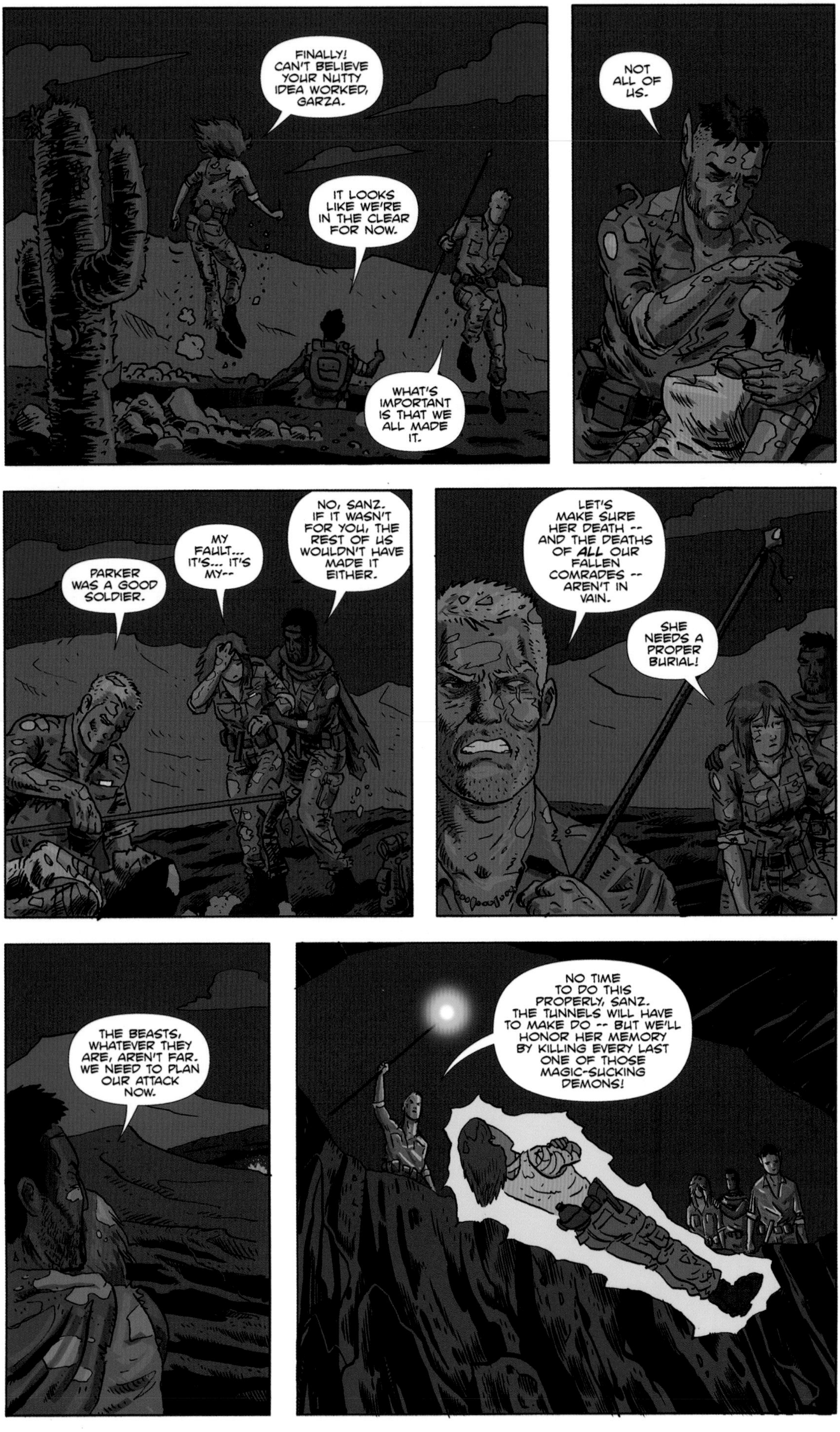
FINALLY! CAN'T BELIEVE YOUR NUTTY IDEA WORKED, GARZA.
IT LOOKS LIKE WE'RE IN THE CLEAR FOR NOW.
WHAT'S IMPORTANT IS THAT WE ALL MADE IT.
NOT ALL OF US.
PARKER WAS A GOOD SOLDIER.
MY FAULT... IT'S... IT'S MY--
NO, SANZ. IF IT WASN'T FOR YOU, THE REST OF US WOULDN'T HAVE MADE IT EITHER.
LET'S MAKE SURE HER DEATH -- AND THE DEATHS OF ALL OUR FALLEN COMRADES -- AREN'T IN VAIN.
SHE NEEDS A PROPER BURIAL!
THE BEASTS, WHATEVER THEY ARE, AREN'T FAR. WE NEED TO PLAN OUR ATTACK NOW.
NO TIME TO DO THIS PROPERLY, SANZ. THE TUNNELS WILL HAVE TO MAKE DO -- BUT WE'LL HONOR HER MEMORY BY KILLING EVERY LAST ONE OF THOSE MAGIC-SUCKING DEMONS!

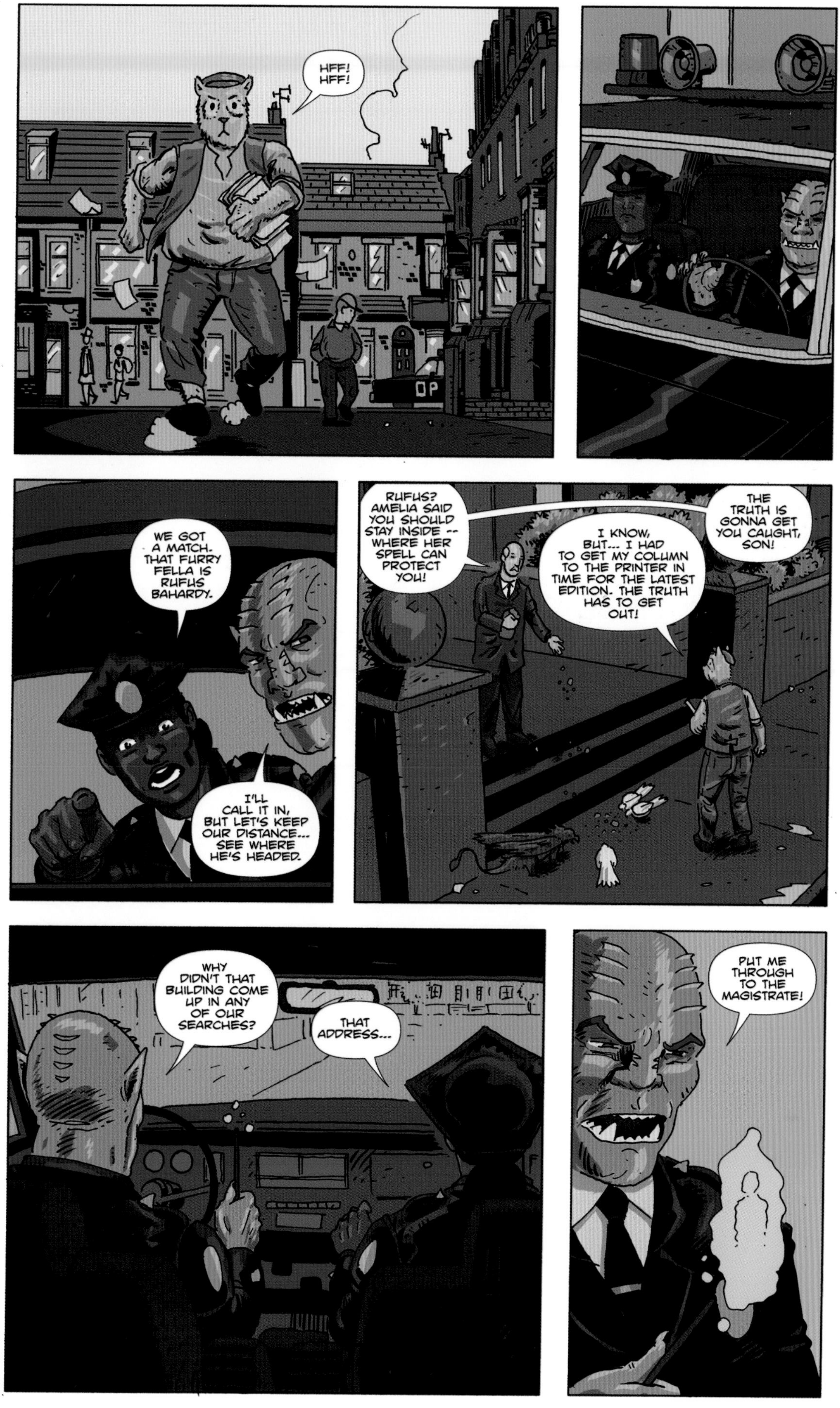
HFF! HFF!
OP
WE GOT A MATCH. THAT FURRY FELLA IS RUFUS BAHARDY.
I'LL CALL IT IN, BUT LET'S KEEP OUR DISTANCE... SEE WHERE HE'S HEADED.
RUFUS? AMELIA SAID YOU SHOULD STAY INSIDE -- WHERE HER SPELL CAN PROTECT YOU!
I KNOW, BUT... I HAD TO GET MY COLUMN TO THE PRINTER IN TIME FOR THE LATEST EDITION. THE TRUTH HAS TO GET OUT!
THE TRUTH IS GONNA GET YOU CAUGHT, SON!
WHY DIDN'T THAT BUILDING COME UP IN ANY OF OUR SEARCHES?
THAT ADDRESS...
PUT ME THROUGH TO THE MAGISTRATE!

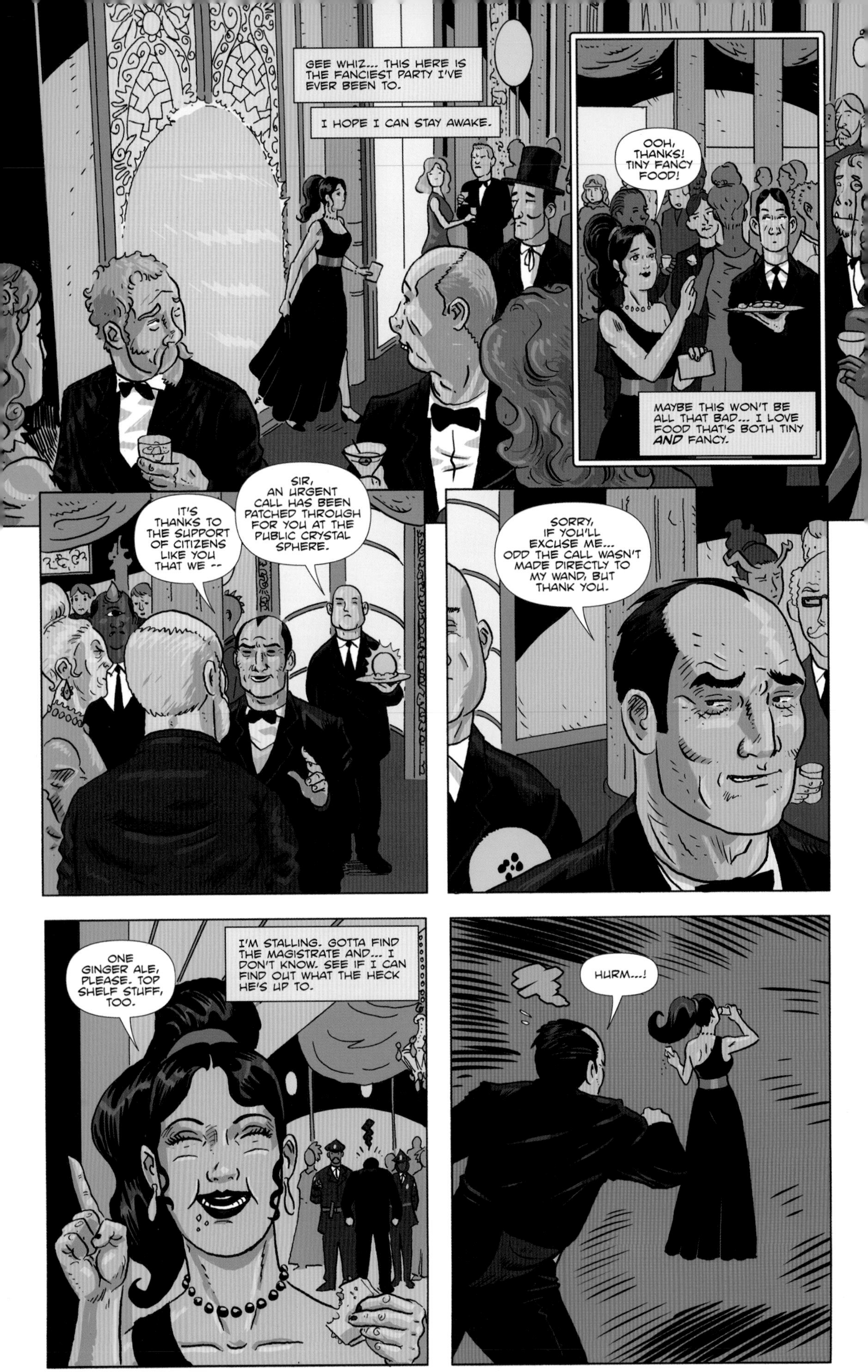
GEE WHIZ... THIS HERE IS THE FANCIEST PARTY I'VE EVER BEEN TO.
I HOPE I CAN STAY AWAKE.
OOH, THANKS! TINY FANCY FOOD!
MAYBE THIS WON'T BE ALL THAT BAD... I LOVE FOOD THAT'S BOTH TINY AND FANCY.
IT'S THANKS TO THE SUPPORT OF CITIZENS LIKE YOU THAT WE --
SIR, AN URGENT CALL HAS BEEN PATCHED THROUGH FOR YOU AT THE PUBLIC CRYSTAL SPHERE.
SORRY, IF YOU'LL EXCUSE ME... ODD THE CALL WASN'T MADE DIRECTLY TO MY WAND, BUT THANK YOU.
ONE GINGER ALE, PLEASE. TOP SHELF STUFF, TOO.
I'M STALLING. GOTTA FIND THE MAGISTRATE AND... I DON'T KNOW. SEE IF I CAN FIND OUT WHAT THE HECK HE'S UP TO.
HURM...!

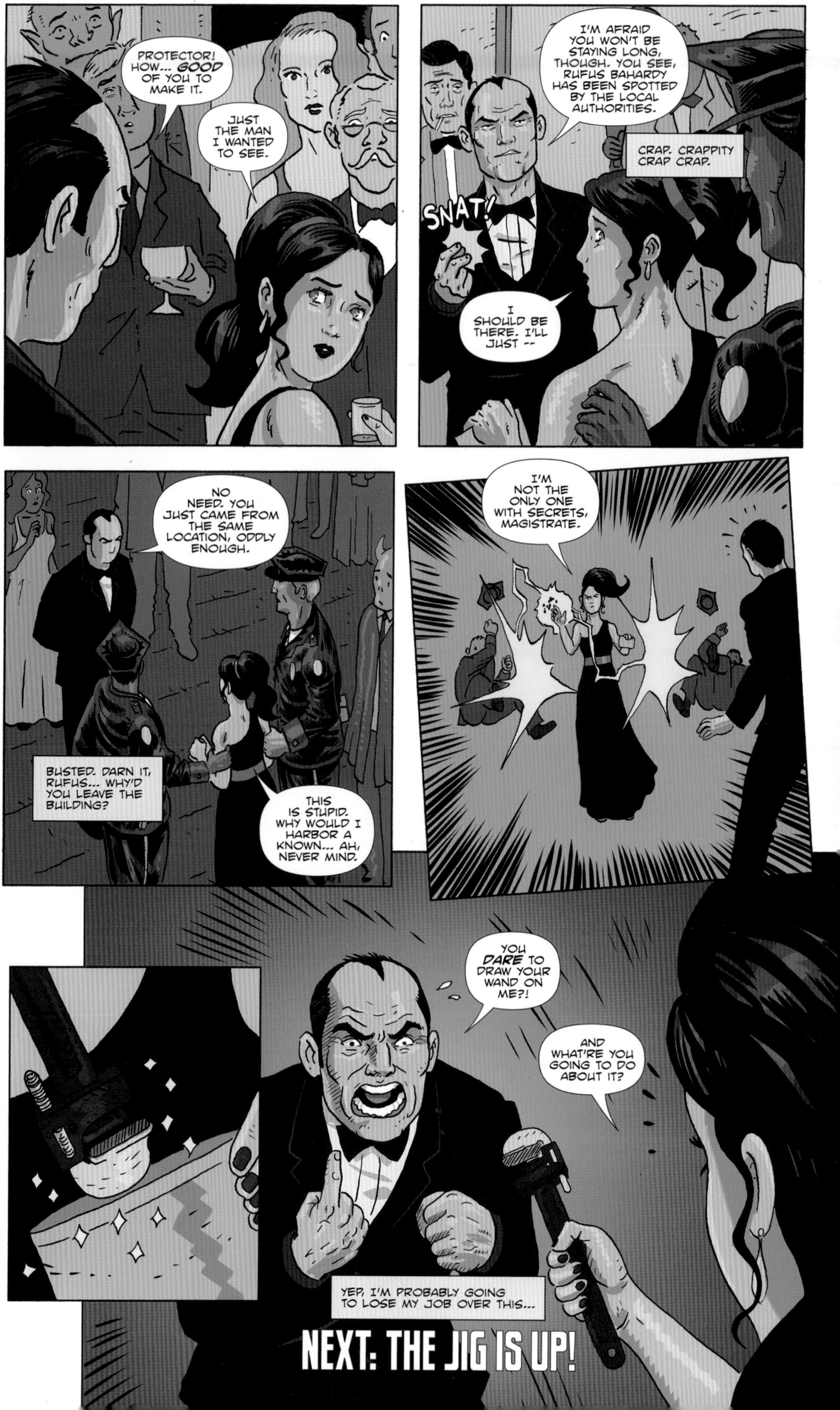
PROTECTOR! HOW... GOOD OF YOU TO MAKE IT.
JUST THE MAN I WANTED TO SEE.
I'M AFRAID YOU WON'T BE STAYING LONG, THOUGH. YOU SEE, RUFUS BAHARDY HAS BEEN SPOTTED BY THE LOCAL AUTHORITIES.
CRAP. CRAPPITY CRAP CRAP.
SNAT!
I SHOULD BE THERE. I'LL JUST --
NO NEED. YOU JUST CAME FROM THE SAME LOCATION, ODDLY ENOUGH.
BUSTED. DARN IT, RUFUS... WHY'D YOU LEAVE THE BUILDING?
THIS IS STUPID. WHY WOULD I HARBOR A KNOWN... AH, NEVER MIND.
I'M NOT THE ONLY ONE WITH SECRETS, MAGISTRATE.
YOU DARE TO DRAW YOUR WAND ON ME?!
AND WHAT'RE YOU GOING TO DO ABOUT IT?
YEP, I'M PROBABLY GOING TO LOSE MY JOB OVER THIS...
NEXT: THE JIG IS UP!

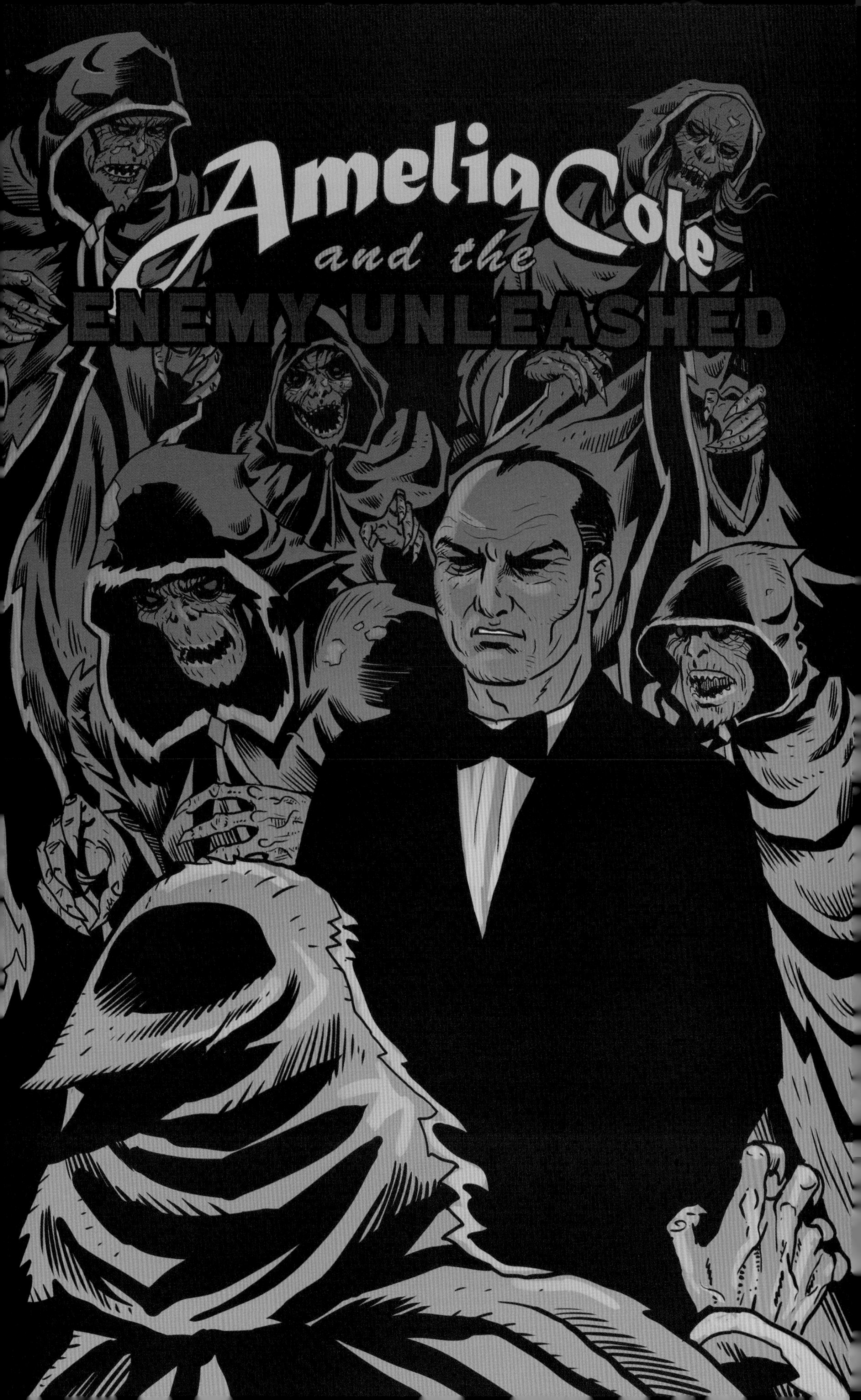
Amelia Cole
and the
ENEMY UNLEASHED

CHAPTER 2

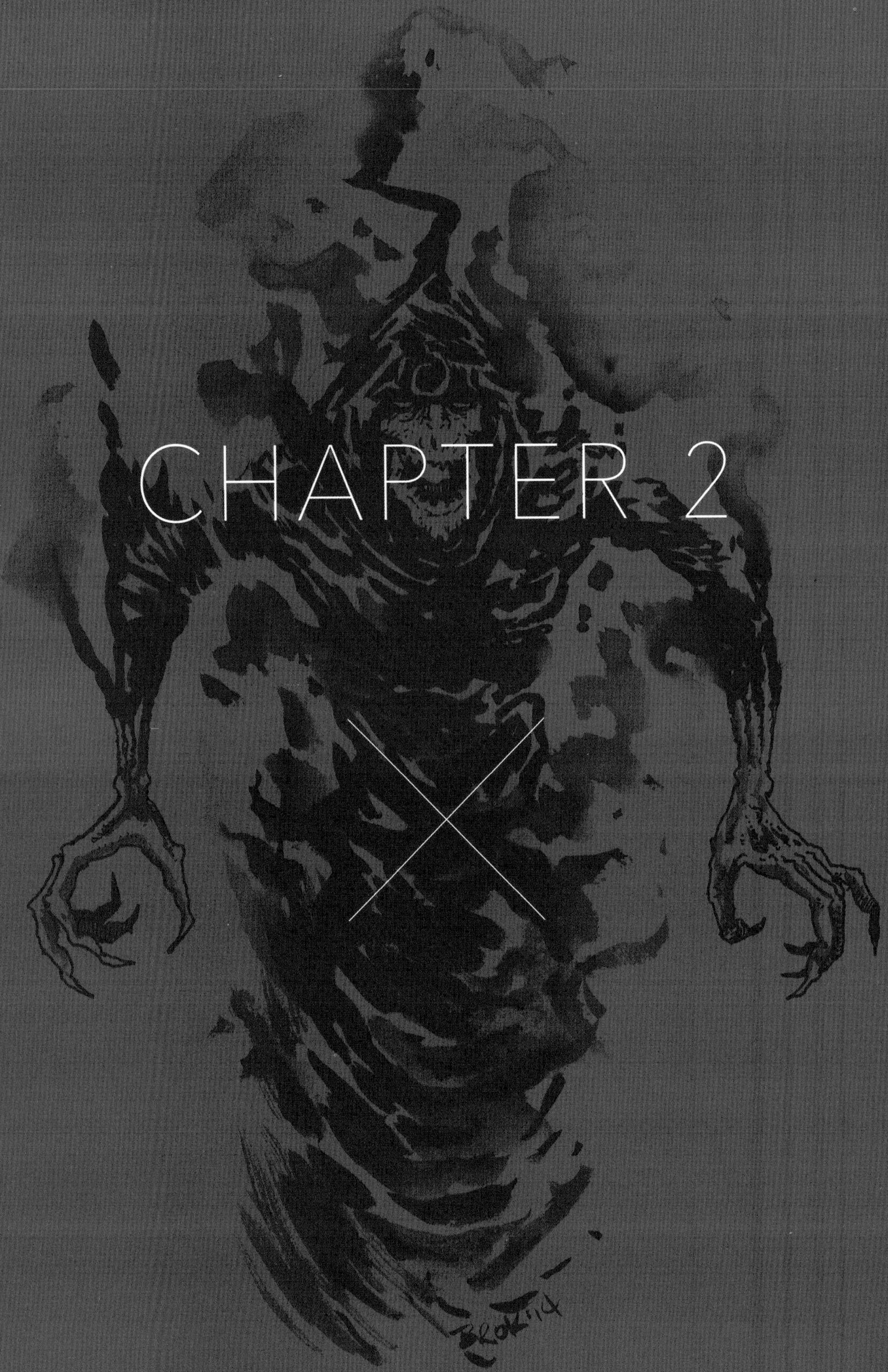

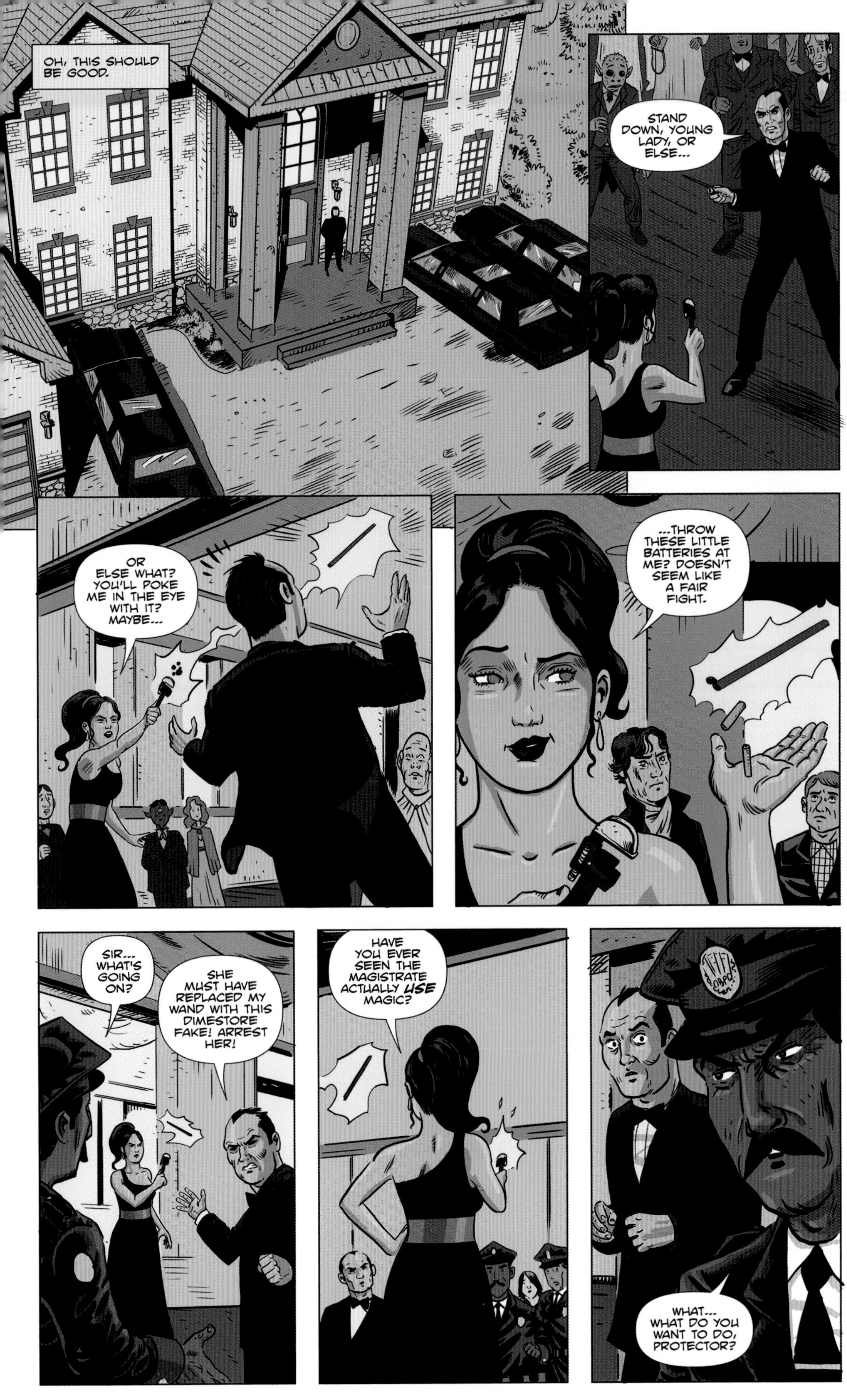
OH, THIS SHOULD BE GOOD.
STAND DOWN, YOUNG LADY, OR ELSE...
OR ELSE WHAT? YOU'LL POKE ME IN THE EYE WITH IT? MAYBE...
...THROW THESE LITTLE BATTERIES AT ME? DOESN'T SEEM LIKE A FAIR FIGHT.
SIR... WHAT'S GOING ON?
SHE MUST HAVE REPLACED MY WAND WITH THIS DIMESTORE FAKE! ARREST HER!
HAVE YOU EVER SEEN THE MAGISTRATE ACTUALLY *USE* MAGIC?
WHAT... WHAT DO YOU WANT TO DO, PROTECTOR?

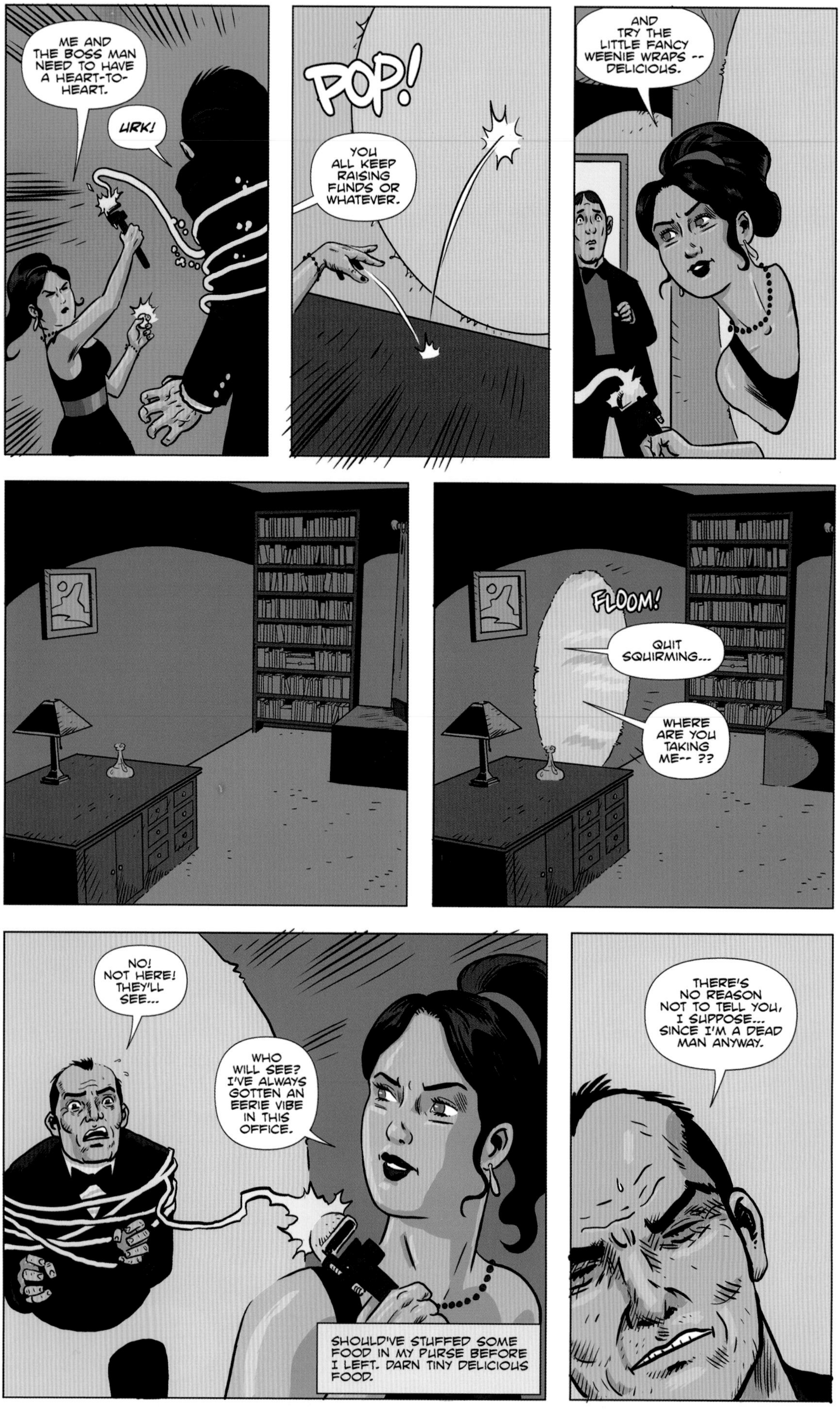
ME AND THE BOSS MAN NEED TO HAVE A HEART-TO-HEART.
URK!
POP!
YOU ALL KEEP RAISING FUNDS OR WHATEVER.
AND TRY THE LITTLE FANCY WEENIE WRAPS -- DELICIOUS.
FLOOM!
QUIT SQUIRMING...
WHERE ARE YOU TAKING ME-- ??
NO! NOT HERE! THEY'LL SEE...
WHO WILL SEE? I'VE ALWAYS GOTTEN AN EERIE VIBE IN THIS OFFICE.
SHOULD'VE STUFFED SOME FOOD IN MY PURSE BEFORE I LEFT. DARN TINY DELICIOUS FOOD.
THERE'S NO REASON NOT TO TELL YOU, I SUPPOSE... SINCE I'M A DEAD MAN ANYWAY.

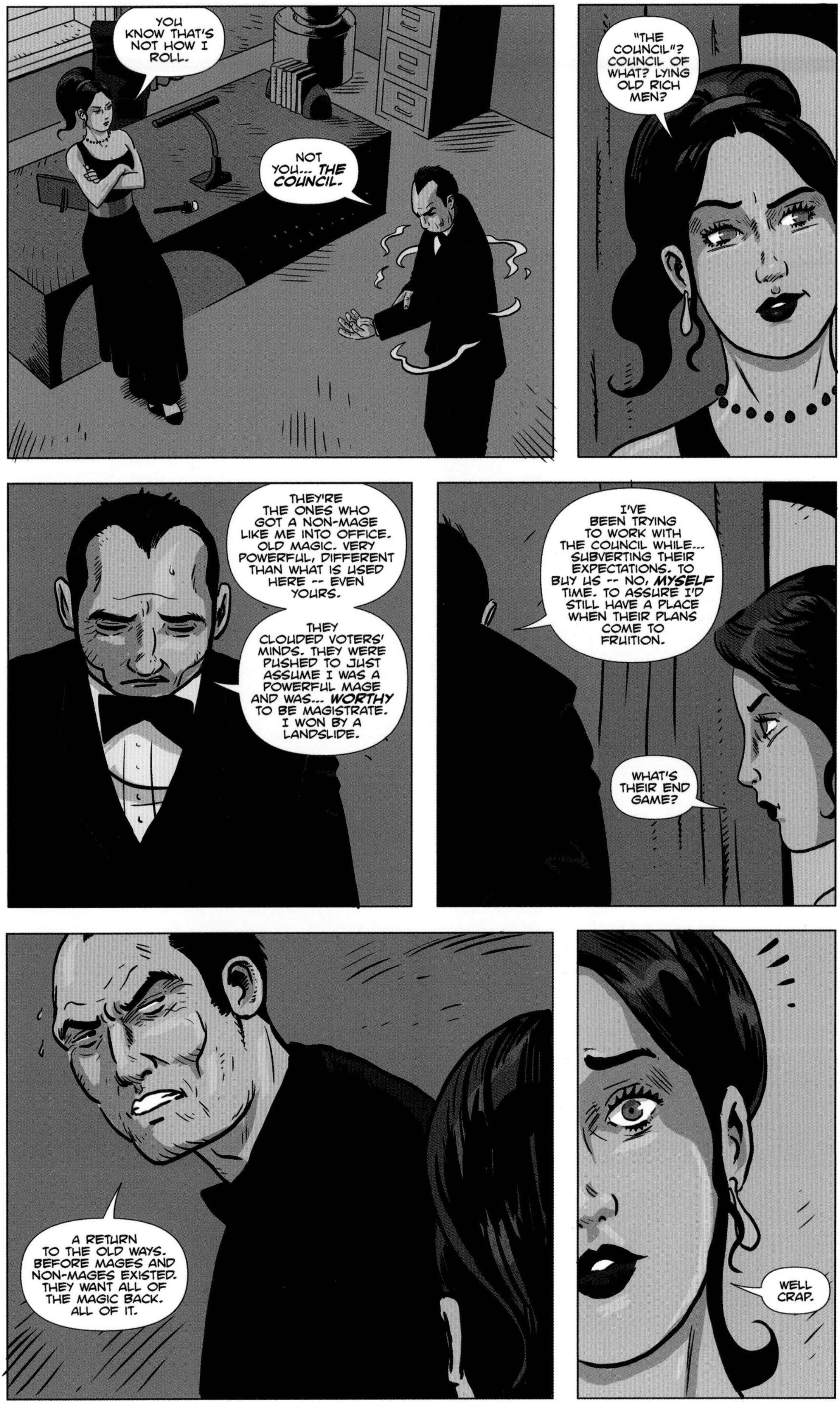
YOU KNOW THAT'S NOT HOW I ROLL.
NOT YOU... THE COUNCIL.
"THE COUNCIL"? COUNCIL OF WHAT? LYING OLD RICH MEN?
THEY'RE THE ONES WHO GOT A NON-MAGE LIKE ME INTO OFFICE. OLD MAGIC. VERY POWERFUL, DIFFERENT THAN WHAT IS USED HERE -- EVEN YOURS.
THEY CLOUDED VOTERS' MINDS. THEY WERE PUSHED TO JUST ASSUME I WAS A POWERFUL MAGE AND WAS... WORTHY TO BE MAGISTRATE. I WON BY A LANDSLIDE.
I'VE BEEN TRYING TO WORK WITH THE COUNCIL WHILE... SUBVERTING THEIR EXPECTATIONS. TO BUY US -- NO, MYSELF TIME. TO ASSURE I'D STILL HAVE A PLACE WHEN THEIR PLANS COME TO FRUITION.
WHAT'S THEIR END GAME?
A RETURN TO THE OLD WAYS. BEFORE MAGES AND NON-MAGES EXISTED. THEY WANT ALL OF THE MAGIC BACK. ALL OF IT.
WELL CRAP.

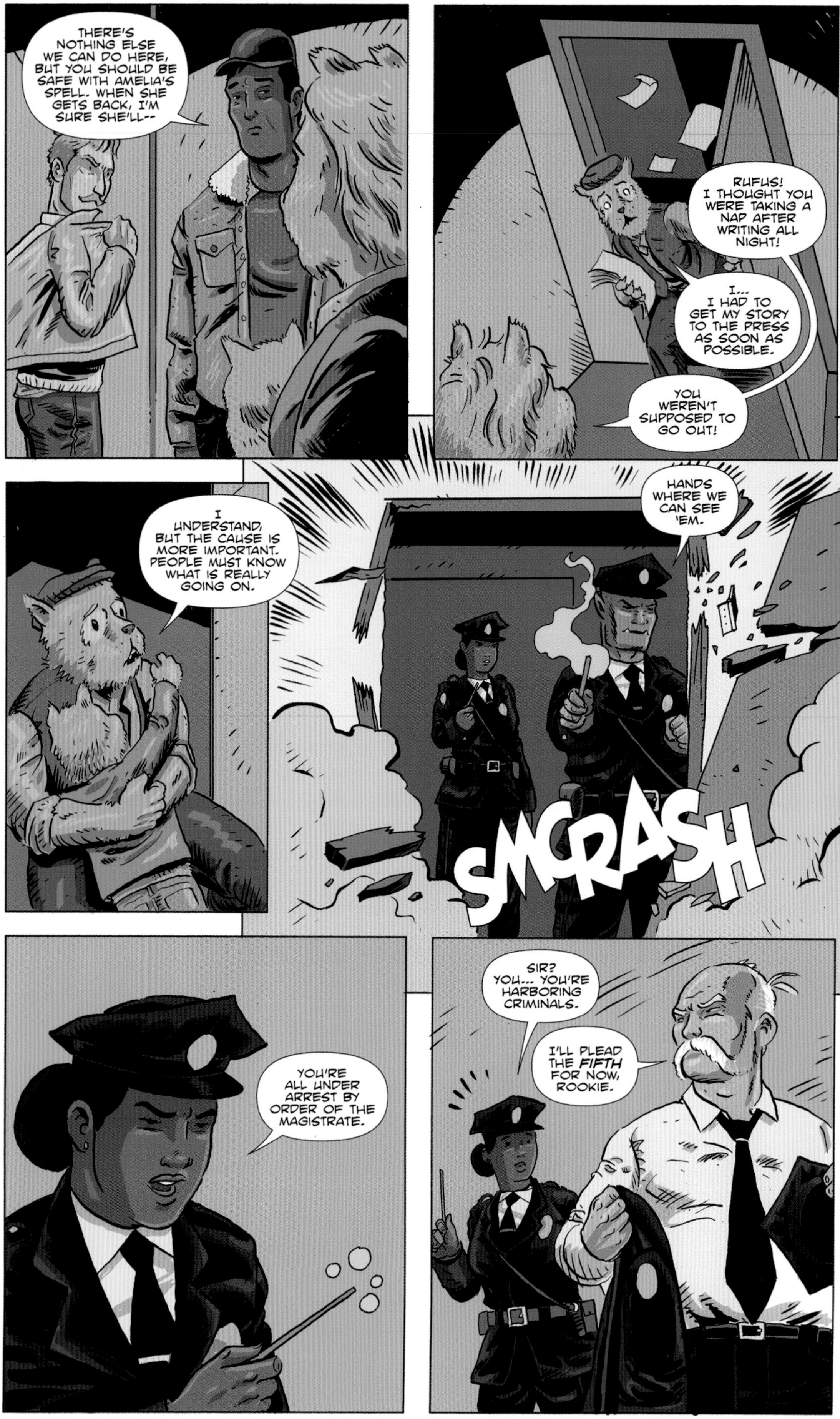
THERE'S NOTHING ELSE WE CAN DO HERE, BUT YOU SHOULD BE SAFE WITH AMELIA'S SPELL. WHEN SHE GETS BACK, I'M SURE SHE'LL--
RUFUS! I THOUGHT YOU WERE TAKING A NAP AFTER WRITING ALL NIGHT!
I... I HAD TO GET MY STORY TO THE PRESS AS SOON AS POSSIBLE.
YOU WEREN'T SUPPOSED TO GO OUT!
I UNDERSTAND, BUT THE CAUSE IS MORE IMPORTANT. PEOPLE MUST KNOW WHAT IS REALLY GOING ON.
HANDS WHERE WE CAN SEE 'EM.
SMCRASH
YOU'RE ALL UNDER ARREST BY ORDER OF THE MAGISTRATE.
SIR? YOU... YOU'RE HARBORING CRIMINALS.
I'LL PLEAD THE FIFTH FOR NOW, ROOKIE.

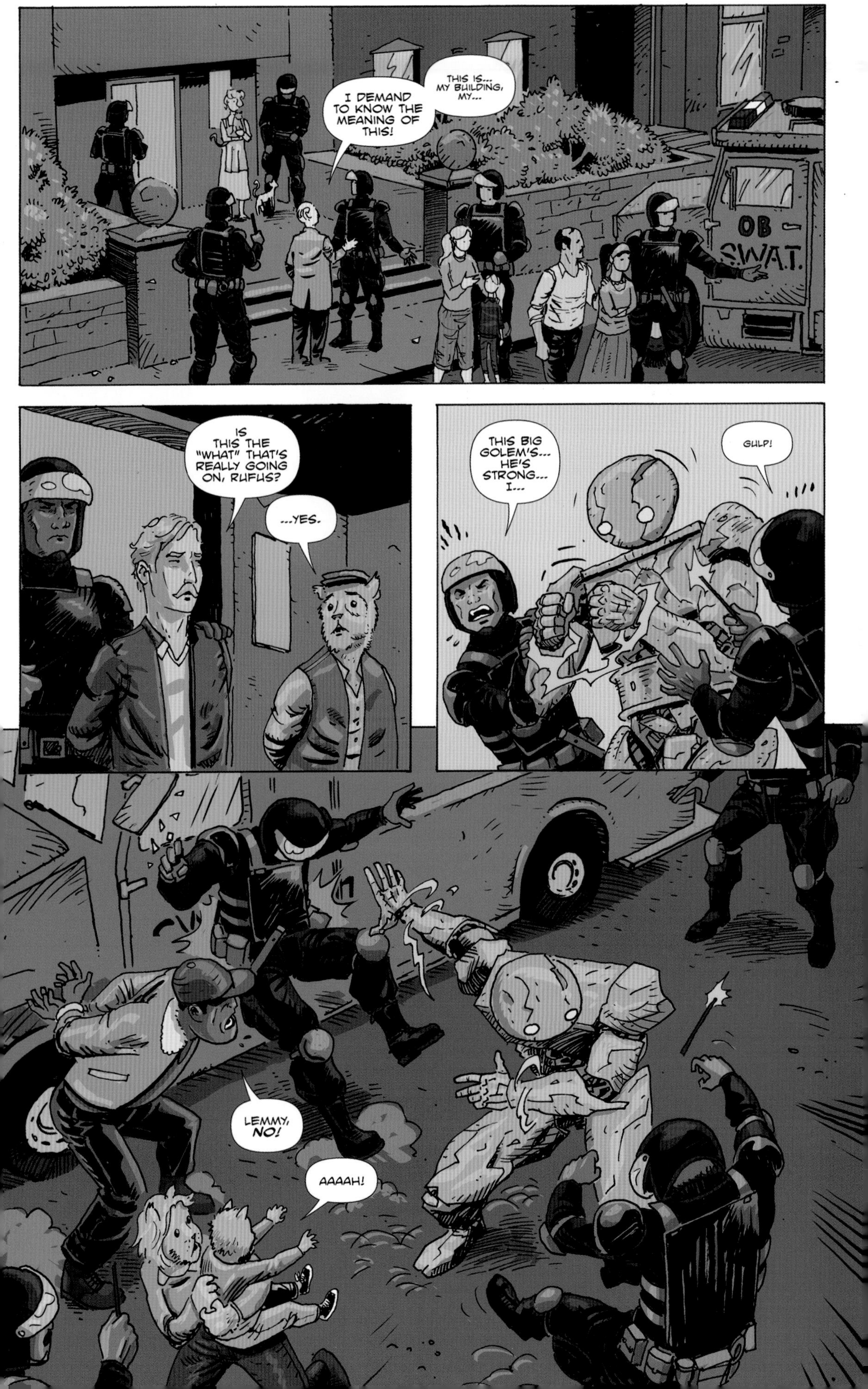

I DEMAND TO KNOW THE MEANING OF THIS!
THIS IS... MY BUILDING, MY...
OB S.W.A.T.
IS THIS THE "WHAT" THAT'S REALLY GOING ON, RUFUS?
...YES.
THIS BIG GOLEM'S... HE'S STRONG... I...
GULP!
LEMMY, NO!
AAAAH!

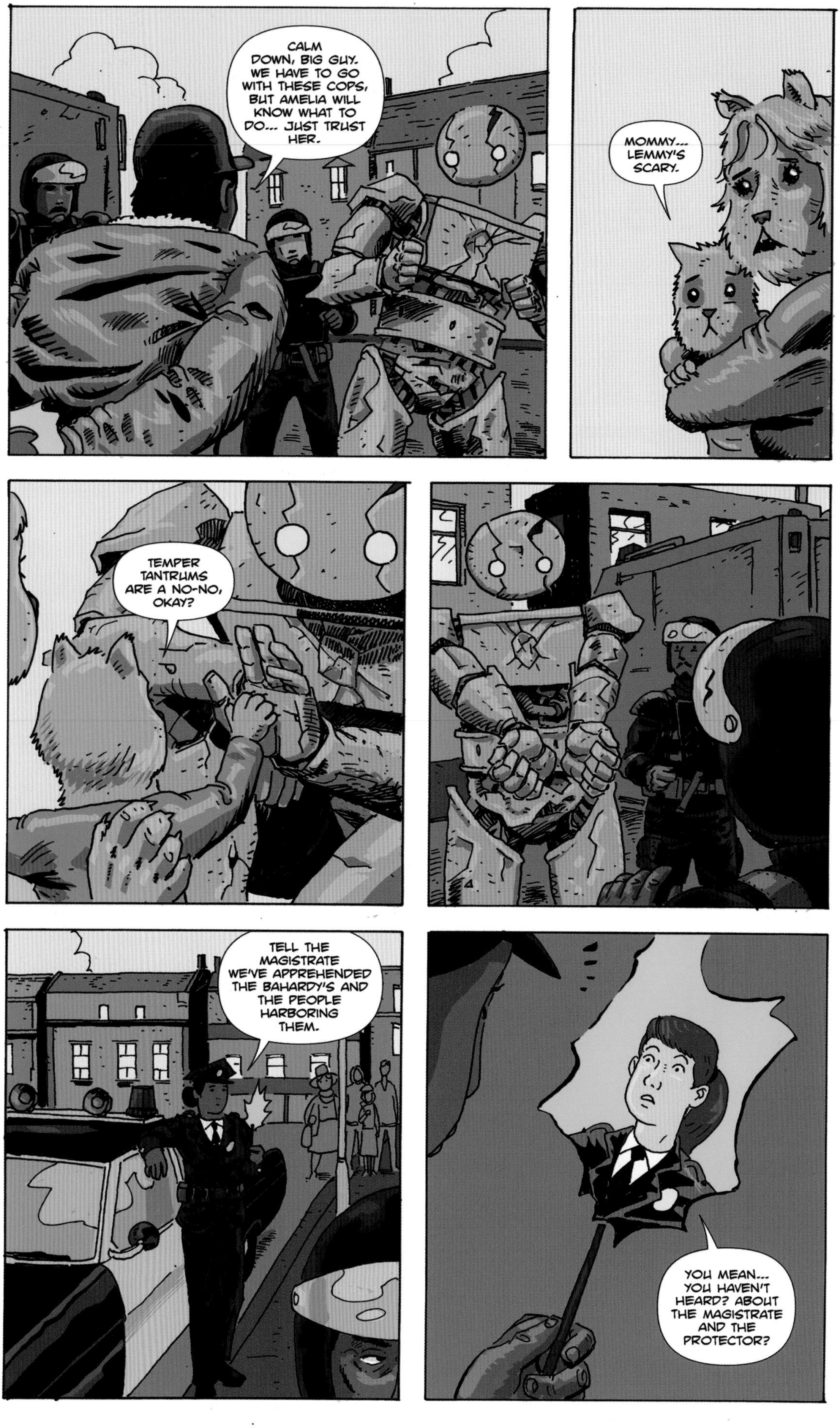
CALM DOWN, BIG GUY. WE HAVE TO GO WITH THESE COPS, BUT AMELIA WILL KNOW WHAT TO DO... JUST TRUST HER.
MOMMY... LEMMY'S SCARY.
TEMPER TANTRUMS ARE A NO-NO, OKAY?
TELL THE MAGISTRATE WE'VE APPREHENDED THE BAHARDY'S AND THE PEOPLE HARBORING THEM.
YOU MEAN... YOU HAVEN'T HEARD? ABOUT THE MAGISTRATE AND THE PROTECTOR?

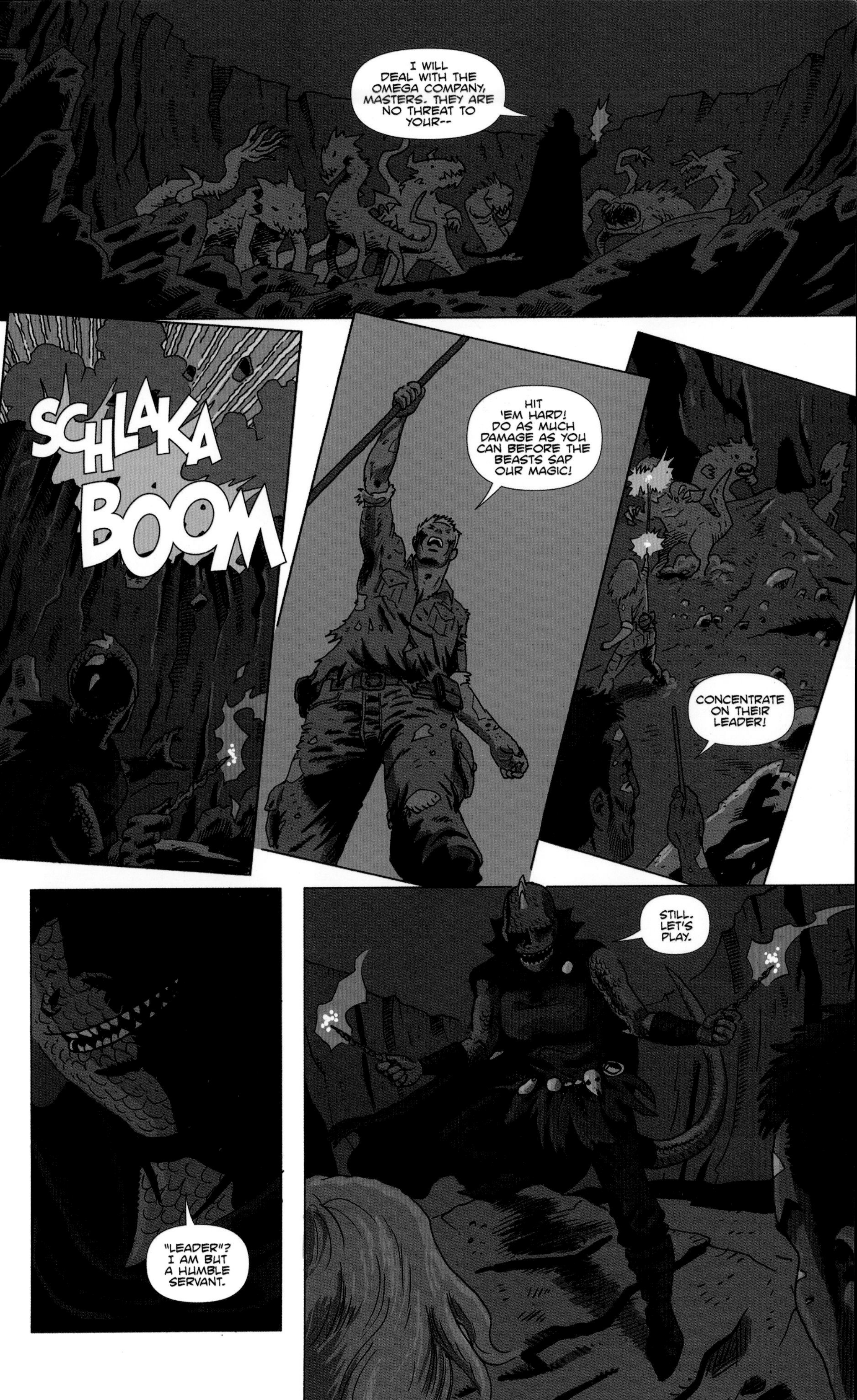
I WILL DEAL WITH THE OMEGA COMPANY, MASTERS. THEY ARE NO THREAT TO YOUR--
SCHLAKA BOOM
HIT 'EM HARD! DO AS MUCH DAMAGE AS YOU CAN BEFORE THE BEASTS SAP OUR MAGIC!
CONCENTRATE ON THEIR LEADER!
"LEADER"? I AM BUT A HUMBLE SERVANT.
STILL. LET'S PLAY.

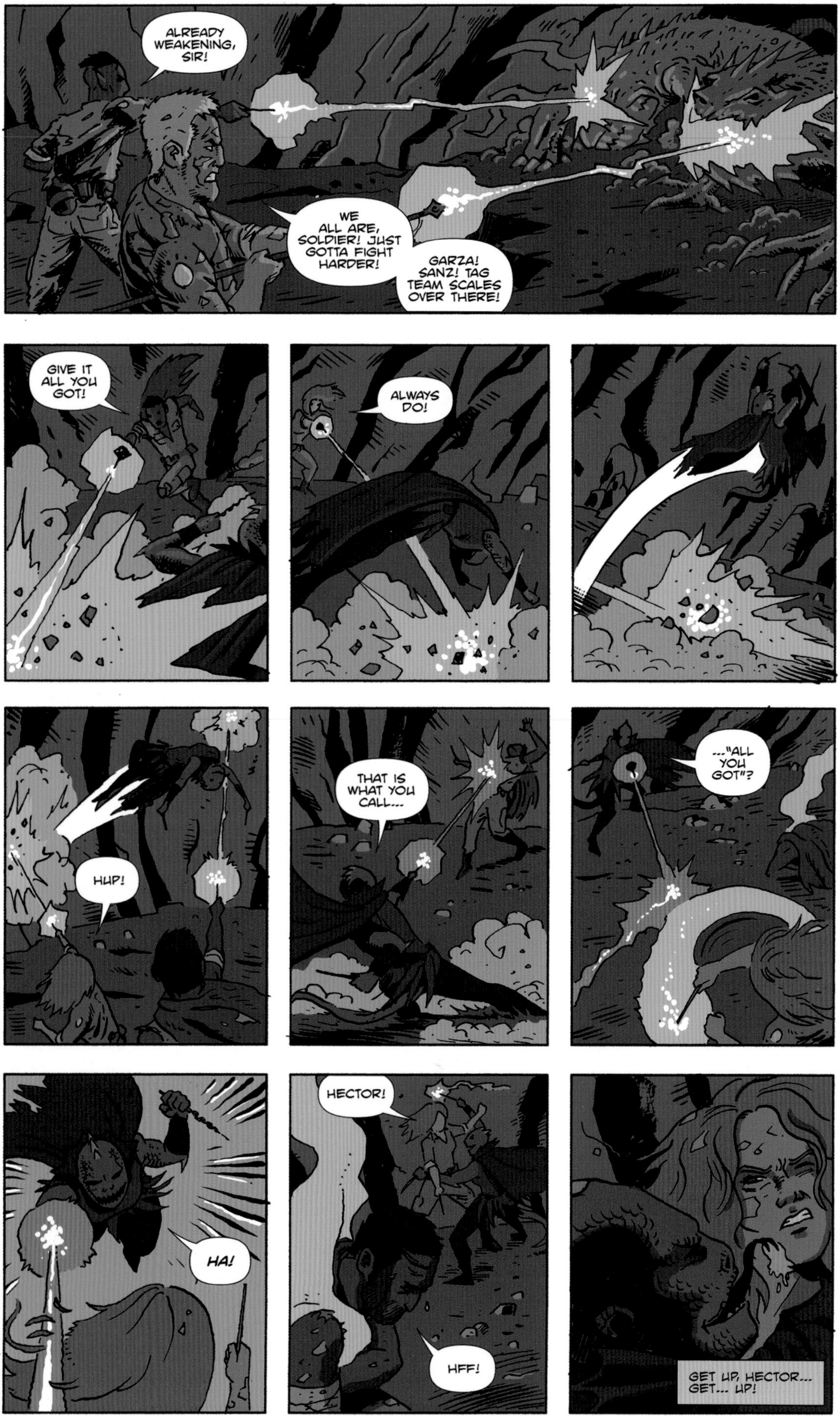
ALREADY WEAKENING, SIR!
WE ALL ARE, SOLDIER! JUST GOTTA FIGHT HARDER!
GARZA! SANZ! TAG TEAM SCALES OVER THERE!
GIVE IT ALL YOU GOT!
ALWAYS DO!
HUP!
THAT IS WHAT YOU CALL...
..."ALL YOU GOT"?
HA!
HECTOR!
HFF!
GET UP, HECTOR... GET... UP!

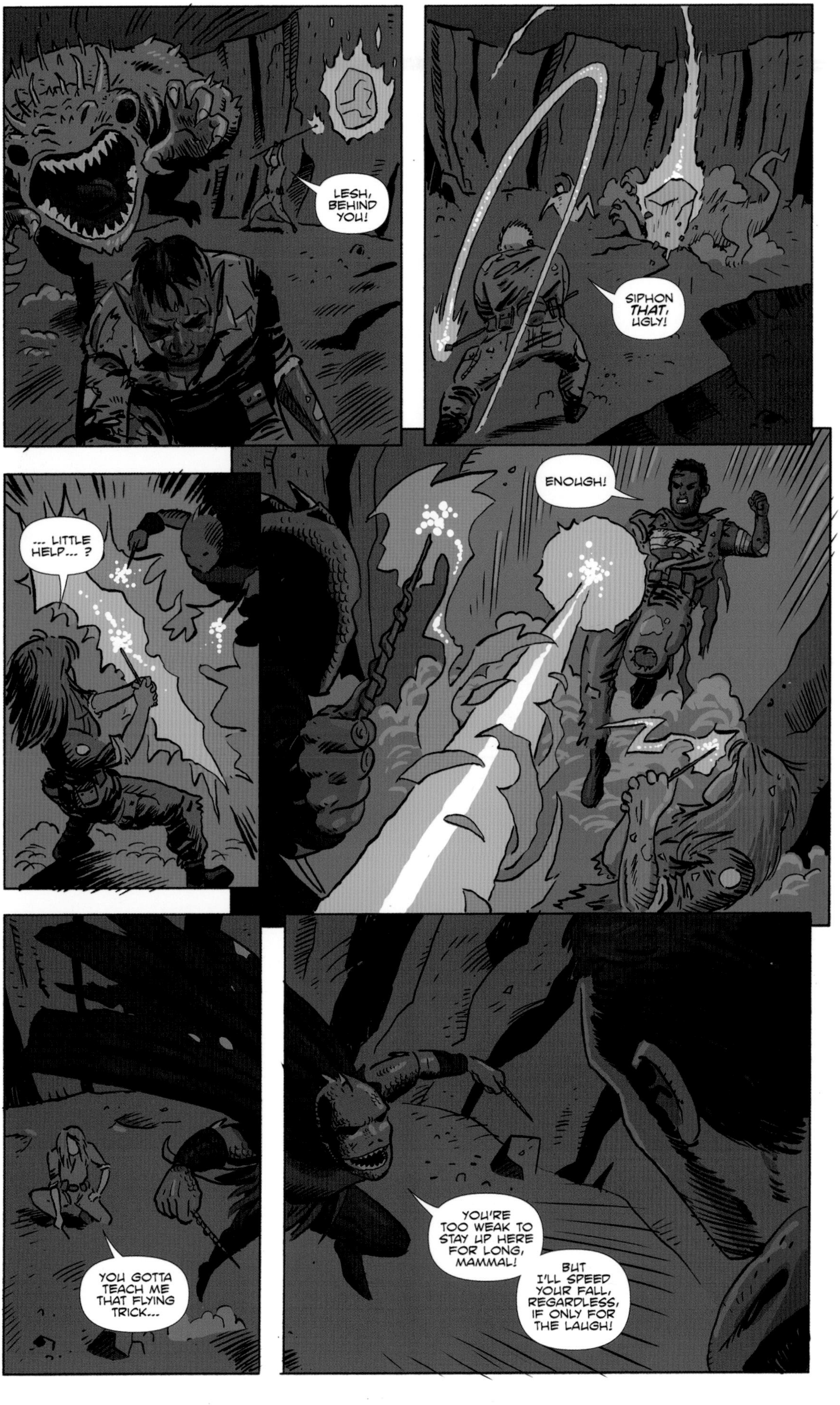
LESH, BEHIND YOU!
SIPHON THAT, UGLY!
... LITTLE HELP... ?
ENOUGH!
YOU GOTTA TEACH ME THAT FLYING TRICK...
YOU'RE TOO WEAK TO STAY UP HERE FOR LONG, MAMMAL!
BUT I'LL SPEED YOUR FALL, REGARDLESS, IF ONLY FOR THE LAUGH!

WEAKNESSES?

NONE! THIS IS NOT SOME FIGHT YOU CAN WIN, GIRL! THE BEST WE CAN DO IS WORK WITH THE COUNCIL TO--

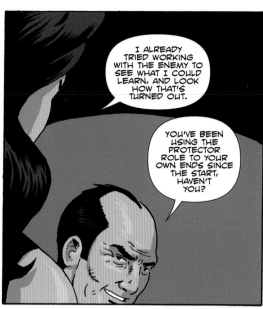

I ALREADY TRIED WORKING WITH THE ENEMY TO SEE WHAT I COULD LEARN, AND LOOK HOW THAT'S TURNED OUT.

YOU'VE BEEN USING THE PROTECTOR ROLE TO YOUR OWN ENDS SINCE THE START, HAVEN'T YOU?

BRILIANT DEDUCTION, GENIUS!

NOW, HOW DO I FIND THESE COUNCIL CREEPERS?

NO NEED TO

TO FIND US, CHILD.

CHILD, WE ARE

ARE NEVER

FAR AWAY.

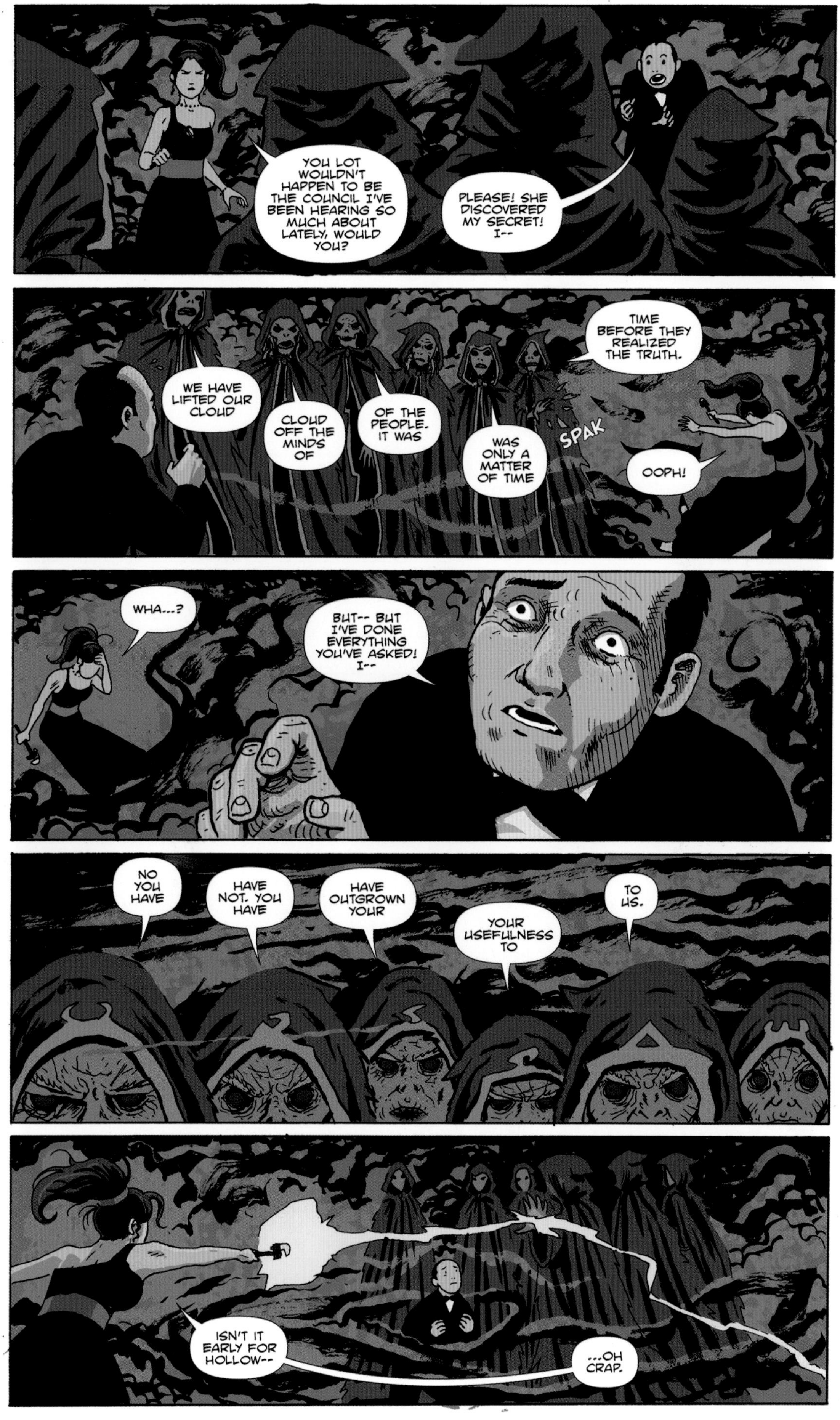
YOU LOT WOULDN'T HAPPEN TO BE THE COUNCIL I'VE BEEN HEARING SO MUCH ABOUT LATELY, WOULD YOU?
PLEASE! SHE DISCOVERED MY SECRET! I--
WE HAVE LIFTED OUR CLOUD
CLOUD OFF THE MINDS OF
OF THE PEOPLE. IT WAS
WAS ONLY A MATTER OF TIME
TIME BEFORE THEY REALIZED THE TRUTH.
SPAK
OOPH!
WHA...?
BUT-- BUT I'VE DONE EVERYTHING YOU'VE ASKED! I--
NO YOU HAVE
HAVE NOT. YOU HAVE
HAVE OUTGROWN YOUR
YOUR USEFULNESS TO
TO US.
ISN'T IT EARLY FOR HOLLOW--
...OH CRAP.

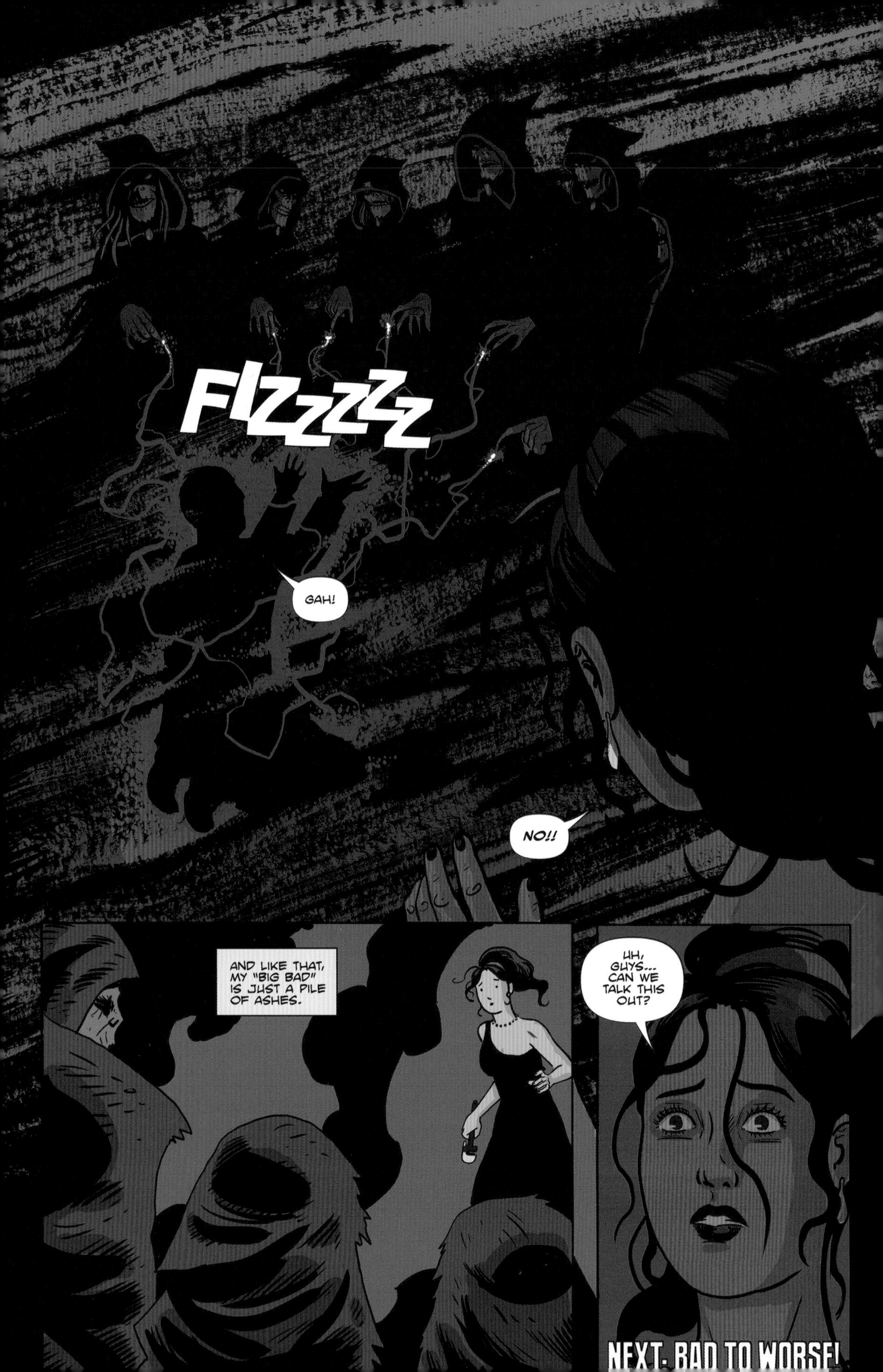
FIZZZZZ
GAH!
NO!!
AND LIKE THAT, MY "BIG BAD" IS JUST A PILE OF ASHES.
UH, GUYS... CAN WE TALK THIS OUT?
NEXT: BAD TO WORSE!

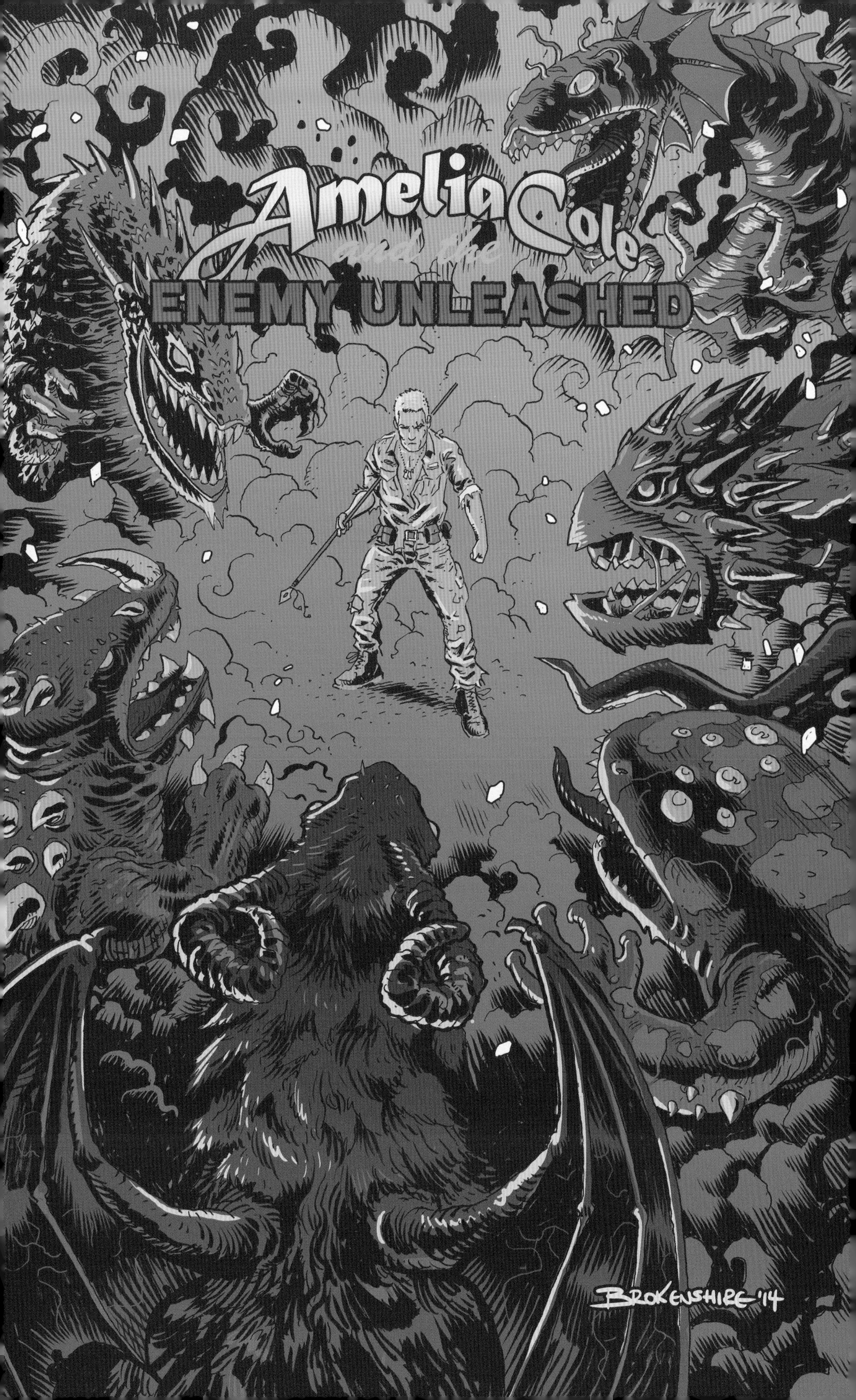
Amelia Cole
and the
ENEMY UNLEASHED
BROKENSHIRE '14

CHAPTER 3

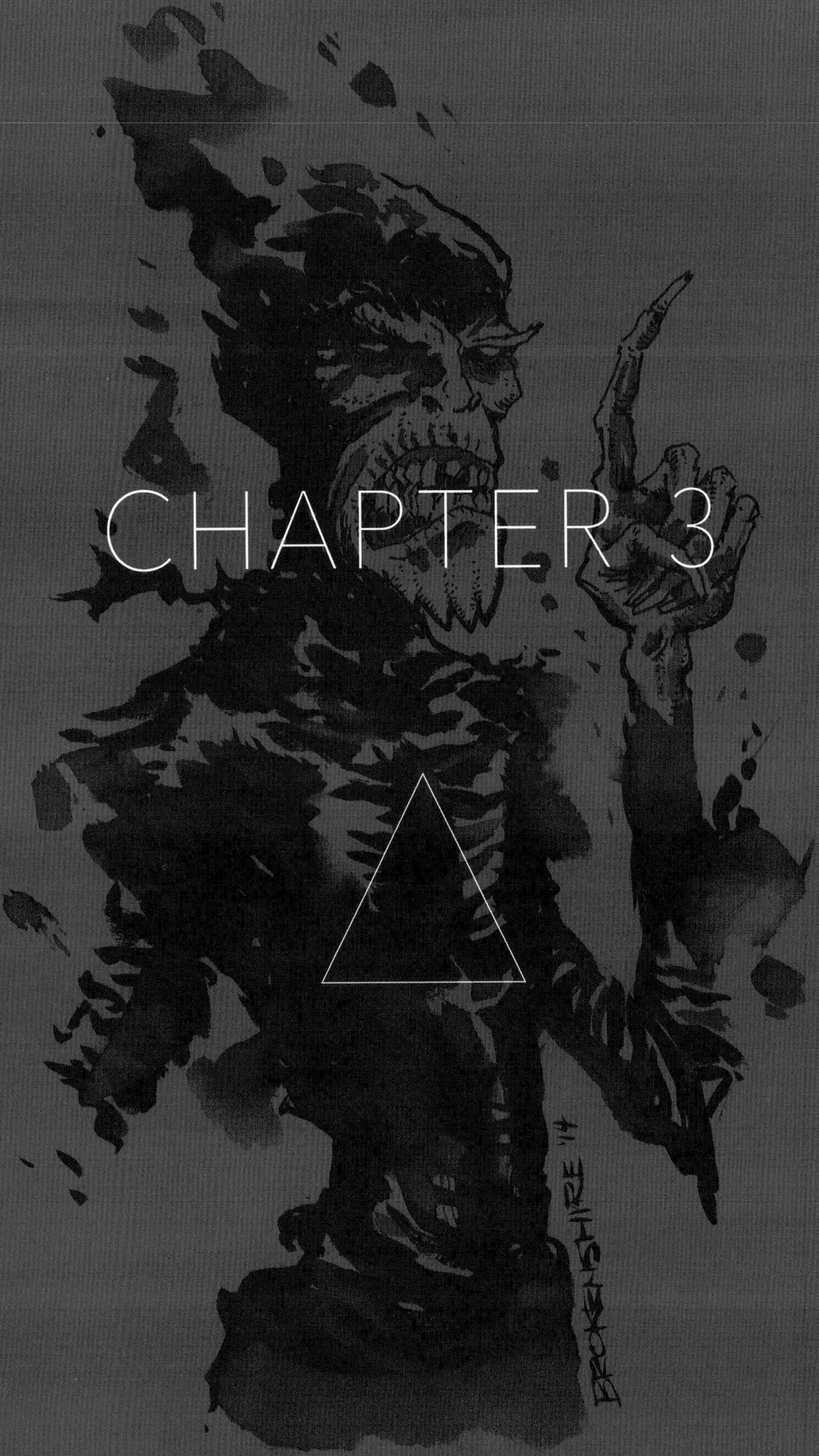

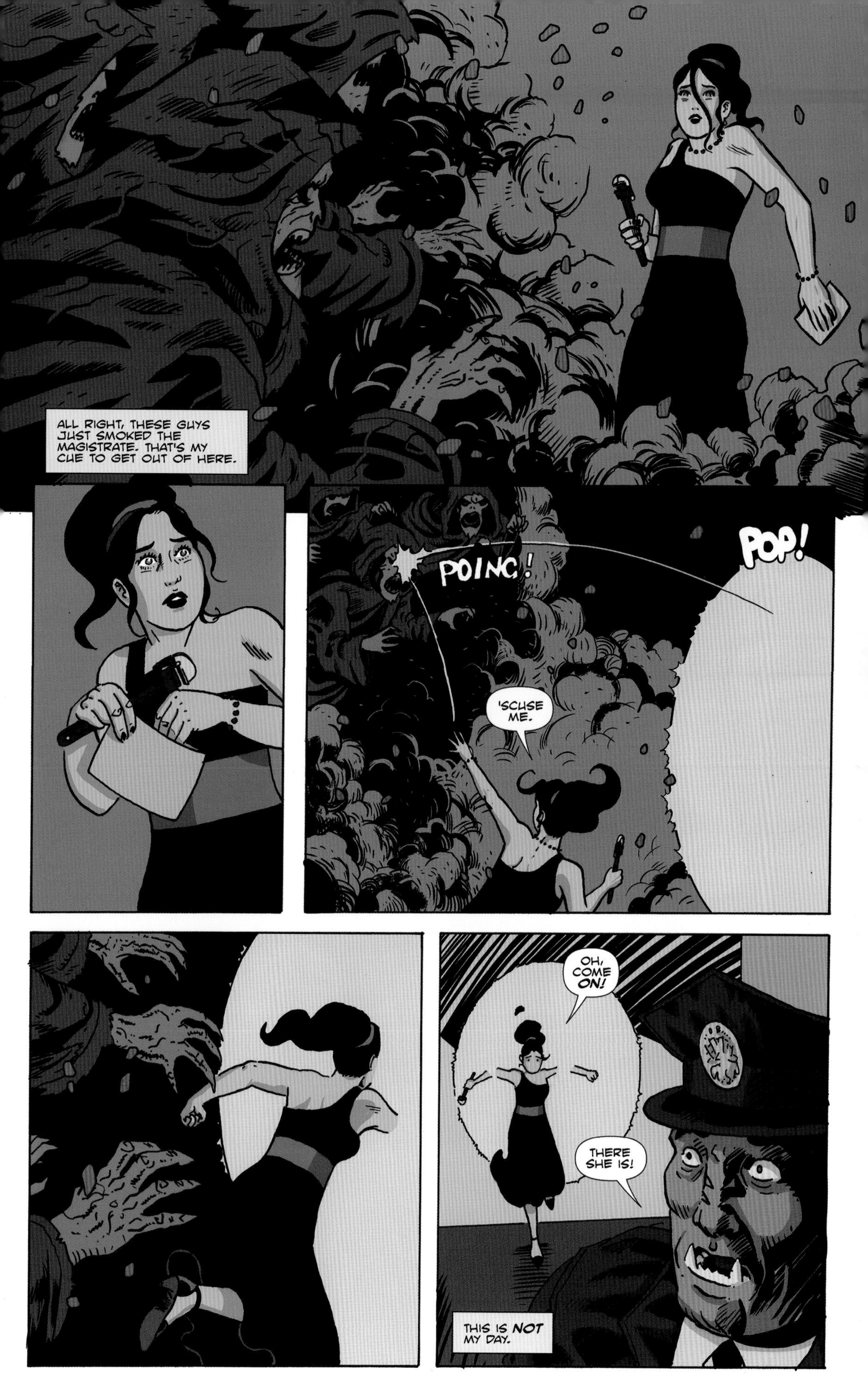
ALL RIGHT, THESE GUYS JUST SMOKED THE MAGISTRATE. THAT'S MY CUE TO GET OUT OF HERE.
POP!
POING!
'SCUSE ME.
OH, COME ON!
THERE SHE IS!
THIS IS NOT MY DAY.

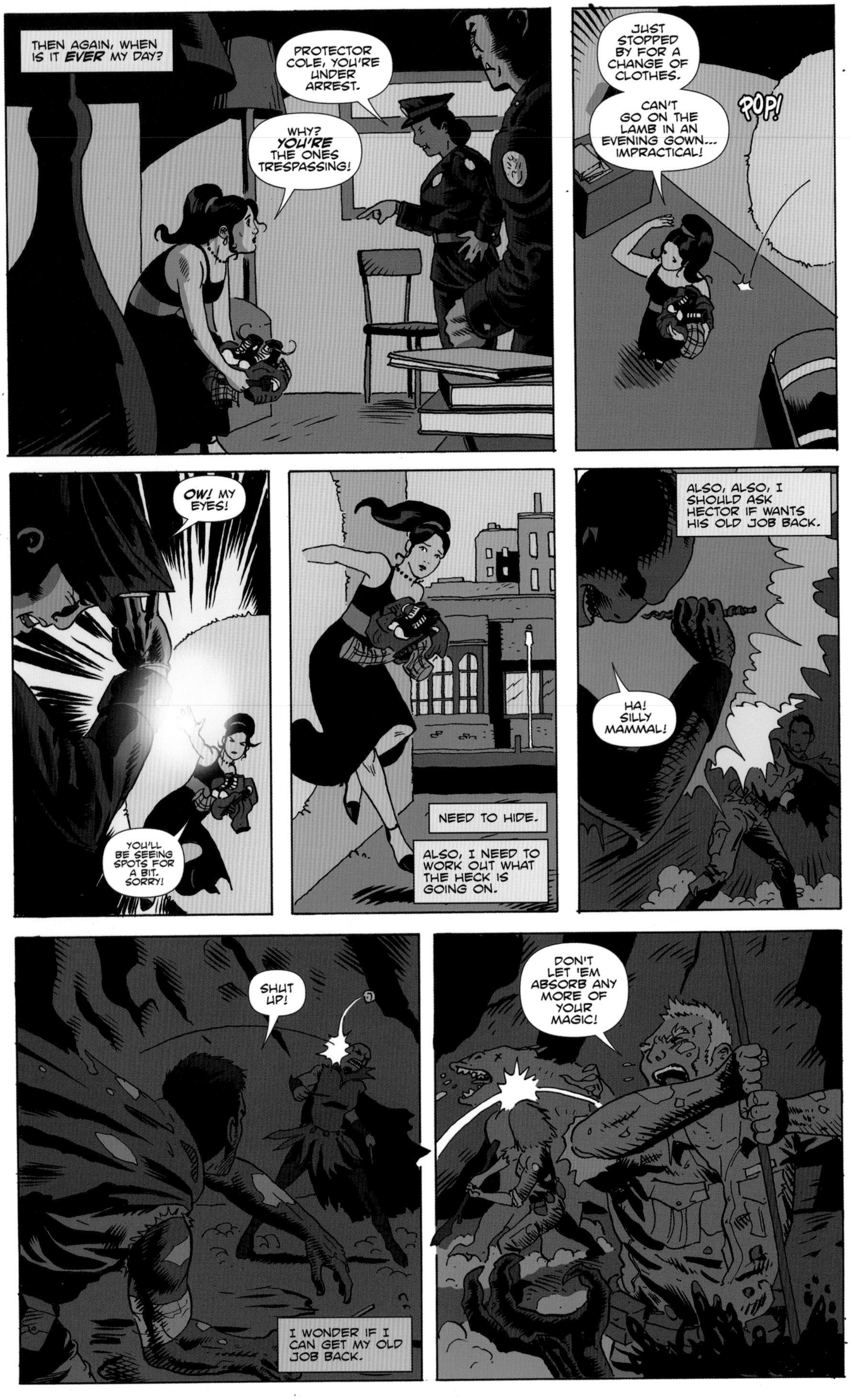
THEN AGAIN, WHEN IS IT EVER MY DAY?
PROTECTOR COLE, YOU'RE UNDER ARREST.
WHY? YOU'RE THE ONES TRESPASSING!
JUST STOPPED BY FOR A CHANGE OF CLOTHES.
CAN'T GO ON THE LAMB IN AN EVENING GOWN... IMPRACTICAL!
POP!
OW! MY EYES!
YOU'LL BE SEEING SPOTS FOR A BIT. SORRY!
NEED TO HIDE.
ALSO, I NEED TO WORK OUT WHAT THE HECK IS GOING ON.
ALSO, ALSO, I SHOULD ASK HECTOR IF WANTS HIS OLD JOB BACK.
HA! SILLY MAMMAL!
SHUT UP!
I WONDER IF I CAN GET MY OLD JOB BACK.
DON'T LET 'EM ABSORB ANY MORE OF YOUR MAGIC!

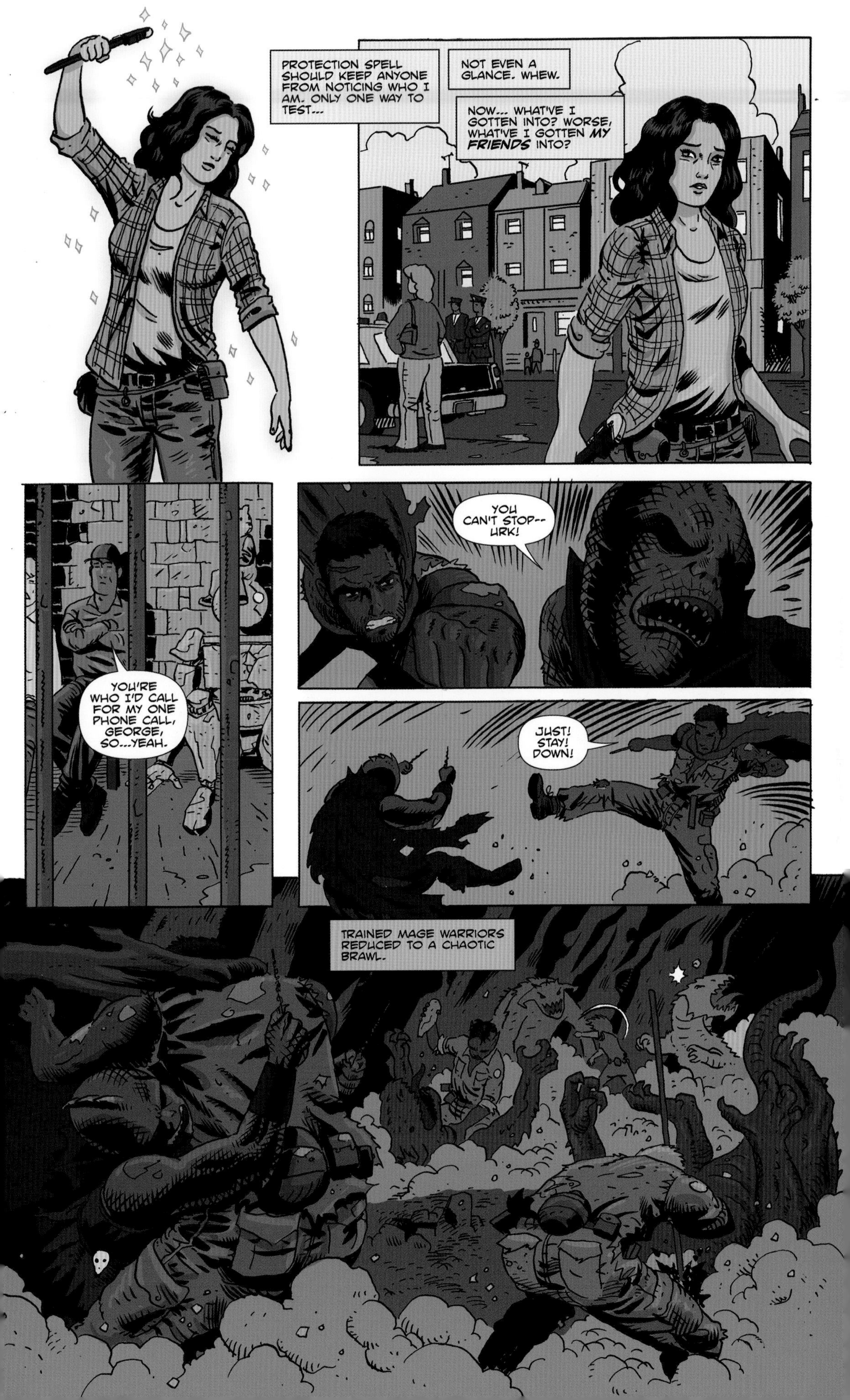
PROTECTION SPELL SHOULD KEEP ANYONE FROM NOTICING WHO I AM. ONLY ONE WAY TO TEST...
NOT EVEN A GLANCE. WHEW.
NOW... WHAT'VE I GOTTEN INTO? WORSE, WHAT'VE I GOTTEN **MY FRIENDS** INTO?
YOU'RE WHO I'D CALL FOR MY ONE PHONE CALL, GEORGE, SO...YEAH.
YOU CAN'T STOP-- URK!
JUST! STAY! DOWN!
TRAINED MAGE WARRIORS REDUCED TO A CHAOTIC BRAWL.

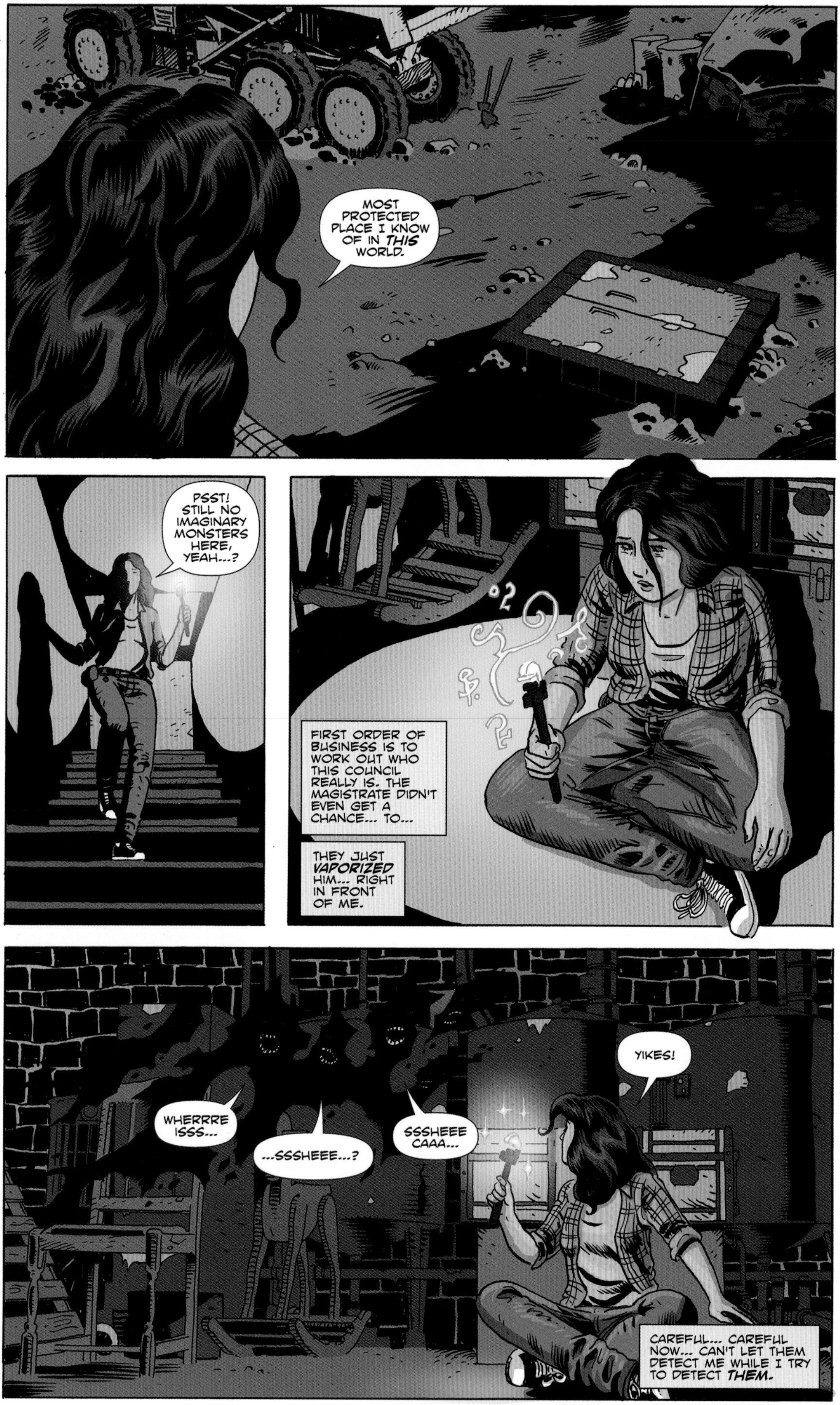
MOST PROTECTED PLACE I KNOW OF IN THIS WORLD.
PSST! STILL NO IMAGINARY MONSTERS HERE, YEAH...?
FIRST ORDER OF BUSINESS IS TO WORK OUT WHO THIS COUNCIL REALLY IS. THE MAGISTRATE DIDN'T EVEN GET A CHANCE... TO...
THEY JUST VAPORIZED HIM... RIGHT IN FRONT OF ME.
YIKES!
WHERRRE ISSS...
...SSSHEEE...?
SSSHEEE CAAA...
CAREFUL... CAREFUL NOW... CAN'T LET THEM DETECT ME WHILE I TRY TO DETECT THEM.

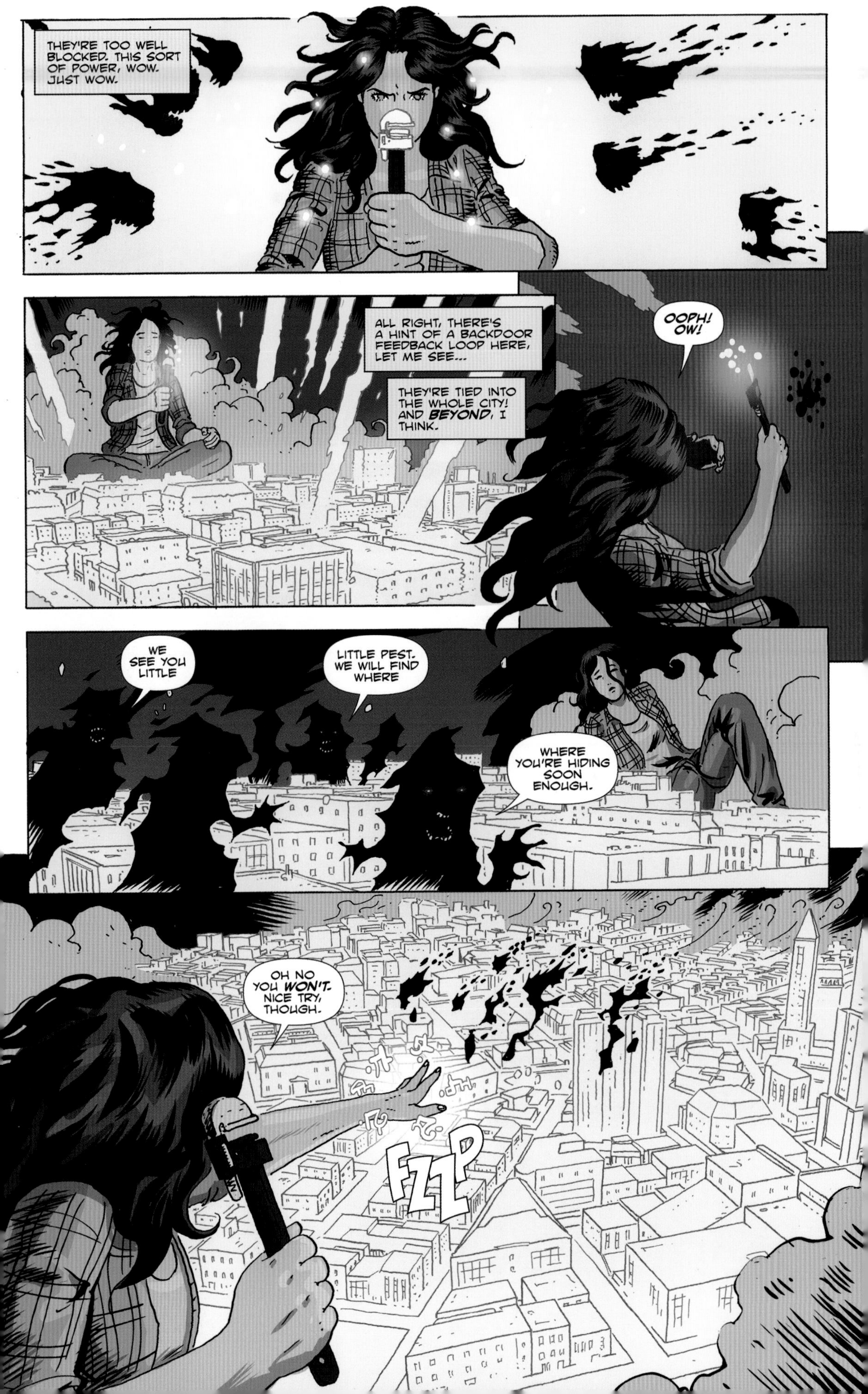
THEY'RE TOO WELL BLOCKED. THIS SORT OF POWER, WOW. JUST WOW.
ALL RIGHT, THERE'S A HINT OF A BACKDOOR FEEDBACK LOOP HERE, LET ME SEE...
THEY'RE TIED INTO THE WHOLE CITY! AND BEYOND, I THINK.
OOPH! OW!
WE SEE YOU LITTLE
LITTLE PEST. WE WILL FIND WHERE
WHERE YOU'RE HIDING SOON ENOUGH.
OH NO YOU WON'T. NICE TRY, THOUGH.
FZZP

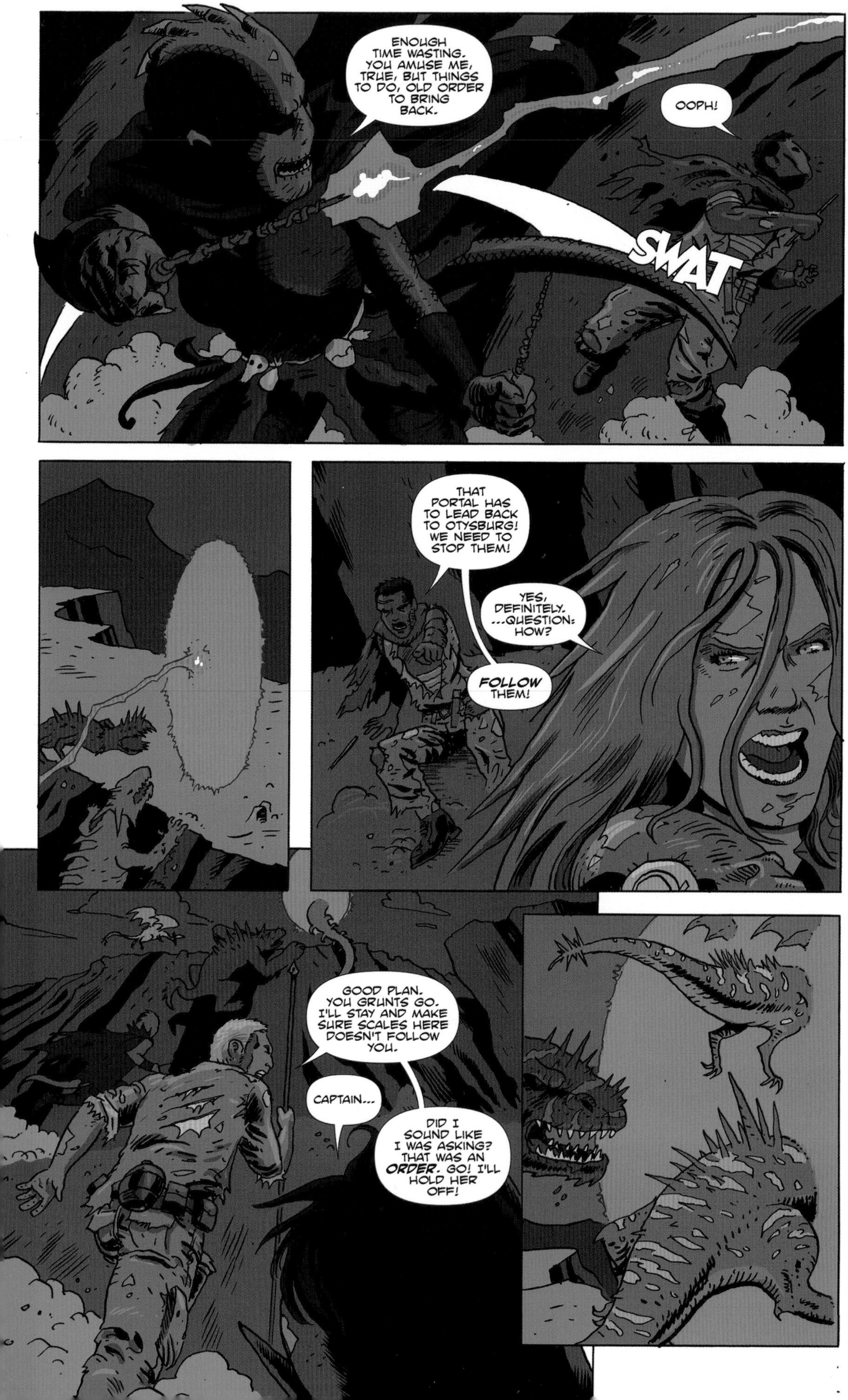

ENOUGH TIME WASTING. YOU AMUSE ME, TRUE, BUT THINGS TO DO, OLD ORDER TO BRING BACK.
OOPH!
SWAT
THAT PORTAL HAS TO LEAD BACK TO OTYSBURG! WE NEED TO STOP THEM!
YES, DEFINITELY. ...QUESTION: HOW?
FOLLOW THEM!
GOOD PLAN. YOU GRUNTS GO. I'LL STAY AND MAKE SURE SCALES HERE DOESN'T FOLLOW YOU.
CAPTAIN...
DID I SOUND LIKE I WAS ASKING? THAT WAS AN ORDER. GO! I'LL HOLD HER OFF!

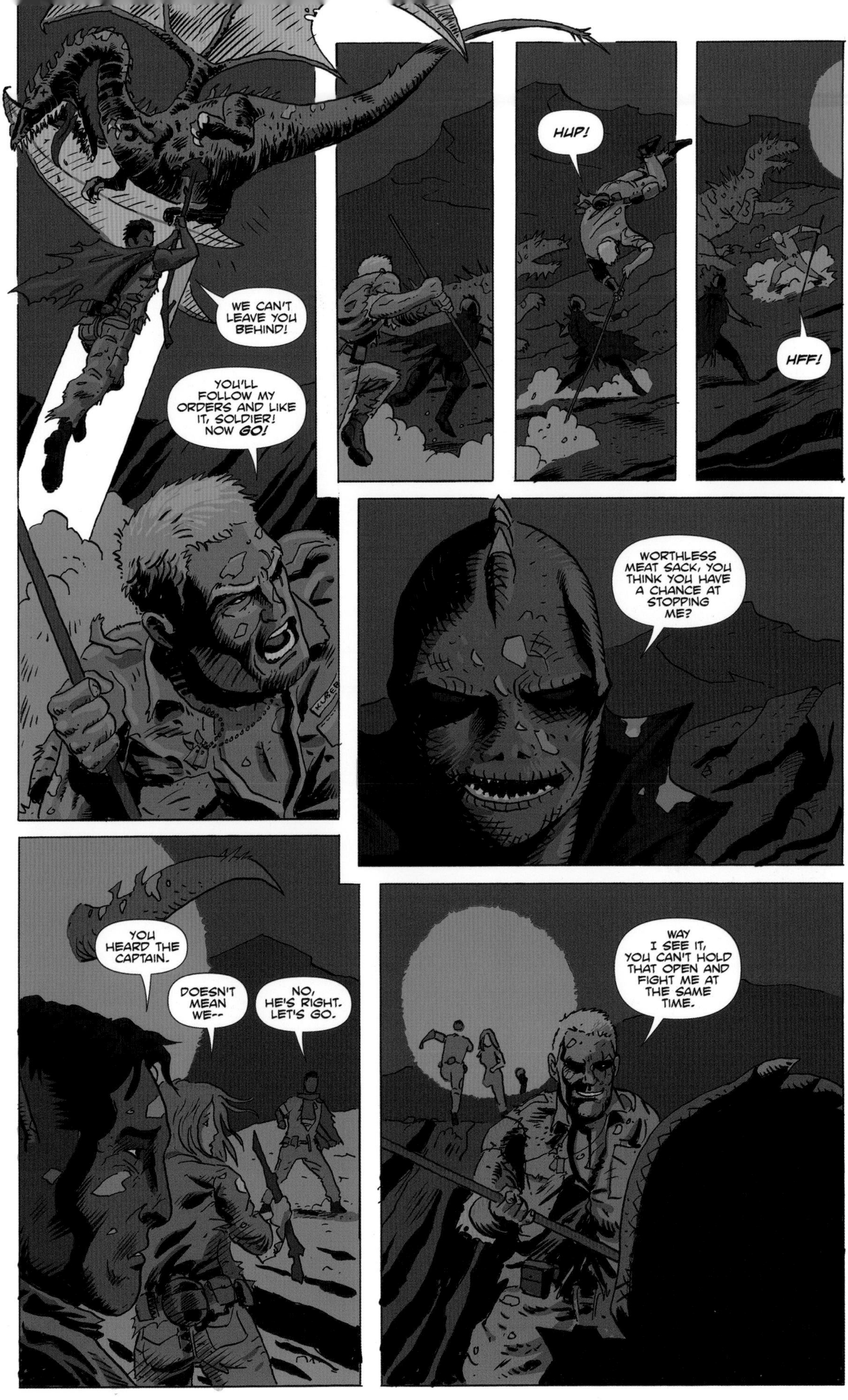
WE CAN'T LEAVE YOU BEHIND!
YOU'LL FOLLOW MY ORDERS AND LIKE IT, SOLDIER! NOW GO!
HUP!
HFF!
WORTHLESS MEAT SACK, YOU THINK YOU HAVE A CHANCE AT STOPPING ME?
YOU HEARD THE CAPTAIN.
DOESN'T MEAN WE--
NO, HE'S RIGHT. LET'S GO.
WAY I SEE IT, YOU CAN'T HOLD THAT OPEN AND FIGHT ME AT THE SAME TIME.

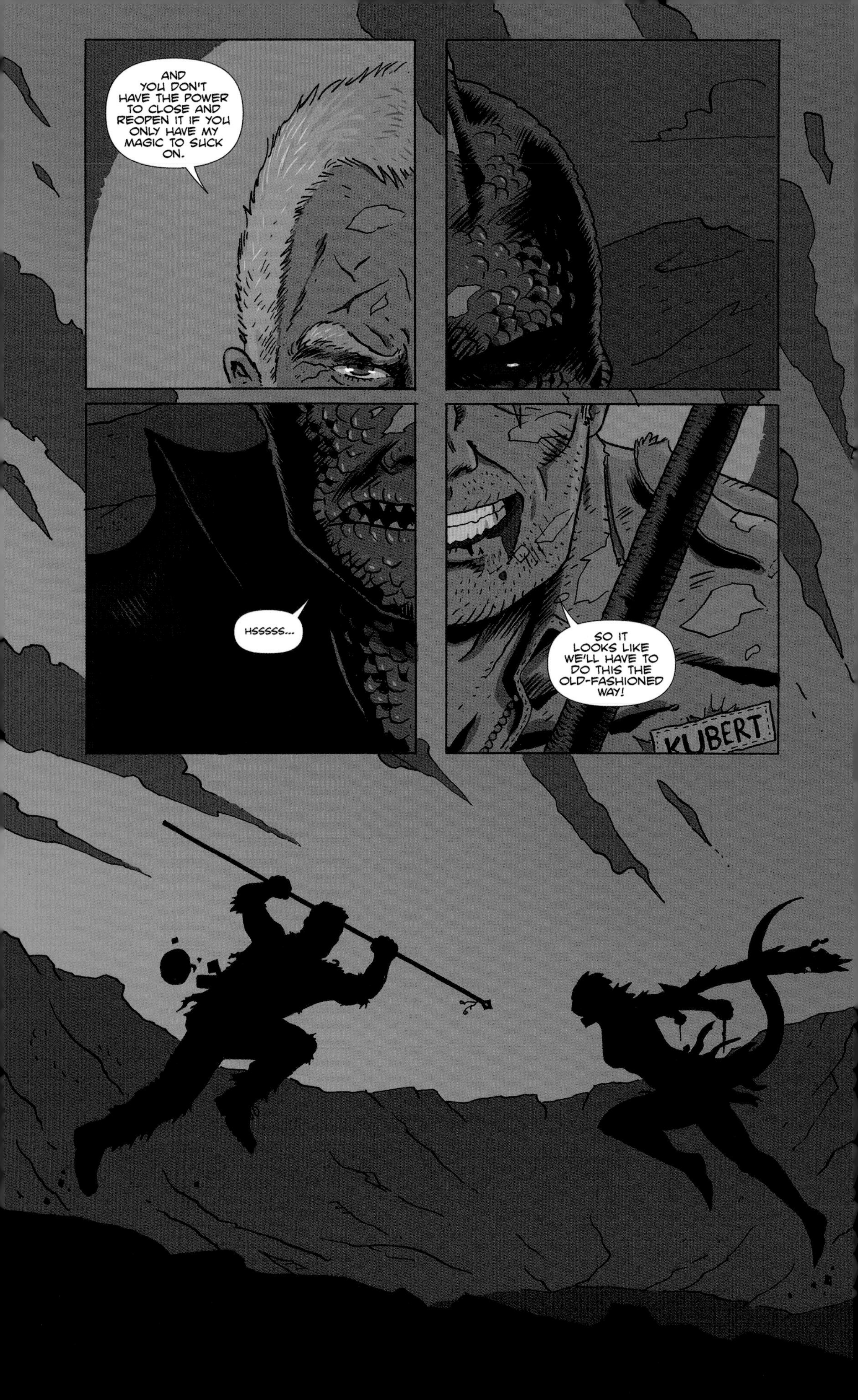
AND YOU DON'T HAVE THE POWER TO CLOSE AND REOPEN IT IF YOU ONLY HAVE MY MAGIC TO SUCK ON.
HSSSSS...
SO IT LOOKS LIKE WE'LL HAVE TO DO THIS THE OLD-FASHIONED WAY!
KUBERT

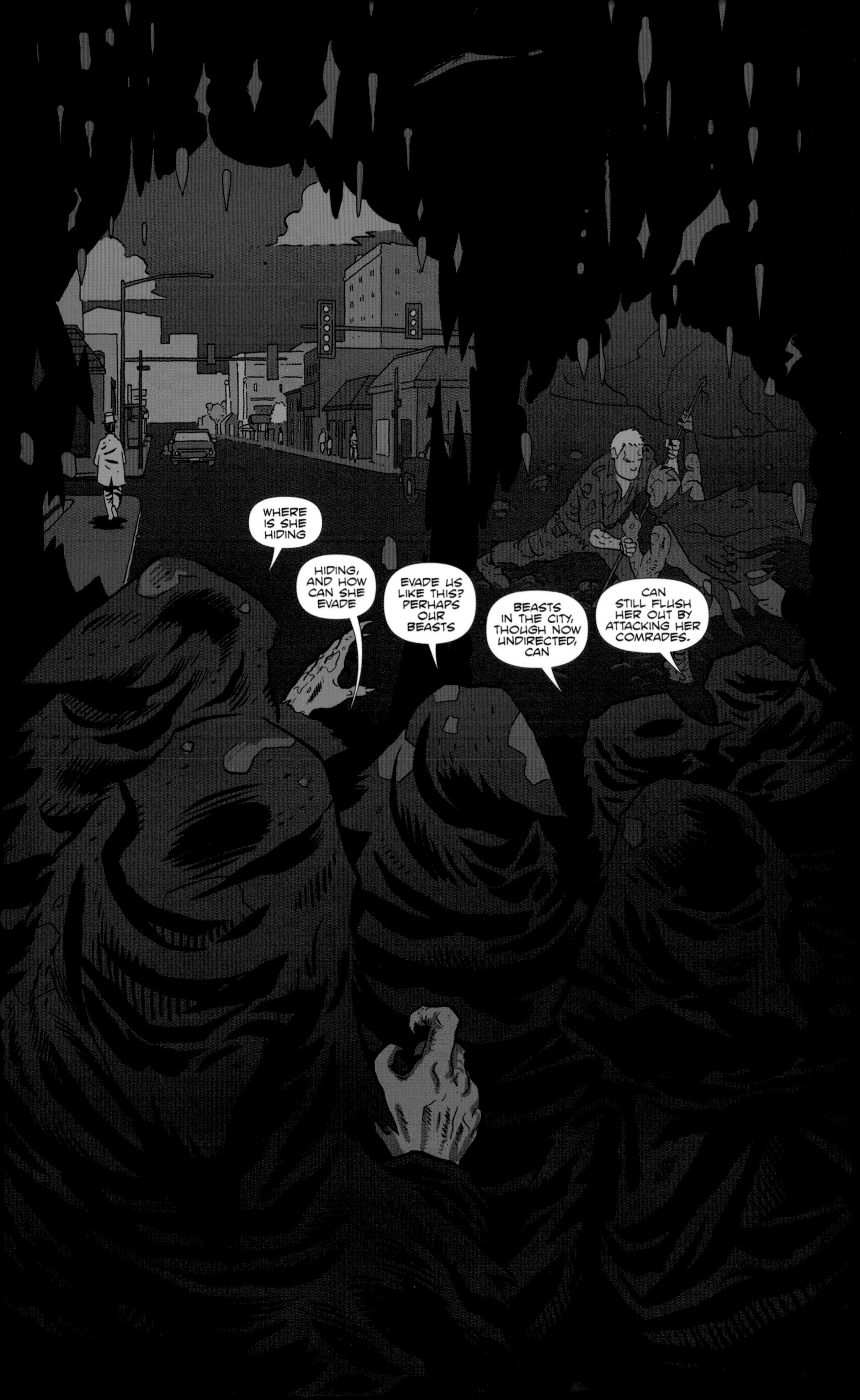
WHERE IS SHE HIDING
HIDING, AND HOW CAN SHE EVADE
EVADE US LIKE THIS? PERHAPS OUR BEASTS
BEASTS IN THE CITY, THOUGH NOW UNDIRECTED, CAN
CAN STILL FLUSH HER OUT BY ATTACKING HER COMRADES.

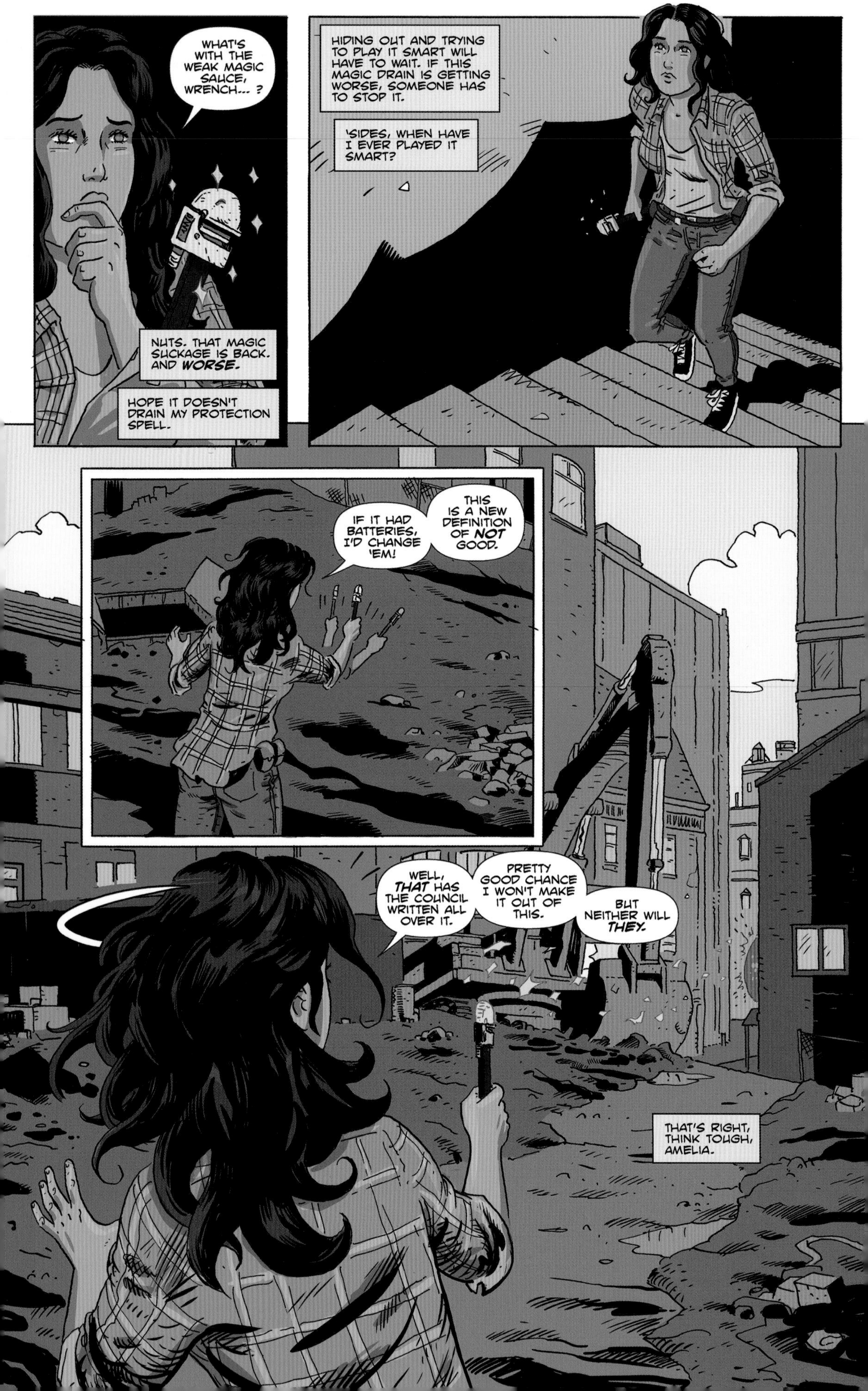
WHAT'S WITH THE WEAK MAGIC SAUCE, WRENCH... ?
NUTS. THAT MAGIC SUCKAGE IS BACK. AND WORSE.
HOPE IT DOESN'T DRAIN MY PROTECTION SPELL.
HIDING OUT AND TRYING TO PLAY IT SMART WILL HAVE TO WAIT. IF THIS MAGIC DRAIN IS GETTING WORSE, SOMEONE HAS TO STOP IT.
'SIDES, WHEN HAVE I EVER PLAYED IT SMART?
THIS IS A NEW DEFINITION OF NOT GOOD.
IF IT HAD BATTERIES, I'D CHANGE 'EM!
WELL, THAT HAS THE COUNCIL WRITTEN ALL OVER IT.
PRETTY GOOD CHANCE I WON'T MAKE IT OUT OF THIS.
BUT NEITHER WILL THEY.
THAT'S RIGHT, THINK TOUGH, AMELIA.

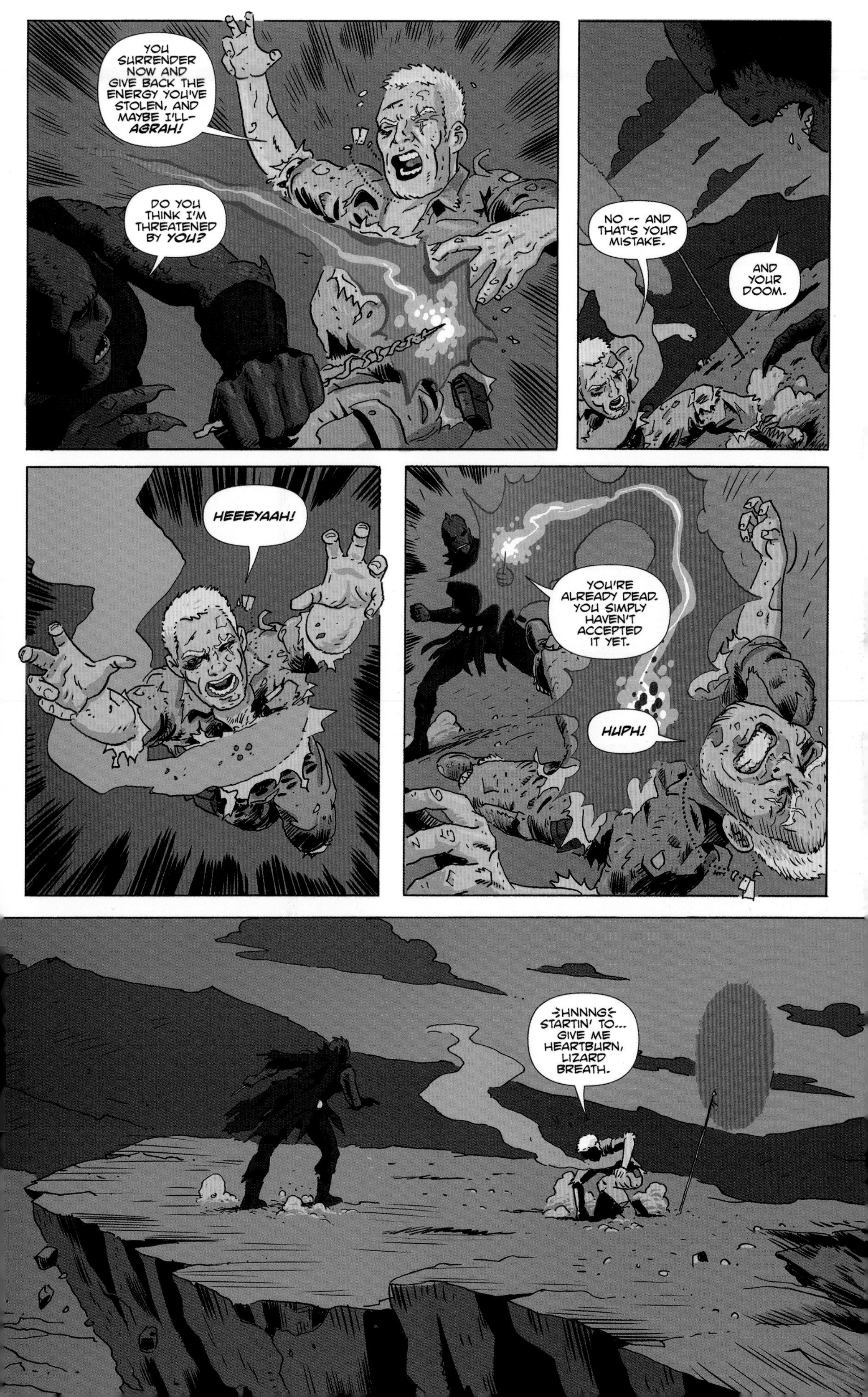
YOU SURRENDER NOW AND GIVE BACK THE ENERGY YOU'VE STOLEN, AND MAYBE I'LL-- AGRAH!
DO YOU THINK I'M THREATENED BY YOU?
NO -- AND THAT'S YOUR MISTAKE.
AND YOUR DOOM.
HEEEYAAH!
YOU'RE ALREADY DEAD. YOU SIMPLY HAVEN'T ACCEPTED IT YET.
HUPH!
HNNNG STARTIN' TO... GIVE ME HEARTBURN, LIZARD BREATH.

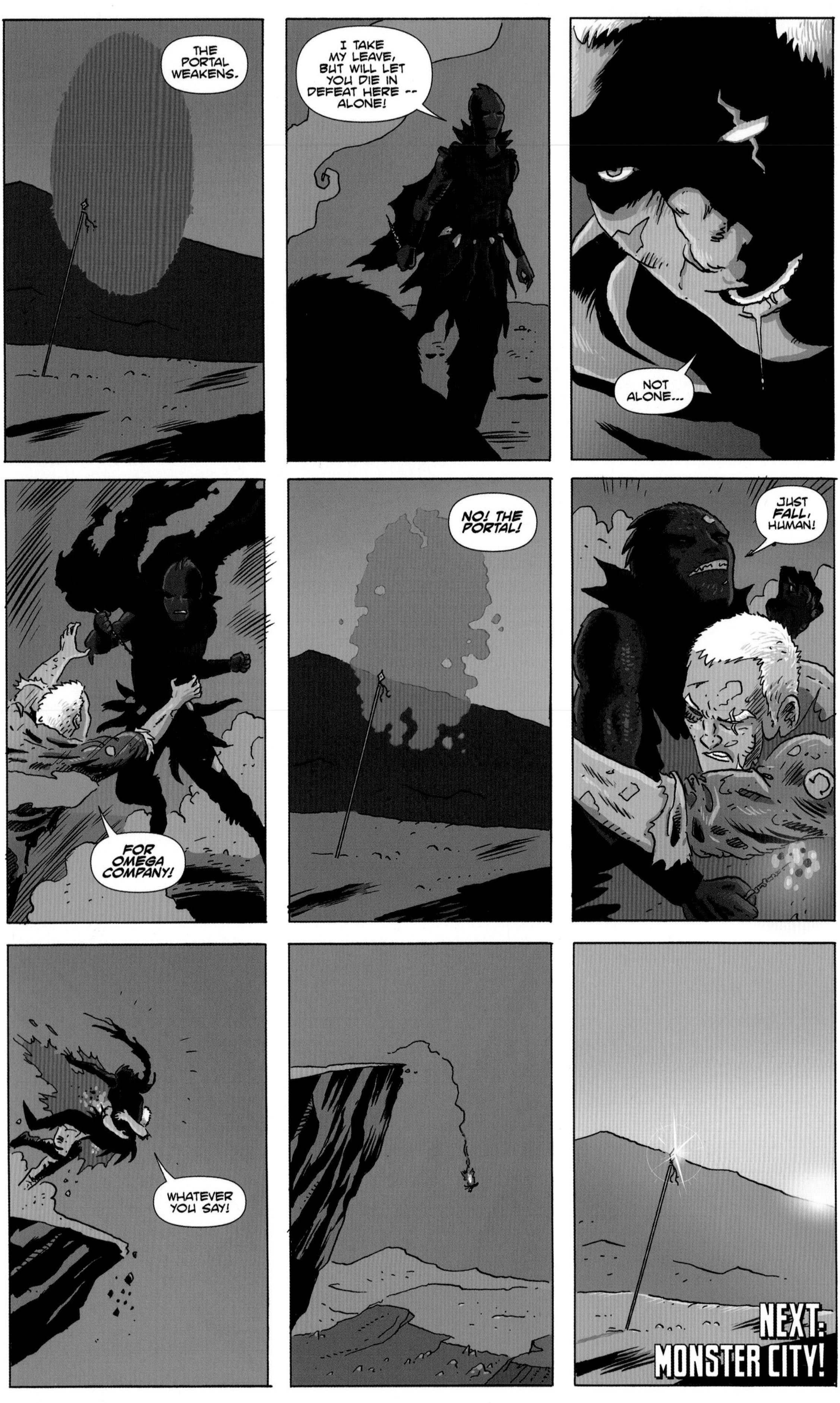
THE PORTAL WEAKENS.
I TAKE MY LEAVE, BUT WILL LET YOU DIE IN DEFEAT HERE -- ALONE!
NOT ALONE...
FOR OMEGA COMPANY!
NO! THE PORTAL!
JUST FALL, HUMAN!
WHATEVER YOU SAY!
NEXT: MONSTER CITY!

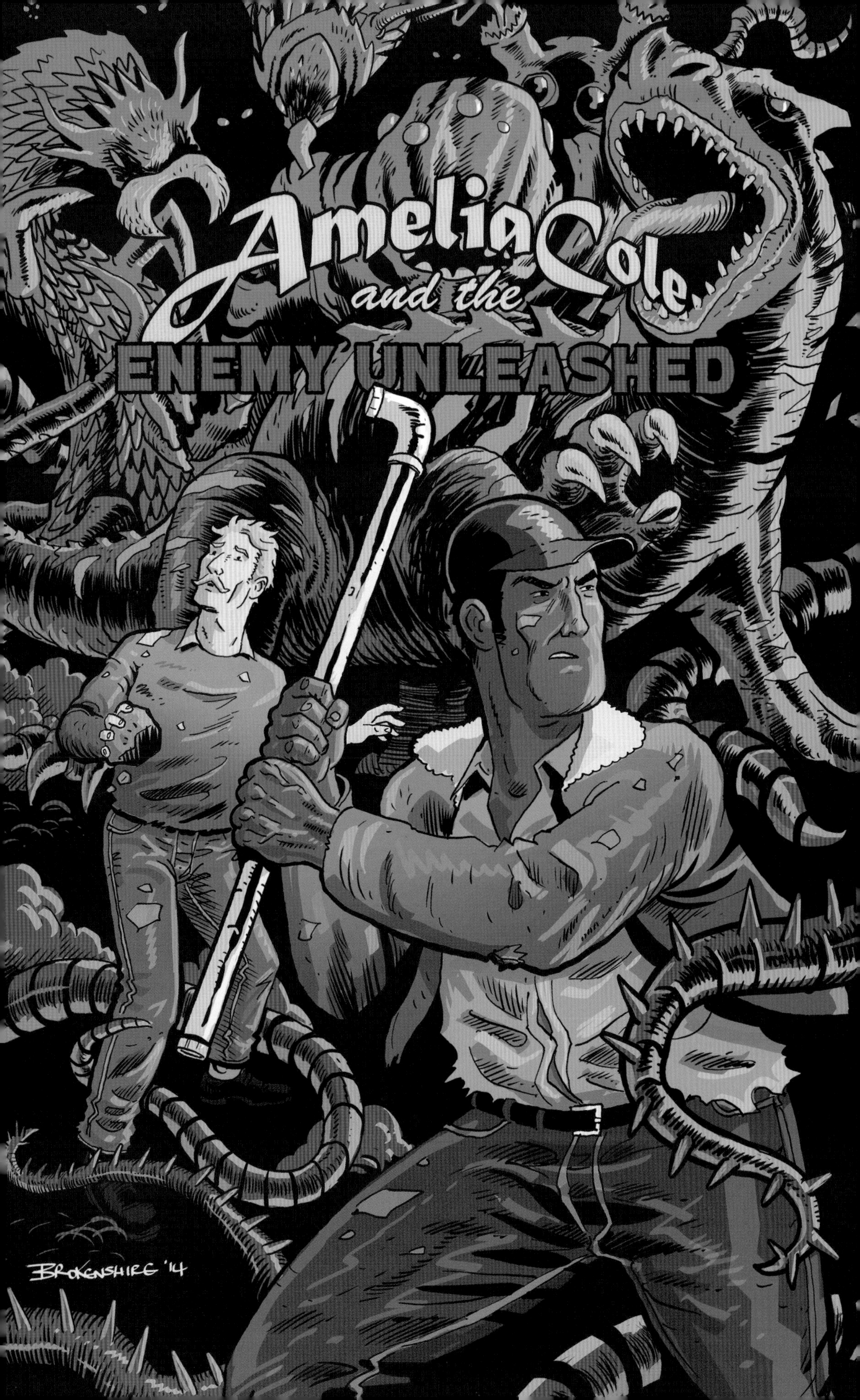
Amelia Cole
and the
ENEMY UNLEASHED
BROKENSHIRE '14

CHAPTER 4

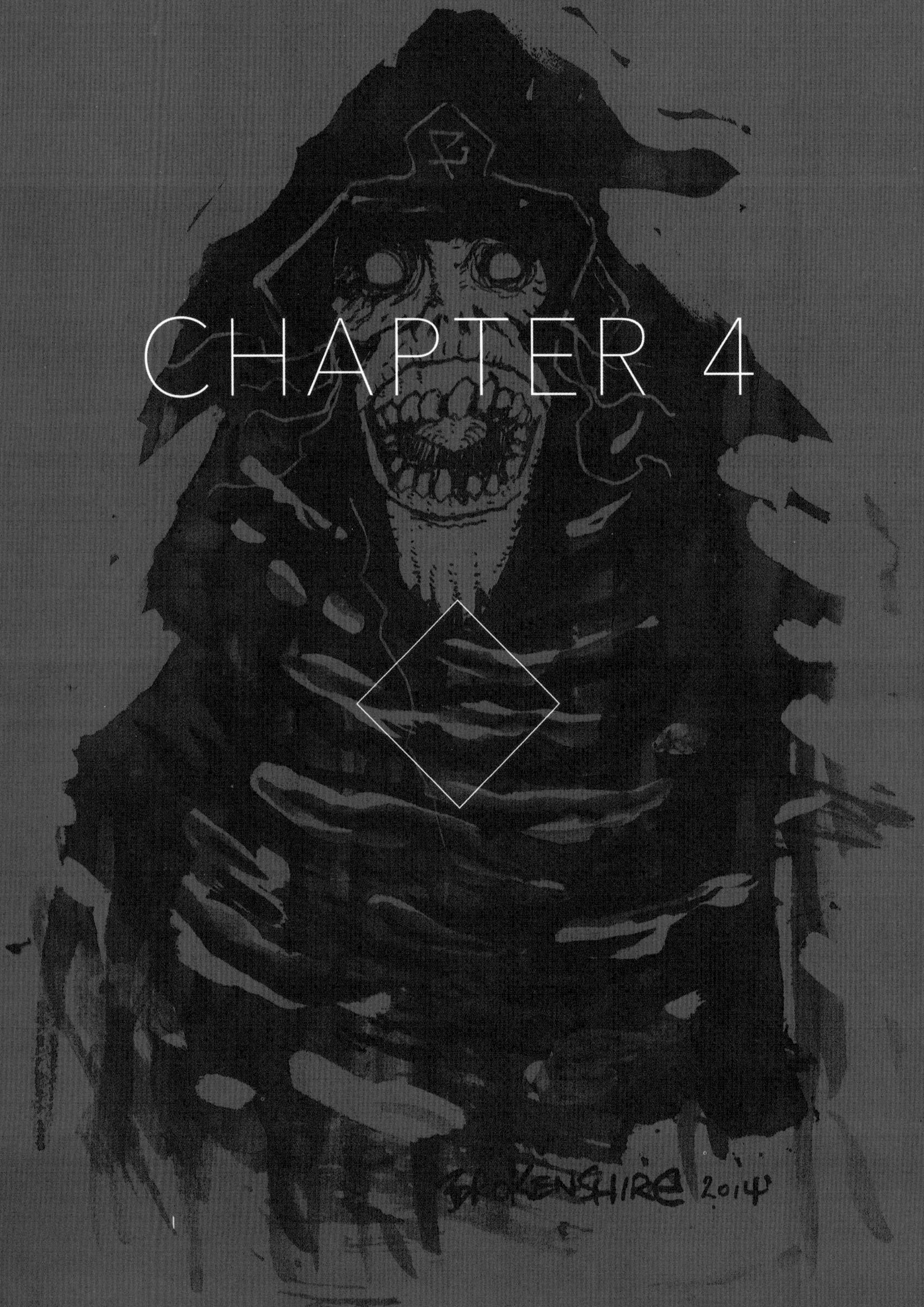
BROKENSHIRE 2014

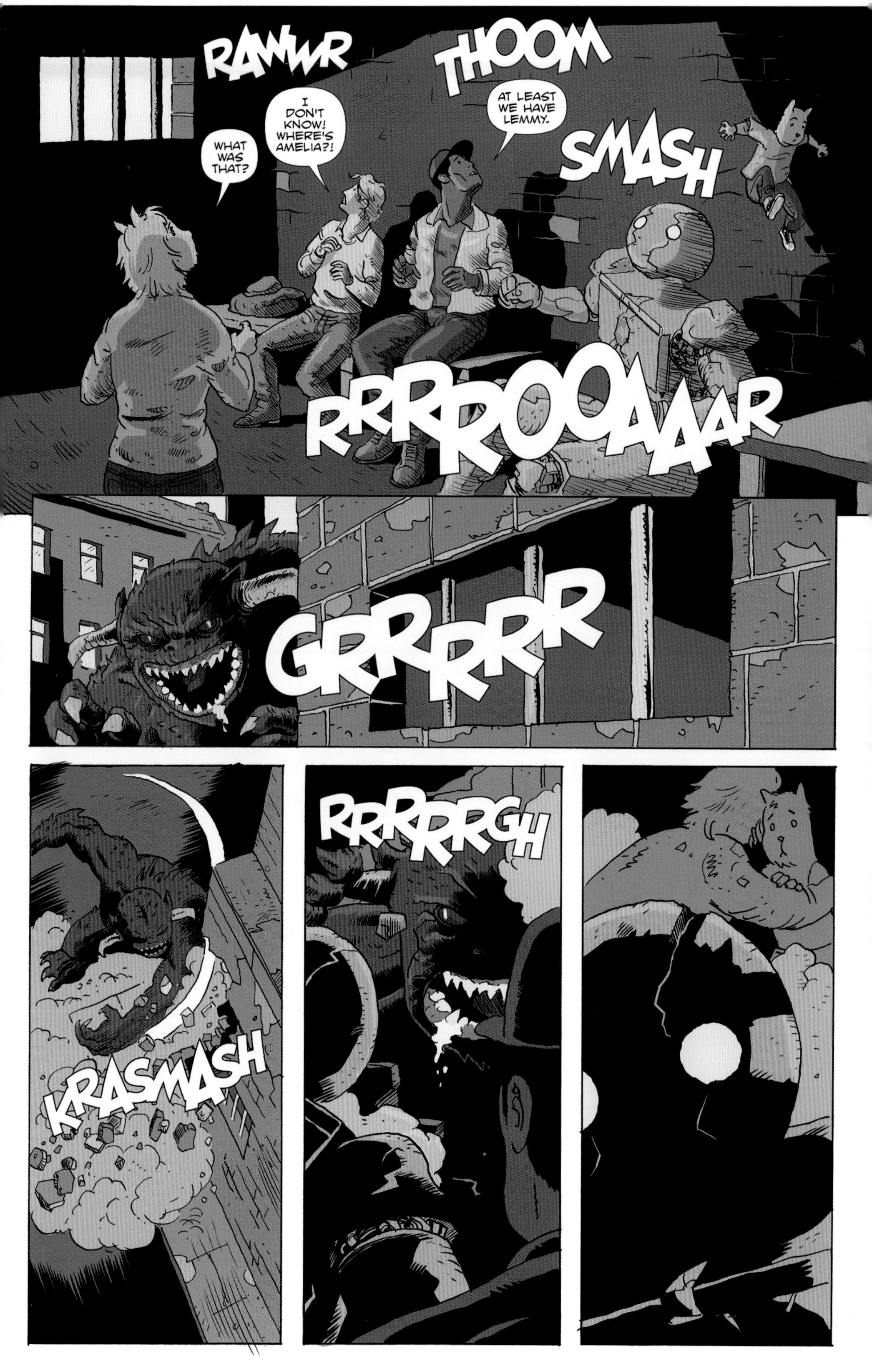
RAWWR
THOOM
WHAT WAS THAT?
I DON'T KNOW! WHERE'S AMELIA?!
AT LEAST WE HAVE LEMMY.
SMASH
RRRRROOAAAAR
GRRRRR
KRASMASH
RRRRRGH

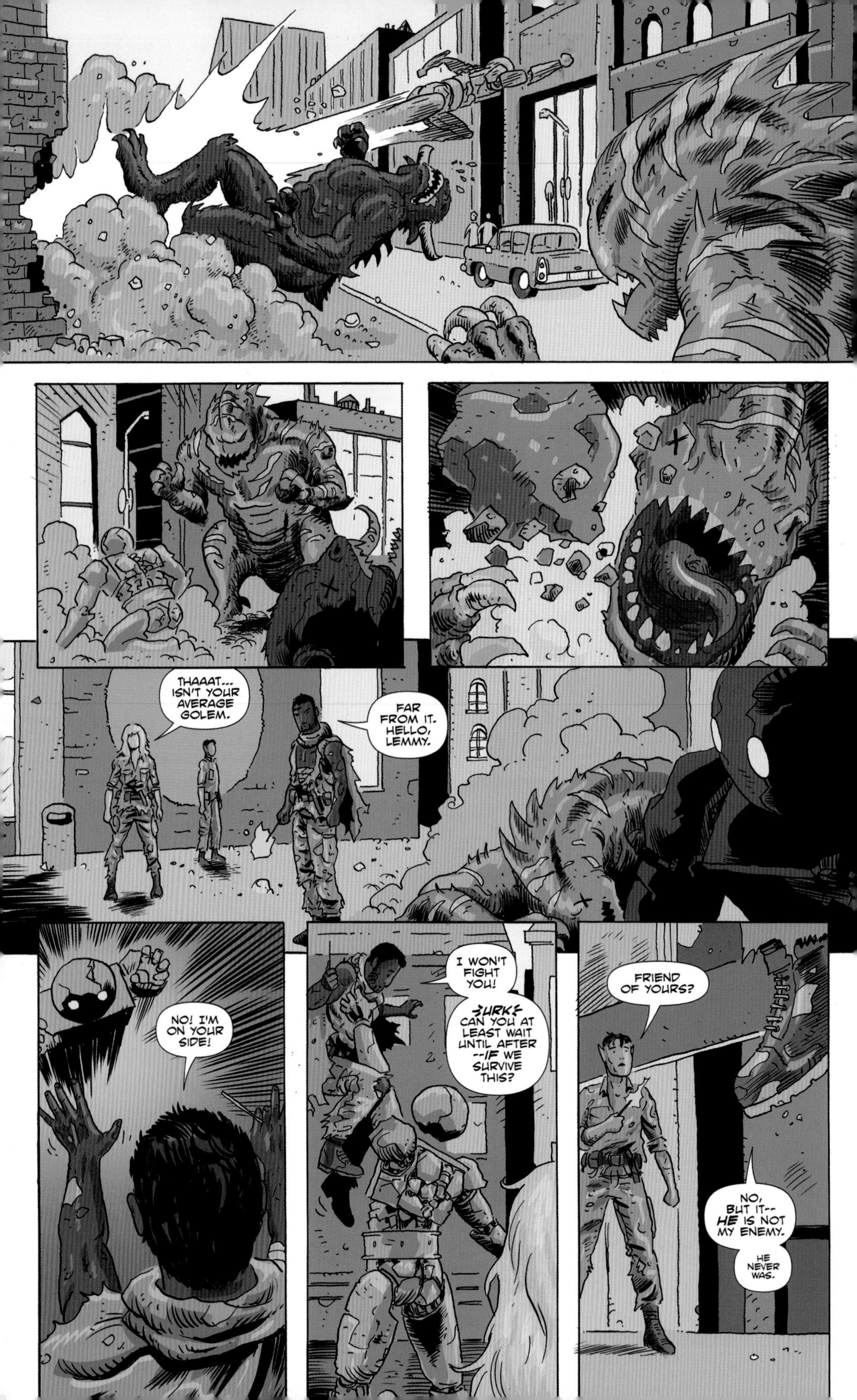
THAAAT... ISN'T YOUR AVERAGE GOLEM.
FAR FROM IT. HELLO, LEMMY.
NO! I'M ON YOUR SIDE!
I WON'T FIGHT YOU!
URK!
CAN YOU AT LEAST WAIT UNTIL AFTER --IF WE SURVIVE THIS?
FRIEND OF YOURS?
NO, BUT IT-- HE IS NOT MY ENEMY.
HE NEVER WAS.

WHO ARE YOU GUYS THEN? I RECOGNIZE THE OLD PROTECTOR, BUT...

AND LIKE HE SAID TO THE BIG GOLEM, MAYBE ALL THIS CAN WAIT UNTIL WE DEAL WITH THE MAGIC DEVOURING MONSTERS.

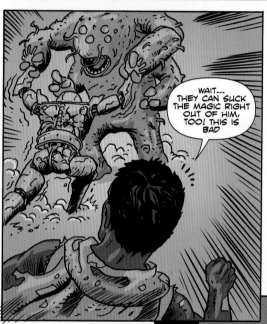

WAIT... THEY CAN SUCK THE MAGIC RIGHT OUT OF HIM, TOO! THIS IS BAD

WE'RE OMEGA COMPANY. THINGS NOT GOING OUR WAY IS STANDARD OPERATING PROCEDURE.

A CHANGE WOULD BE NICE, THOUGH.

WE NEED AMELIA!

THAT'S WHAT I'VE BEEN SAYING!

SO, THEY FEED OFF OF MAGIC?

GOOD THING WE LOT DON'T HAVE ANY.

NOT SURE THAT'S A "GOOD" THING...

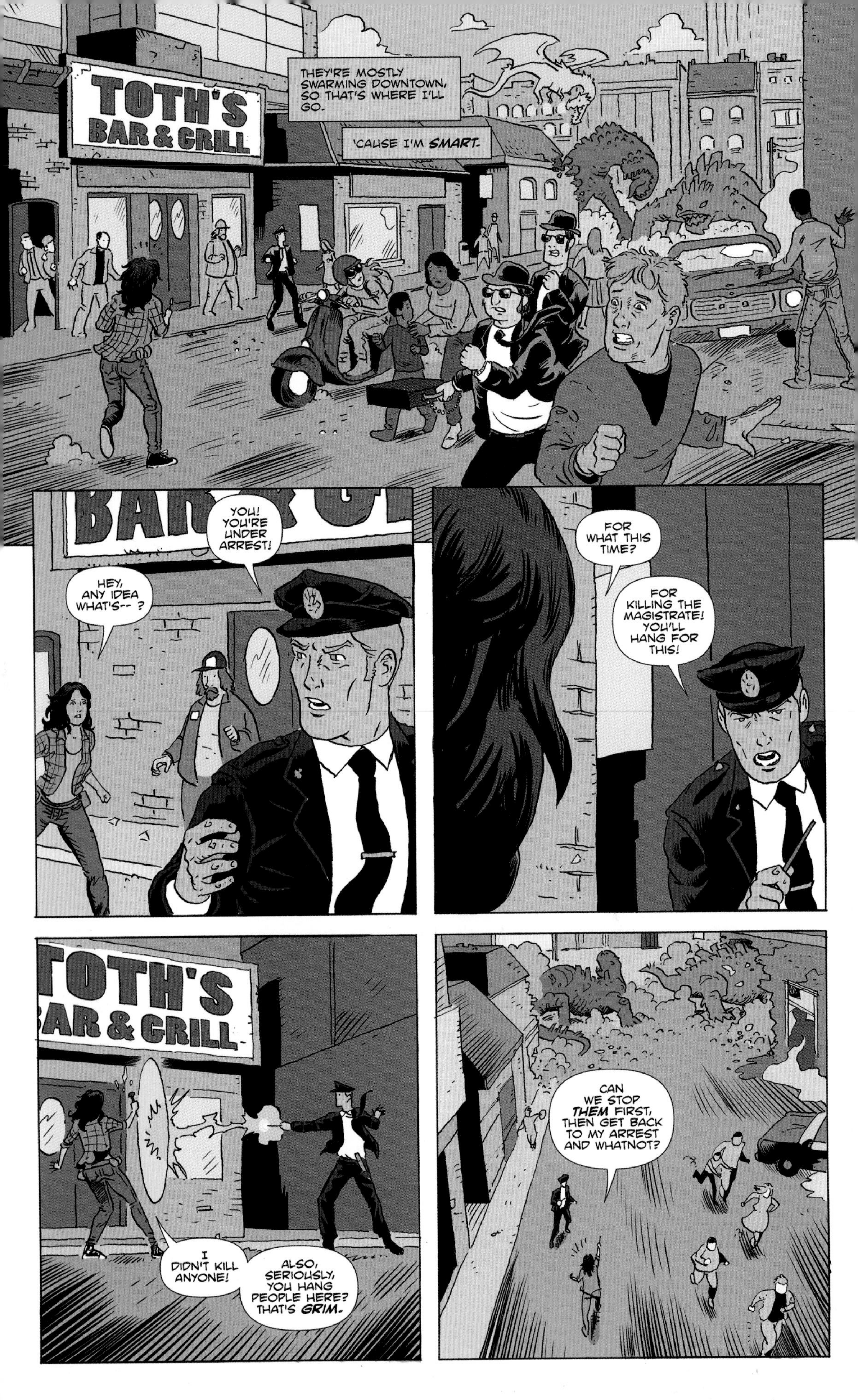
TOTH'S BAR & GRILL
THEY'RE MOSTLY SWARMING DOWNTOWN, SO THAT'S WHERE I'LL GO.
'CAUSE I'M SMART.
HEY, ANY IDEA WHAT'S-- ?
YOU! YOU'RE UNDER ARREST!
FOR WHAT THIS TIME?
FOR KILLING THE MAGISTRATE! YOU'LL HANG FOR THIS!
TOTH'S BAR & GRILL
I DIDN'T KILL ANYONE!
ALSO, SERIOUSLY, YOU HANG PEOPLE HERE? THAT'S GRIM.
CAN WE STOP THEM FIRST, THEN GET BACK TO MY ARREST AND WHATNOT?

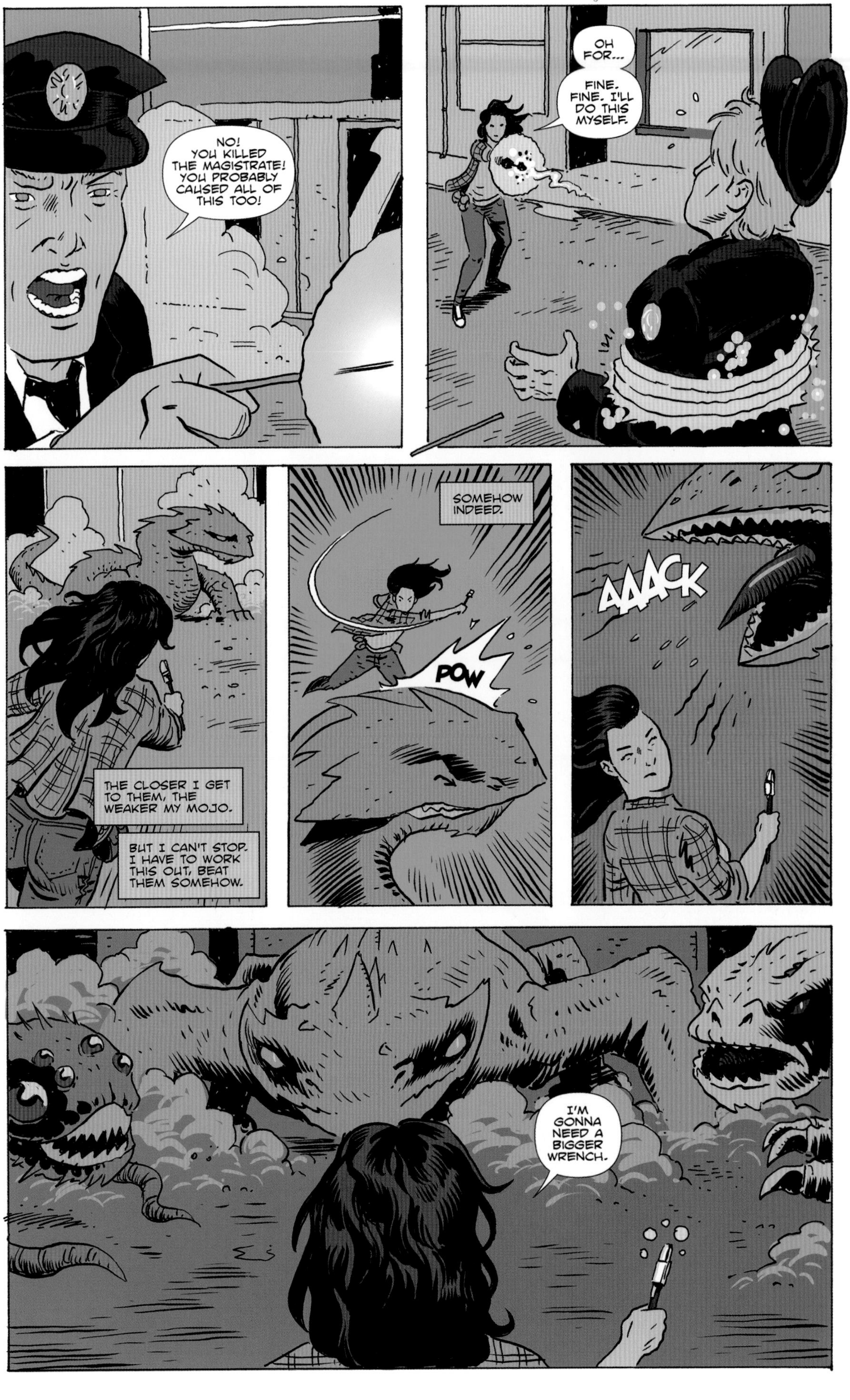
NO! YOU KILLED THE MAGISTRATE! YOU PROBABLY CAUSED ALL OF THIS TOO!
OH FOR...
FINE. FINE. I'LL DO THIS MYSELF.
THE CLOSER I GET TO THEM, THE WEAKER MY MOJO.
BUT I CAN'T STOP. I HAVE TO WORK THIS OUT, BEAT THEM SOMEHOW.
SOMEHOW INDEED.
POW
AAACK
I'M GONNA NEED A BIGGER WRENCH.

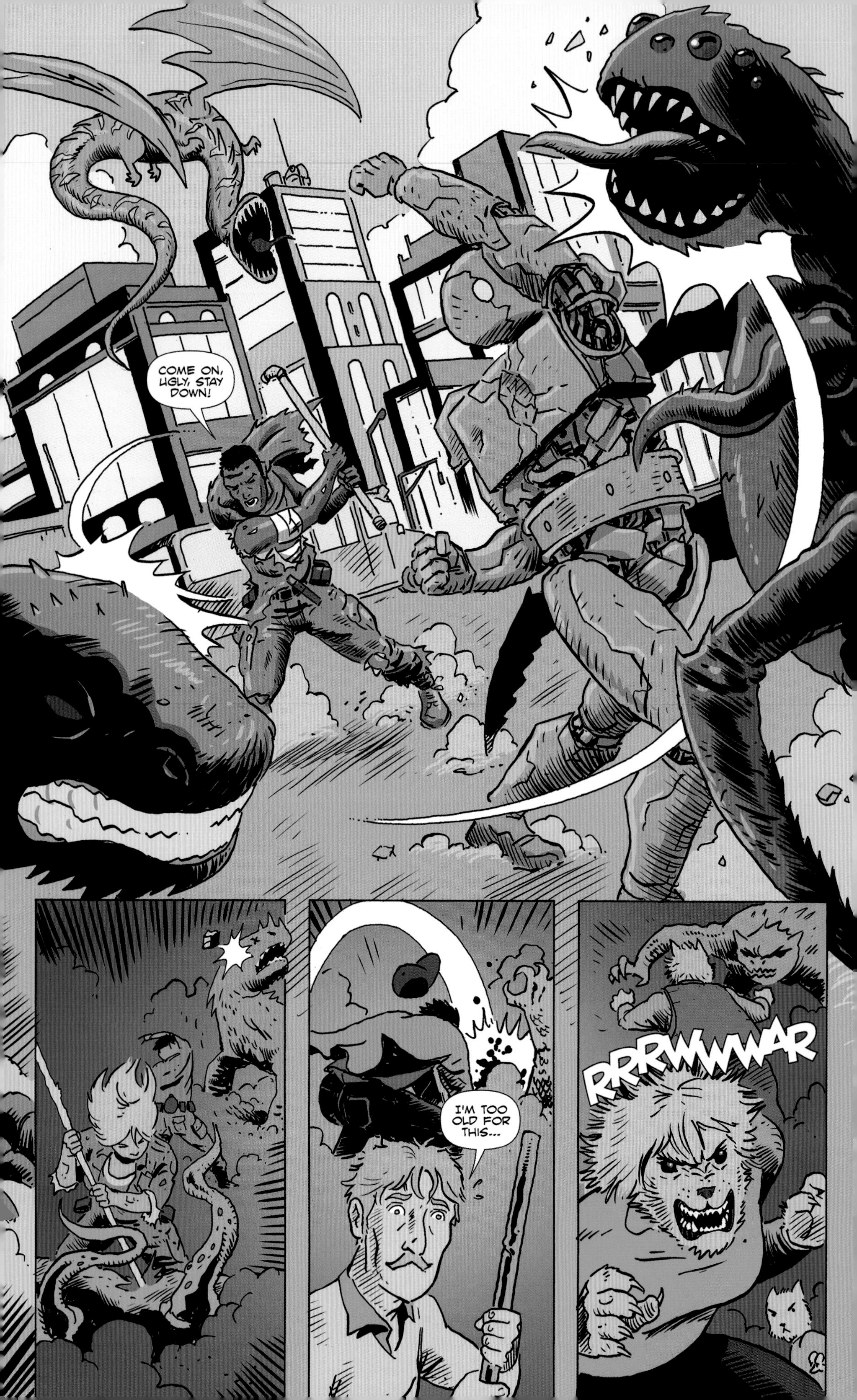
COME ON, UGLY, STAY DOWN!
I'M TOO OLD FOR THIS...
RRRWWWAR

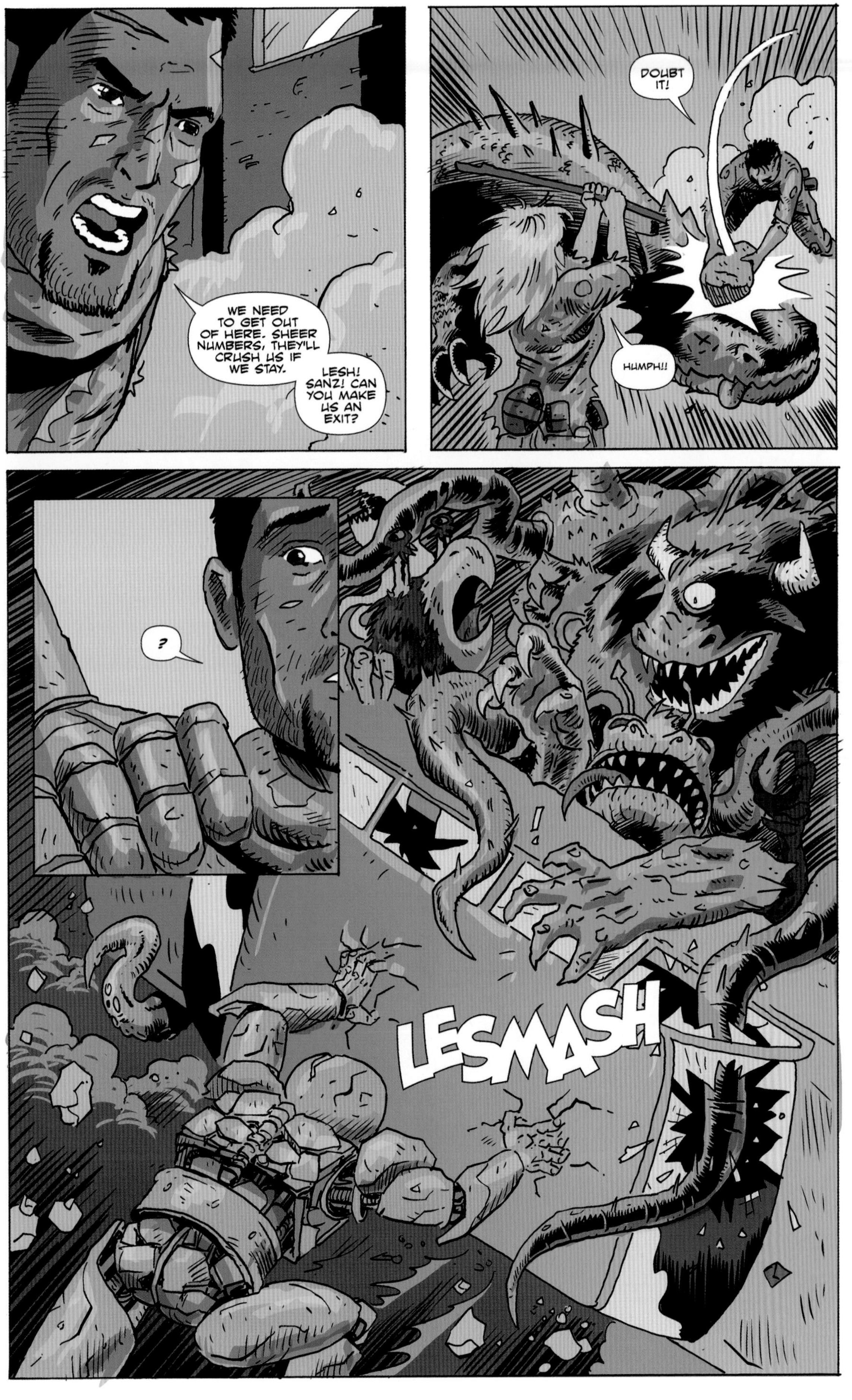
WE NEED TO GET OUT OF HERE. SHEER NUMBERS, THEY'LL CRUSH US IF WE STAY.
LESH! SANZ! CAN YOU MAKE US AN EXIT?
DOUBT IT!
HUMPH!!
?
LESMASH

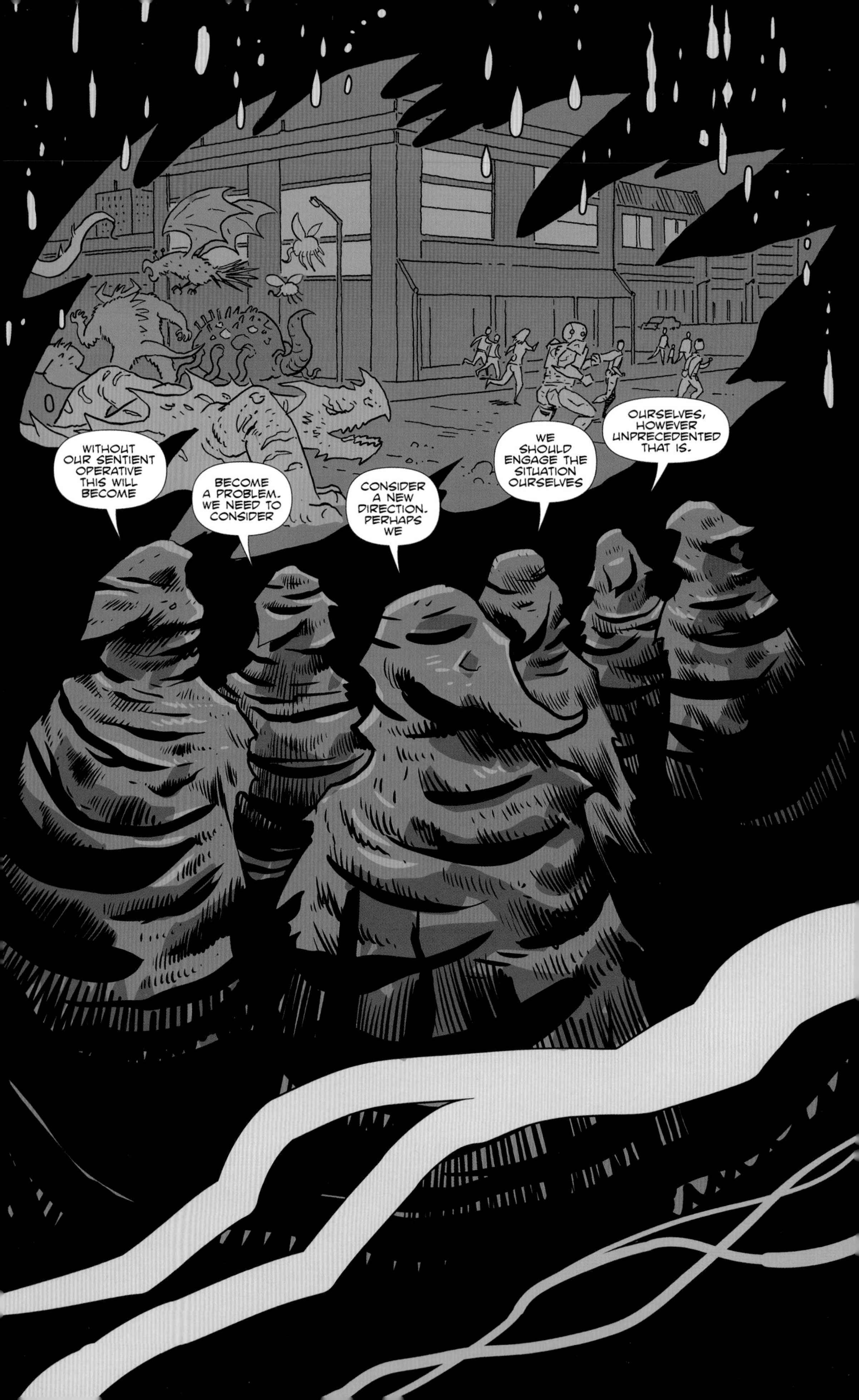
WITHOUT OUR SENTIENT OPERATIVE THIS WILL BECOME
BECOME A PROBLEM. WE NEED TO CONSIDER
CONSIDER A NEW DIRECTION. PERHAPS WE
WE SHOULD ENGAGE THE SITUATION OURSELVES
OURSELVES, HOWEVER UNPRECEDENTED THAT IS.

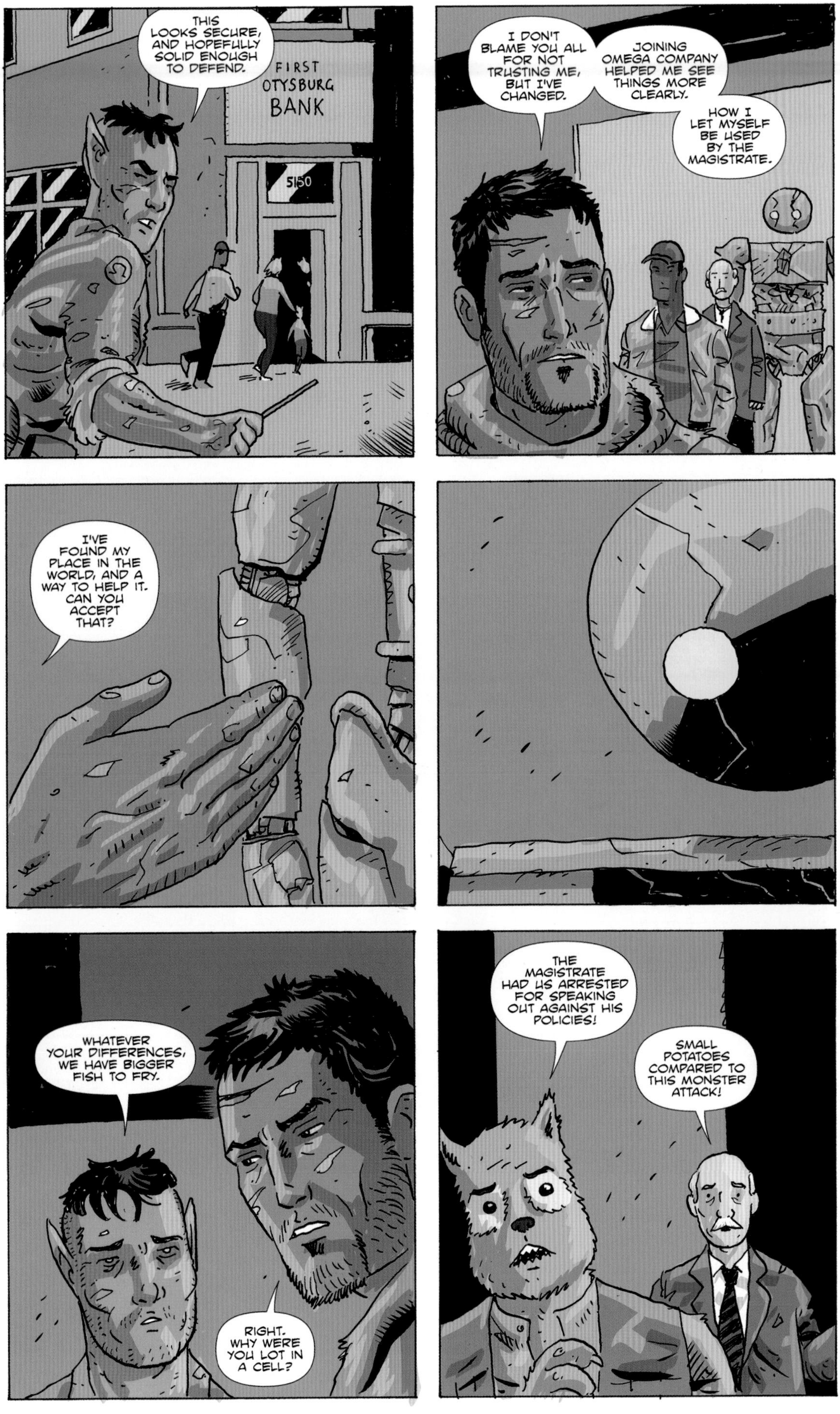
THIS LOOKS SECURE, AND HOPEFULLY SOLID ENOUGH TO DEFEND.
FIRST OTYSBURG BANK
5150
I DON'T BLAME YOU ALL FOR NOT TRUSTING ME, BUT I'VE CHANGED.
JOINING OMEGA COMPANY HELPED ME SEE THINGS MORE CLEARLY.
HOW I LET MYSELF BE USED BY THE MAGISTRATE.
I'VE FOUND MY PLACE IN THE WORLD, AND A WAY TO HELP IT. CAN YOU ACCEPT THAT?
WHATEVER YOUR DIFFERENCES, WE HAVE BIGGER FISH TO FRY.
RIGHT. WHY WERE YOU LOT IN A CELL?
THE MAGISTRATE HAD US ARRESTED FOR SPEAKING OUT AGAINST HIS POLICIES!
SMALL POTATOES COMPARED TO THIS MONSTER ATTACK!

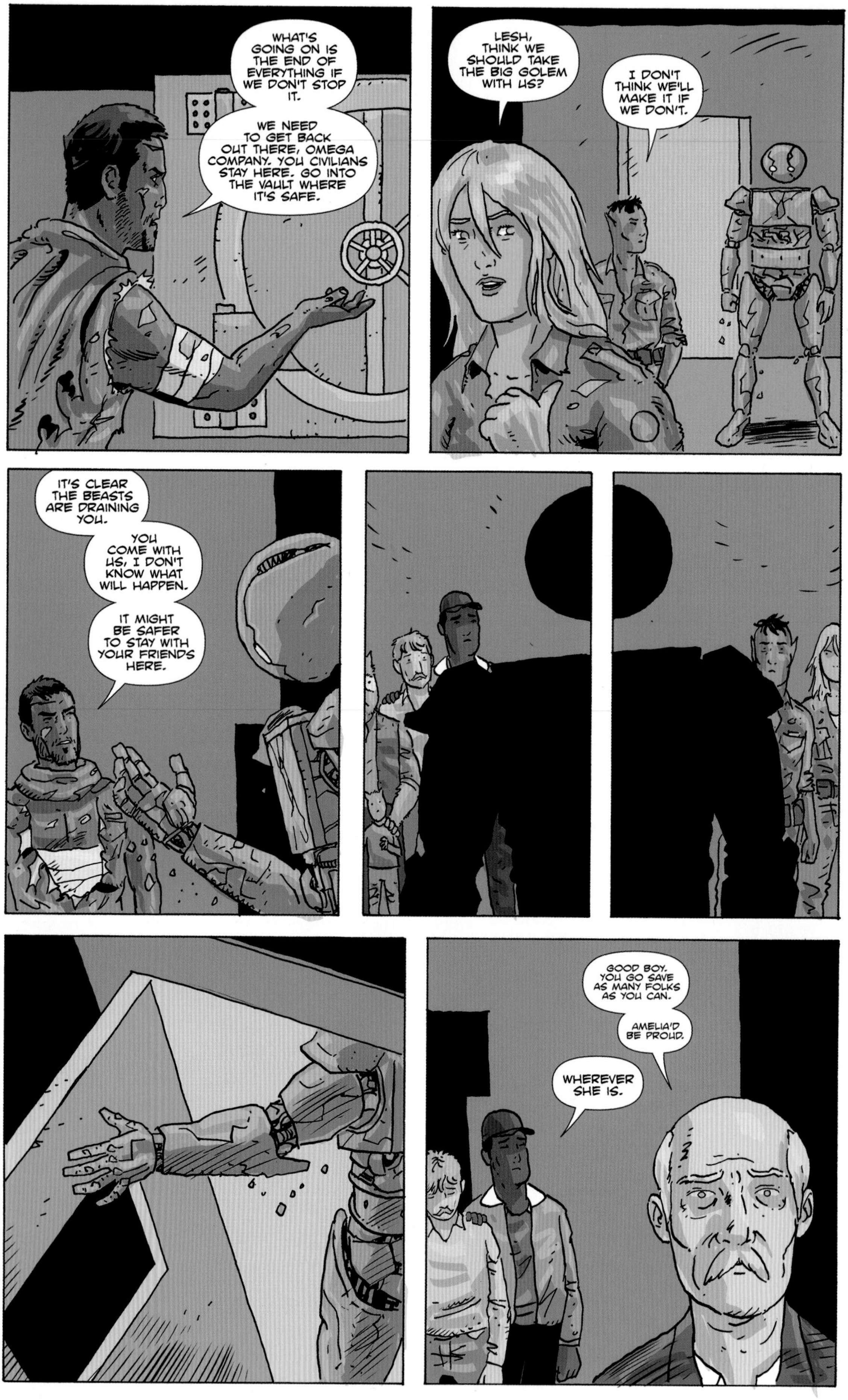
WHAT'S GOING ON IS THE END OF EVERYTHING IF WE DON'T STOP IT.
WE NEED TO GET BACK OUT THERE, OMEGA COMPANY. YOU CIVILIANS STAY HERE. GO INTO THE VAULT WHERE IT'S SAFE.
LESH, THINK WE SHOULD TAKE THE BIG GOLEM WITH US?
I DON'T THINK WE'LL MAKE IT IF WE DON'T.
IT'S CLEAR THE BEASTS ARE DRAINING YOU.
YOU COME WITH US, I DON'T KNOW WHAT WILL HAPPEN.
IT MIGHT BE SAFER TO STAY WITH YOUR FRIENDS HERE.
GOOD BOY. YOU GO SAVE AS MANY FOLKS AS YOU CAN.
AMELIA'D BE PROUD.
WHEREVER SHE IS.

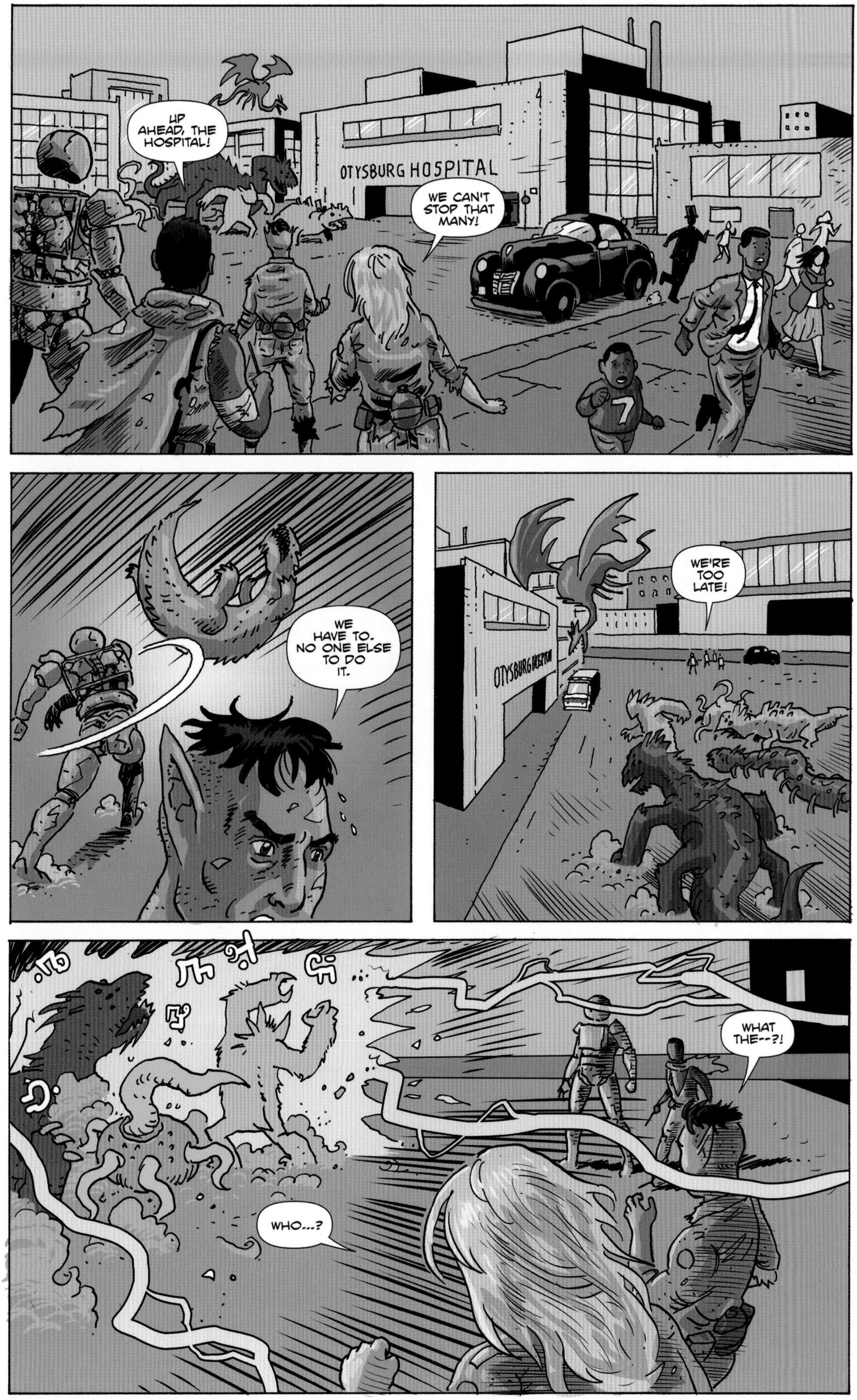
UP AHEAD, THE HOSPITAL!
OTYSBURG HOSPITAL
WE CAN'T STOP THAT MANY!
7
WE HAVE TO. NO ONE ELSE TO DO IT.
OTYSBURG
WE'RE TOO LATE!
WHAT THE--?!
WHO...?

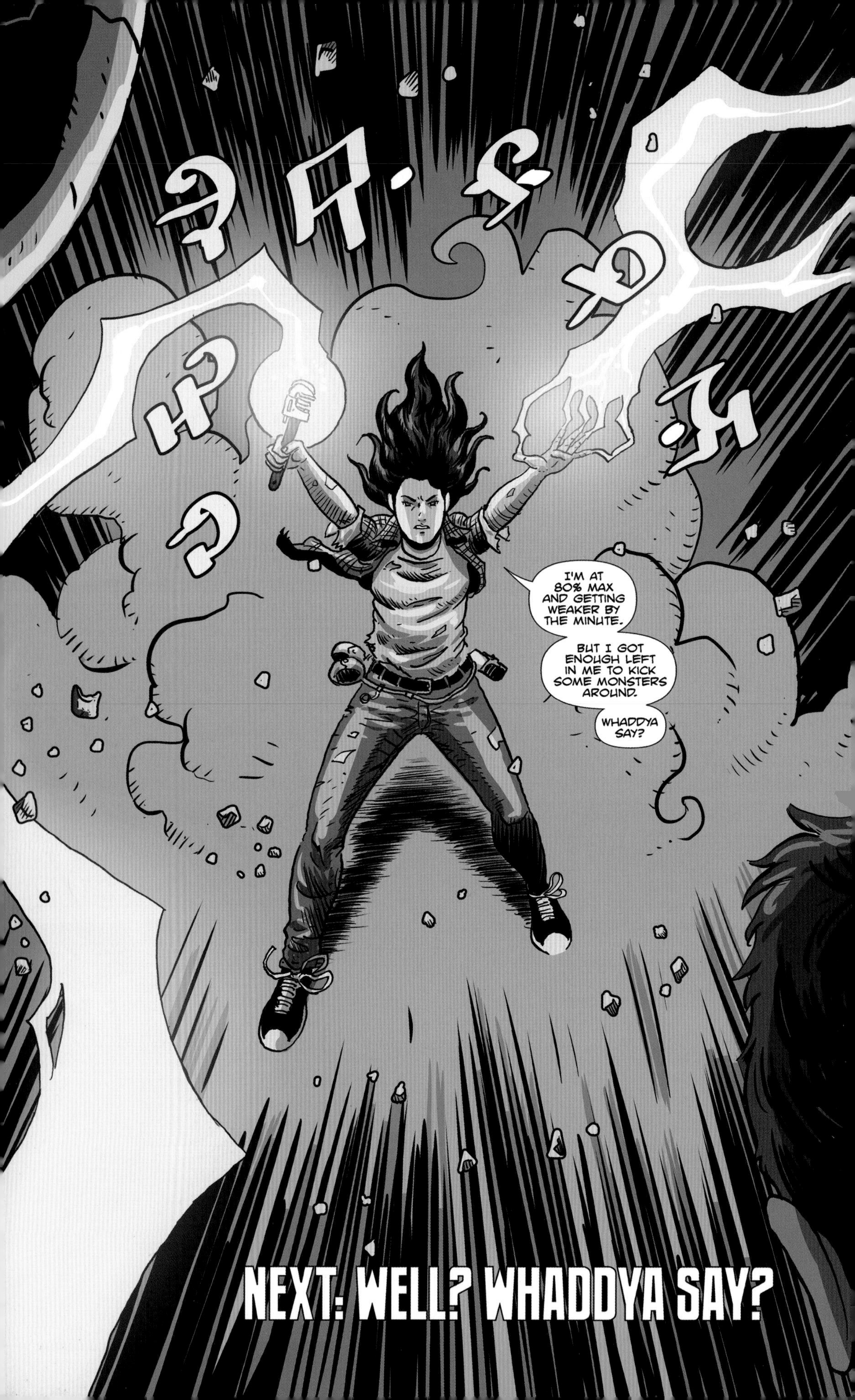
I'M AT 80% MAX AND GETTING WEAKER BY THE MINUTE.
BUT I GOT ENOUGH LEFT IN ME TO KICK SOME MONSTERS AROUND.
WHADDYA SAY?
NEXT: WELL? WHADDYA SAY?

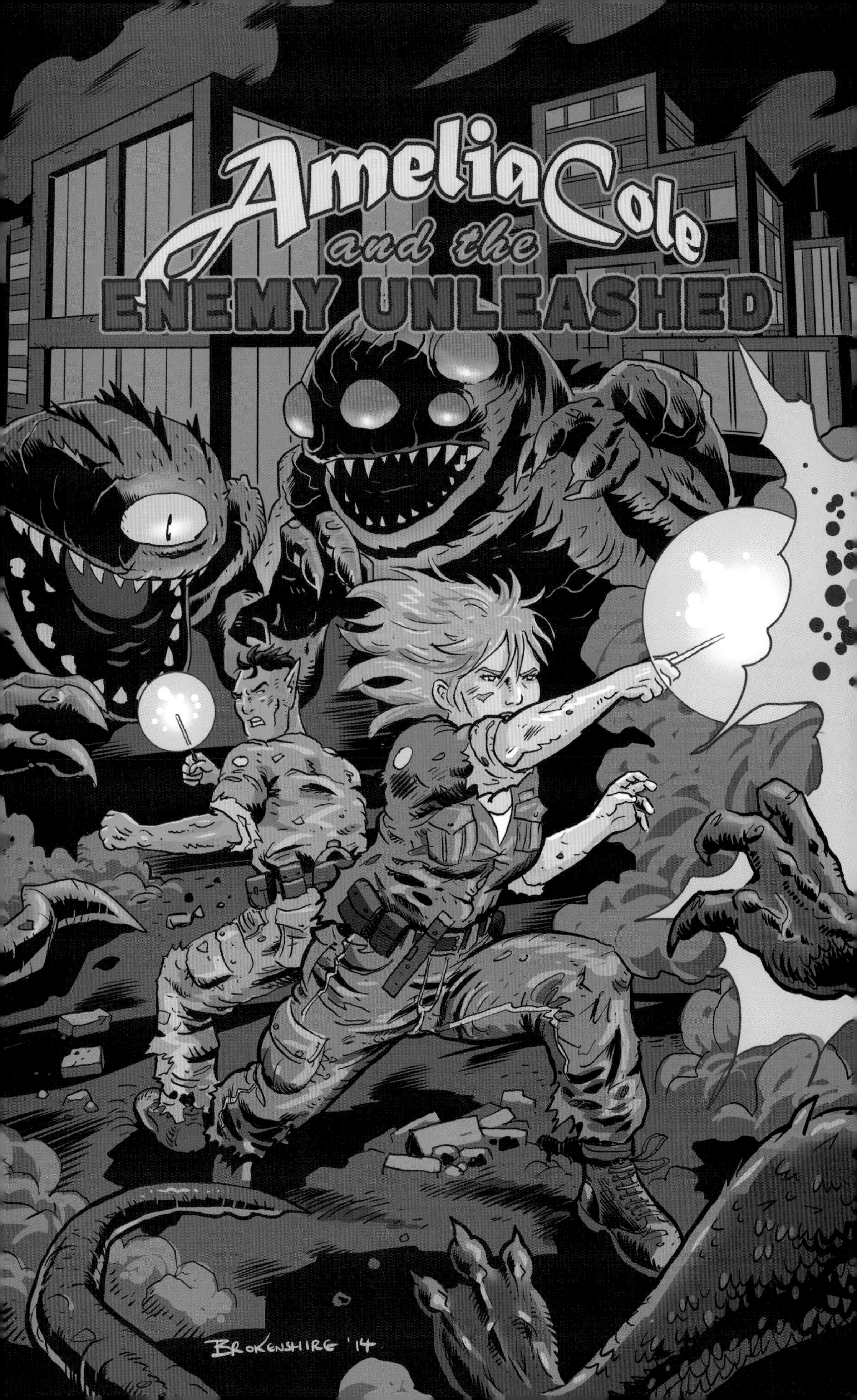
Amelia Cole
and the
ENEMY UNLEASHED
BROKENSHIRE '14

CHAPTER 5

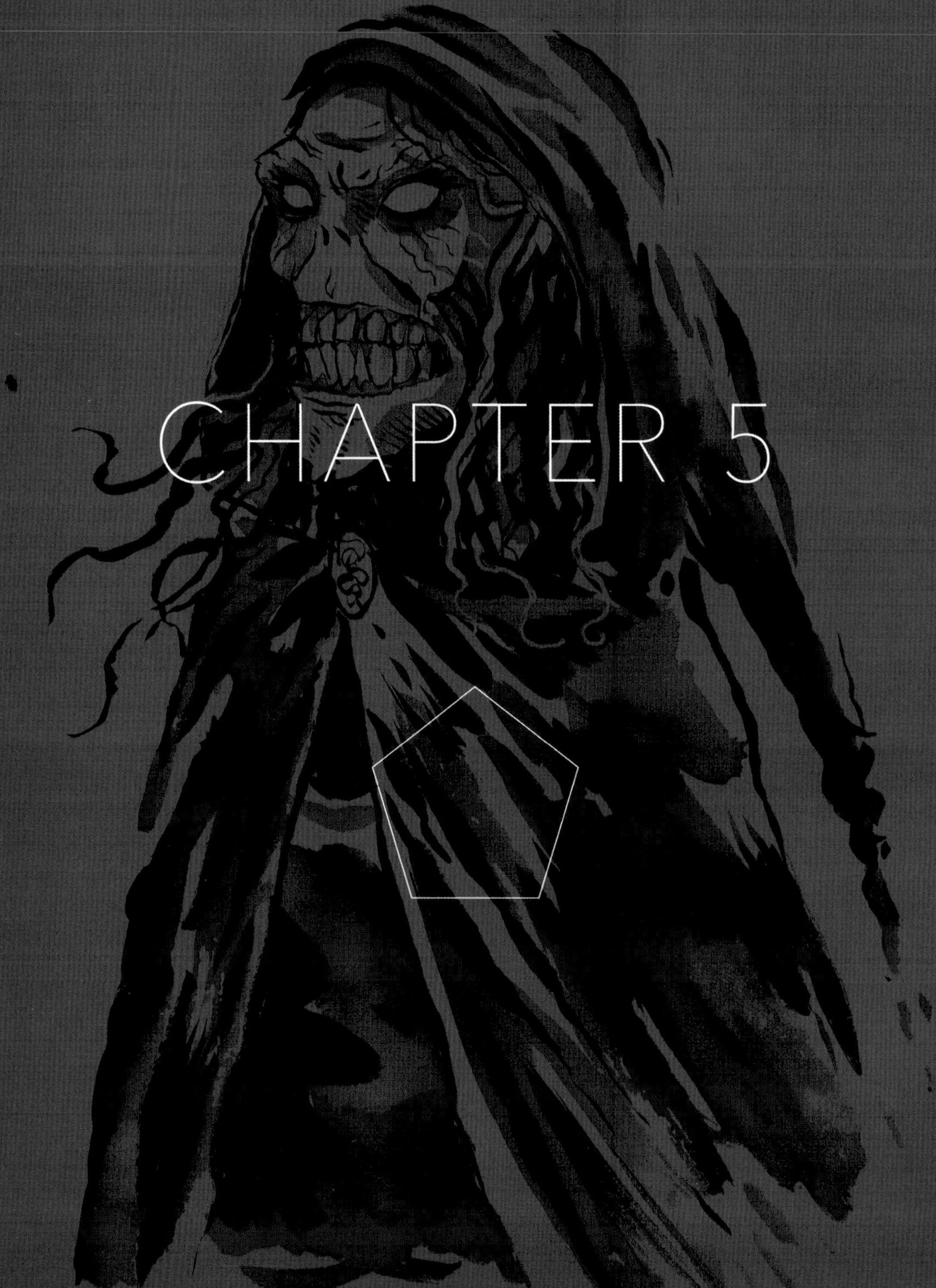
BROKENSHIRE '14

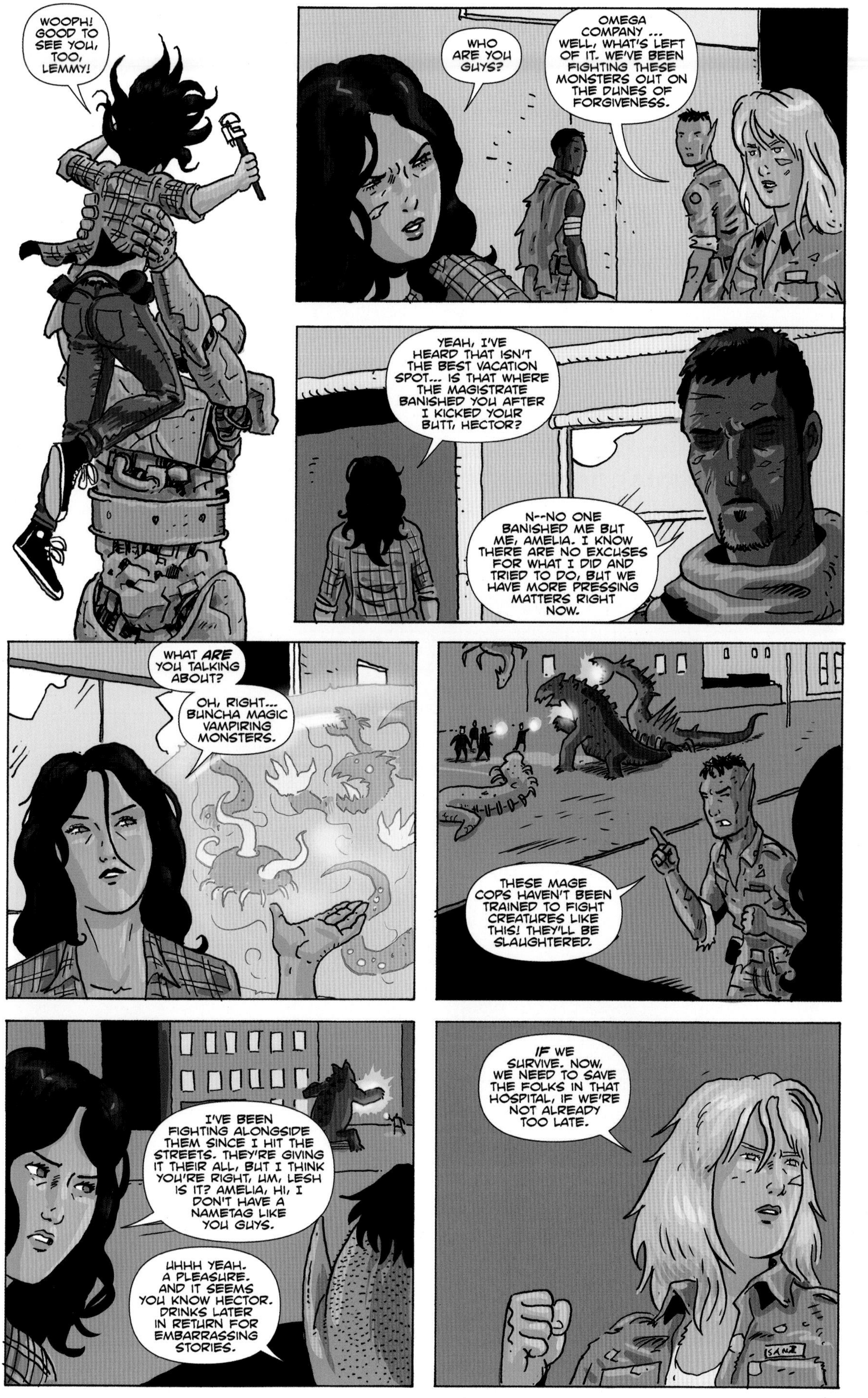
WOOPH! GOOD TO SEE YOU, TOO, LEMMY!
WHO ARE YOU GUYS?
OMEGA COMPANY ... WELL, WHAT'S LEFT OF IT. WE'VE BEEN FIGHTING THESE MONSTERS OUT ON THE DUNES OF FORGIVENESS.
YEAH, I'VE HEARD THAT ISN'T THE BEST VACATION SPOT... IS THAT WHERE THE MAGISTRATE BANISHED YOU AFTER I KICKED YOUR BUTT, HECTOR?
N--NO ONE BANISHED ME BUT ME, AMELIA. I KNOW THERE ARE NO EXCUSES FOR WHAT I DID AND TRIED TO DO, BUT WE HAVE MORE PRESSING MATTERS RIGHT NOW.
WHAT *ARE* YOU TALKING ABOUT?
OH, RIGHT... BUNCHA MAGIC VAMPIRING MONSTERS.
THESE MAGE COPS HAVEN'T BEEN TRAINED TO FIGHT CREATURES LIKE THIS! THEY'LL BE SLAUGHTERED.
I'VE BEEN FIGHTING ALONGSIDE THEM SINCE I HIT THE STREETS. THEY'RE GIVING IT THEIR ALL, BUT I THINK YOU'RE RIGHT, UM, LESH IS IT? AMELIA, HI, I DON'T HAVE A NAMETAG LIKE YOU GUYS.
UHHH YEAH. A PLEASURE. AND IT SEEMS YOU KNOW HECTOR. DRINKS LATER IN RETURN FOR EMBARRASSING STORIES.
IF WE SURVIVE. NOW, WE NEED TO SAVE THE FOLKS IN THAT HOSPITAL, IF WE'RE NOT ALREADY TOO LATE.
SANZ

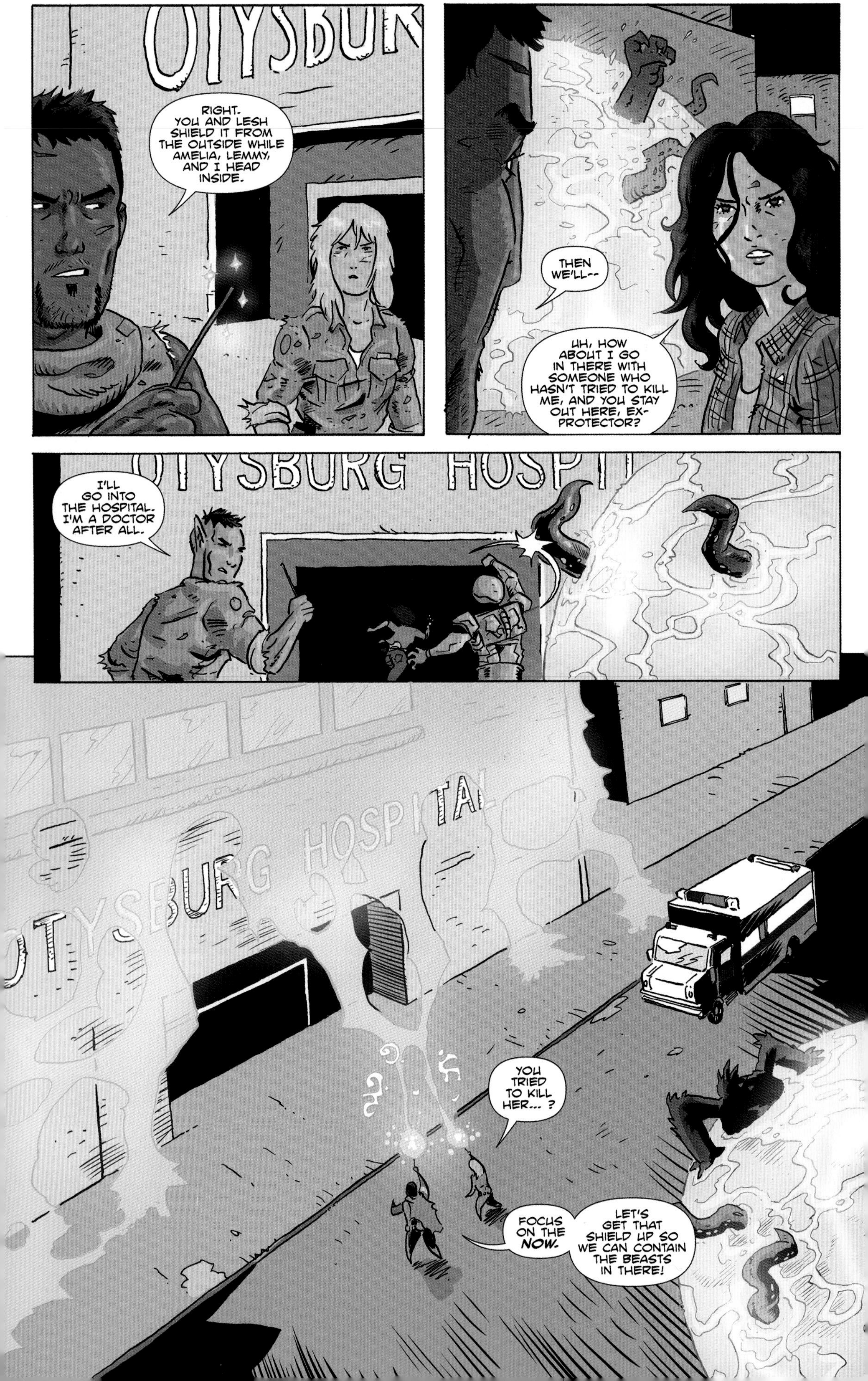
OTYSBUR
RIGHT. YOU AND LESH SHIELD IT FROM THE OUTSIDE WHILE AMELIA, LEMMY, AND I HEAD INSIDE.
THEN WE'LL--
UH, HOW ABOUT I GO IN THERE WITH SOMEONE WHO HASN'T TRIED TO KILL ME, AND YOU STAY OUT HERE, EX-PROTECTOR?
OTYSBURG HOSPIT
I'LL GO INTO THE HOSPITAL. I'M A DOCTOR AFTER ALL.
OTYSBURG HOSPITAL
YOU TRIED TO KILL HER... ?
FOCUS ON THE NOW.
LET'S GET THAT SHIELD UP SO WE CAN CONTAIN THE BEASTS IN THERE!

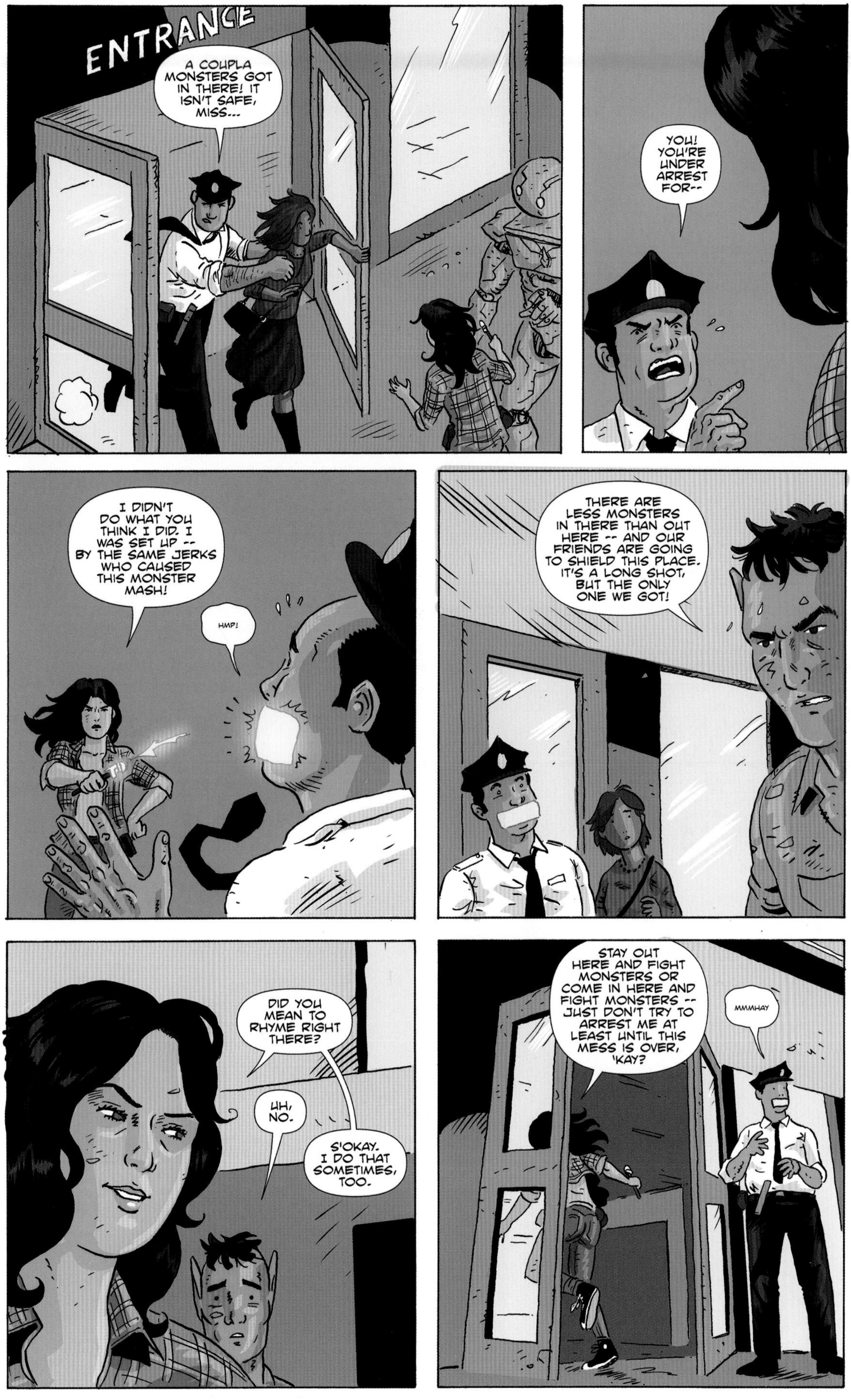
ENTRANCE
A COUPLA MONSTERS GOT IN THERE! IT ISN'T SAFE, MISS...
YOU! YOU'RE UNDER ARREST FOR--
I DIDN'T DO WHAT YOU THINK I DID. I WAS SET UP -- BY THE SAME JERKS WHO CAUSED THIS MONSTER MASH!
HMP!
THERE ARE LESS MONSTERS IN THERE THAN OUT HERE -- AND OUR FRIENDS ARE GOING TO SHIELD THIS PLACE. IT'S A LONG SHOT, BUT THE ONLY ONE WE GOT!
DID YOU MEAN TO RHYME RIGHT THERE?
UH, NO.
S'OKAY. I DO THAT SOMETIMES, TOO.
STAY OUT HERE AND FIGHT MONSTERS OR COME IN HERE AND FIGHT MONSTERS -- JUST DON'T TRY TO ARREST ME AT LEAST UNTIL THIS MESS IS OVER, 'KAY?
MMMHAY

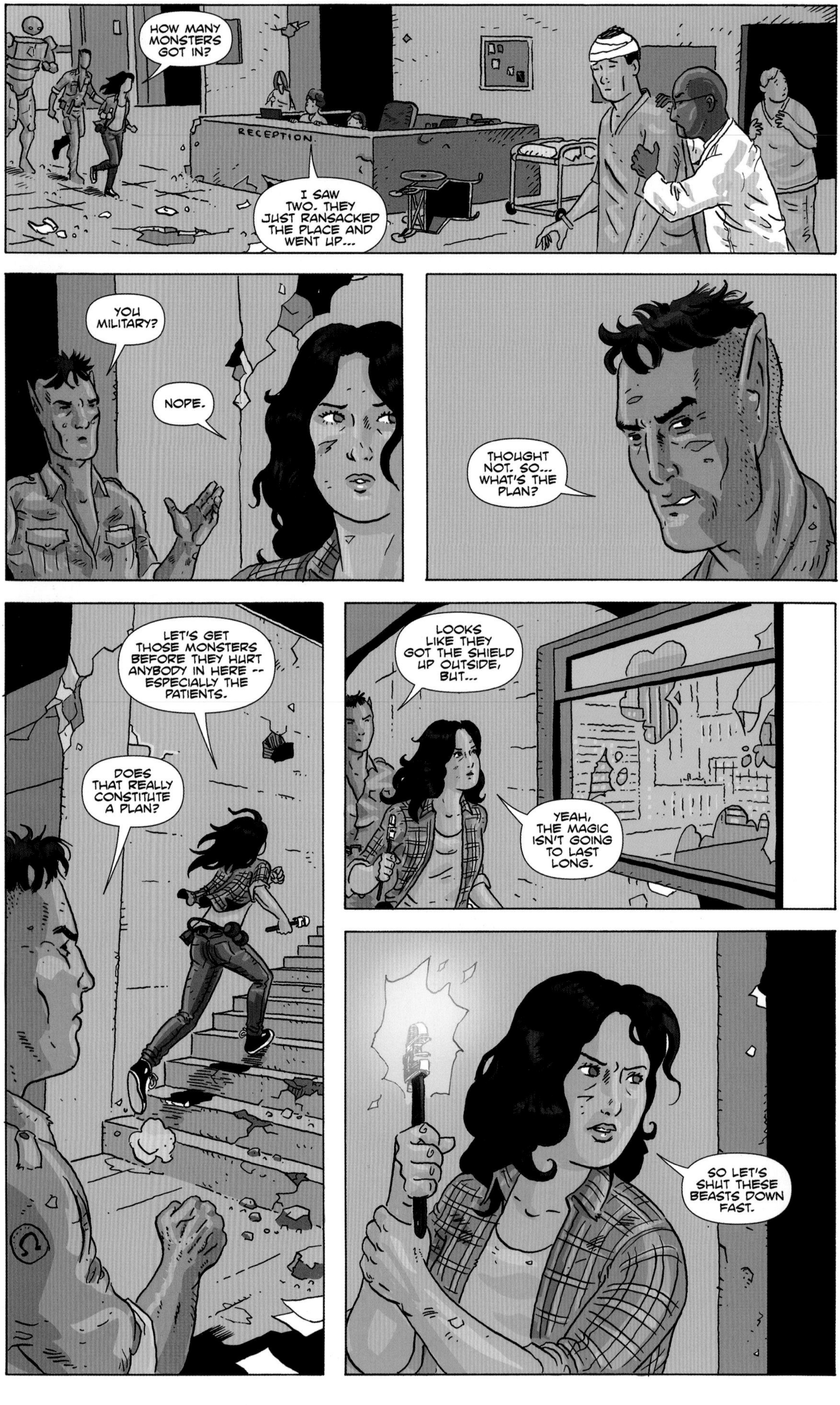
HOW MANY MONSTERS GOT IN?
I SAW TWO. THEY JUST RANSACKED THE PLACE AND WENT UP...
RECEPTION
YOU MILITARY?
NOPE.
THOUGHT NOT. SO... WHAT'S THE PLAN?
LET'S GET THOSE MONSTERS BEFORE THEY HURT ANYBODY IN HERE -- ESPECIALLY THE PATIENTS.
DOES THAT REALLY CONSTITUTE A PLAN?
LOOKS LIKE THEY GOT THE SHIELD UP OUTSIDE, BUT...
YEAH, THE MAGIC ISN'T GOING TO LAST LONG.
SO LET'S SHUT THESE BEASTS DOWN FAST.

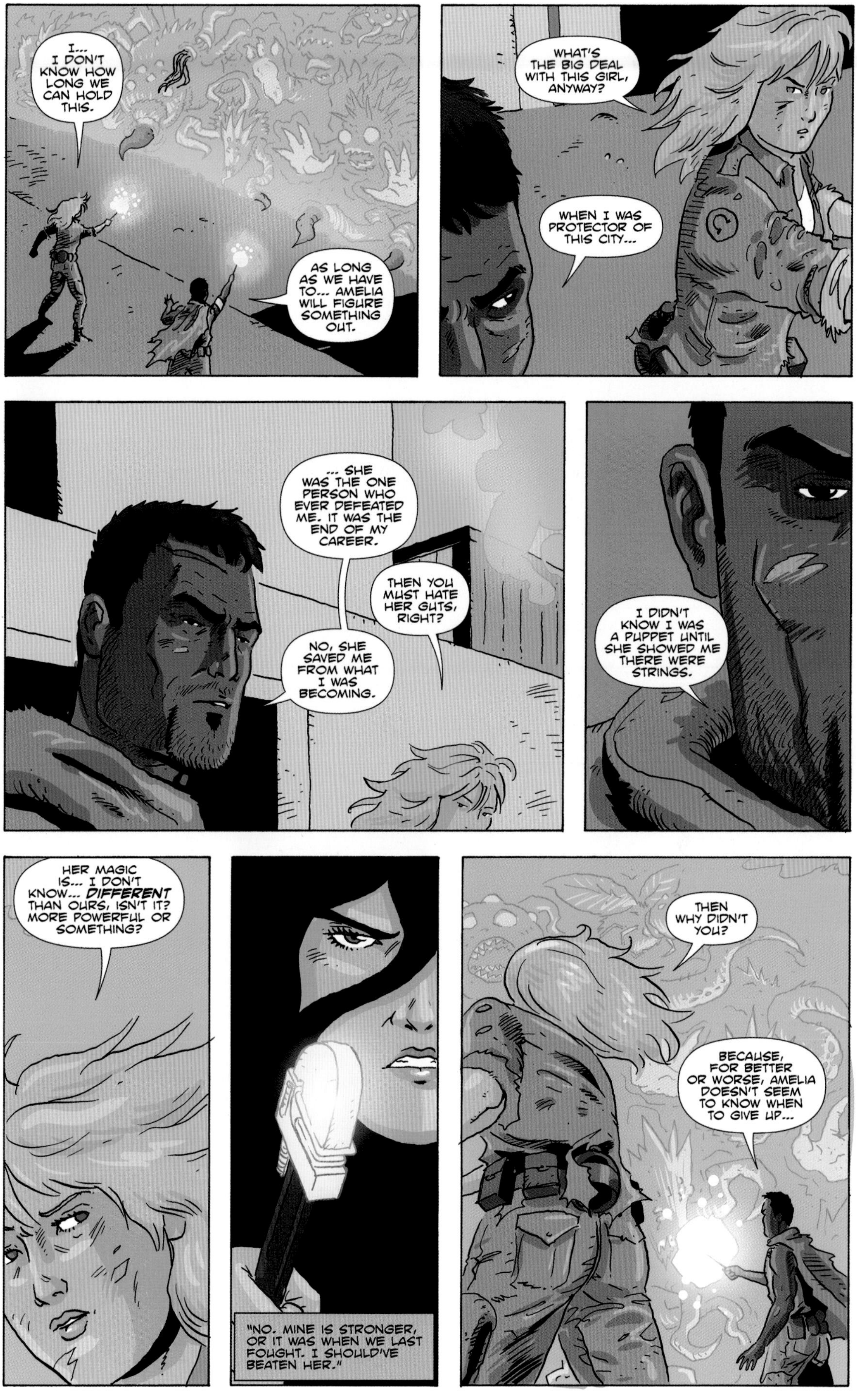
I... I DON'T KNOW HOW LONG WE CAN HOLD THIS.
AS LONG AS WE HAVE TO... AMELIA WILL FIGURE SOMETHING OUT.
WHAT'S THE BIG DEAL WITH THIS GIRL, ANYWAY?
WHEN I WAS PROTECTOR OF THIS CITY...
... SHE WAS THE ONE PERSON WHO EVER DEFEATED ME. IT WAS THE END OF MY CAREER.
THEN YOU MUST HATE HER GUTS, RIGHT?
NO, SHE SAVED ME FROM WHAT I WAS BECOMING.
I DIDN'T KNOW I WAS A PUPPET UNTIL SHE SHOWED ME THERE WERE STRINGS.
HER MAGIC IS... I DON'T KNOW... *DIFFERENT* THAN OURS, ISN'T IT? MORE POWERFUL OR SOMETHING?
"NO. MINE IS STRONGER, OR IT WAS WHEN WE LAST FOUGHT. I SHOULD'VE BEATEN HER."
THEN WHY DIDN'T YOU?
BECAUSE, FOR BETTER OR WORSE, AMELIA DOESN'T SEEM TO KNOW WHEN TO GIVE UP...

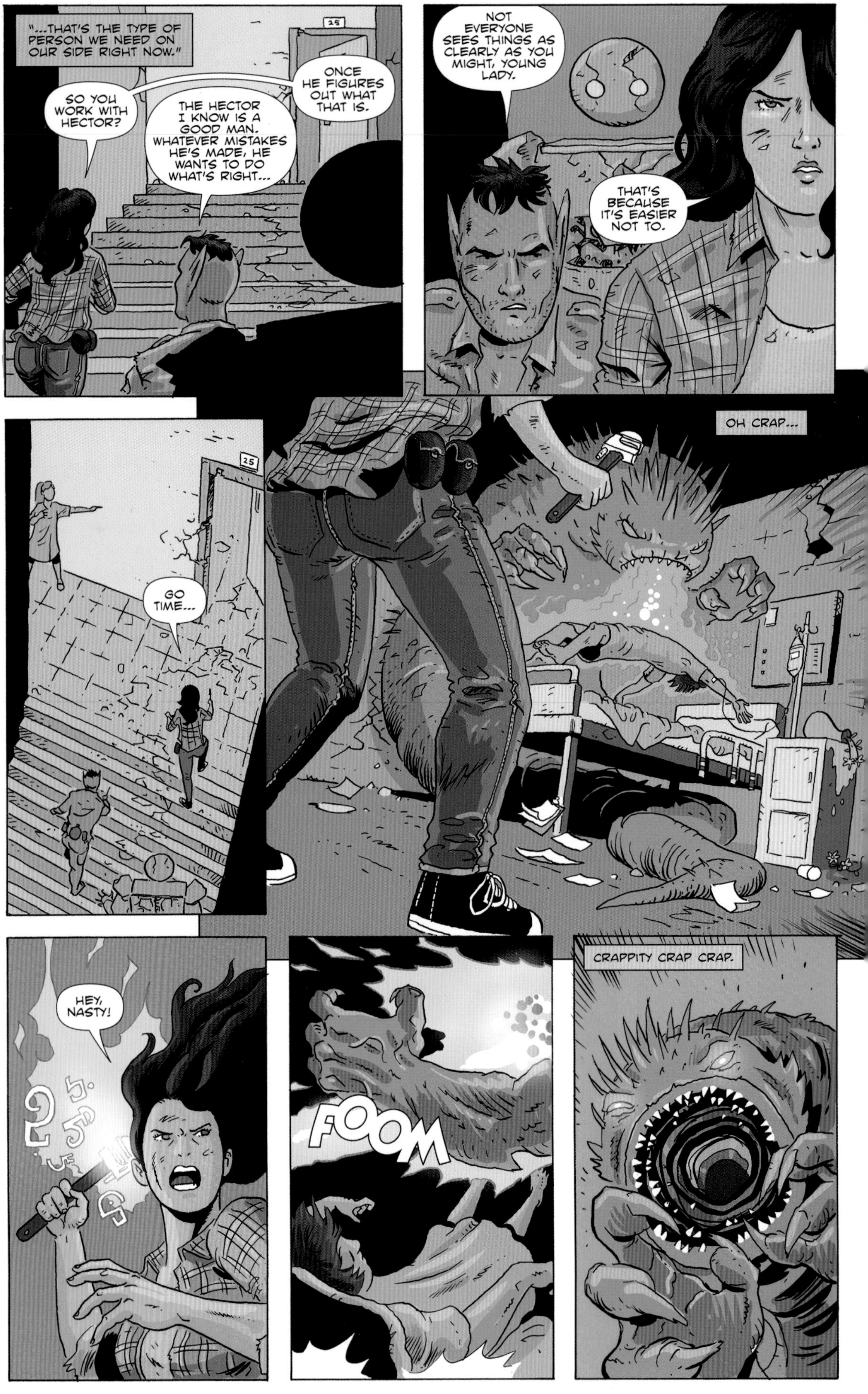
"...THAT'S THE TYPE OF PERSON WE NEED ON OUR SIDE RIGHT NOW."
SO YOU WORK WITH HECTOR?
THE HECTOR I KNOW IS A GOOD MAN. WHATEVER MISTAKES HE'S MADE, HE WANTS TO DO WHAT'S RIGHT...
ONCE HE FIGURES OUT WHAT THAT IS.
25
NOT EVERYONE SEES THINGS AS CLEARLY AS YOU MIGHT, YOUNG LADY.
THAT'S BECAUSE IT'S EASIER NOT TO.
25
GO TIME...
OH CRAP...
HEY, NASTY!
FOOM
CRAPPITY CRAP CRAP.

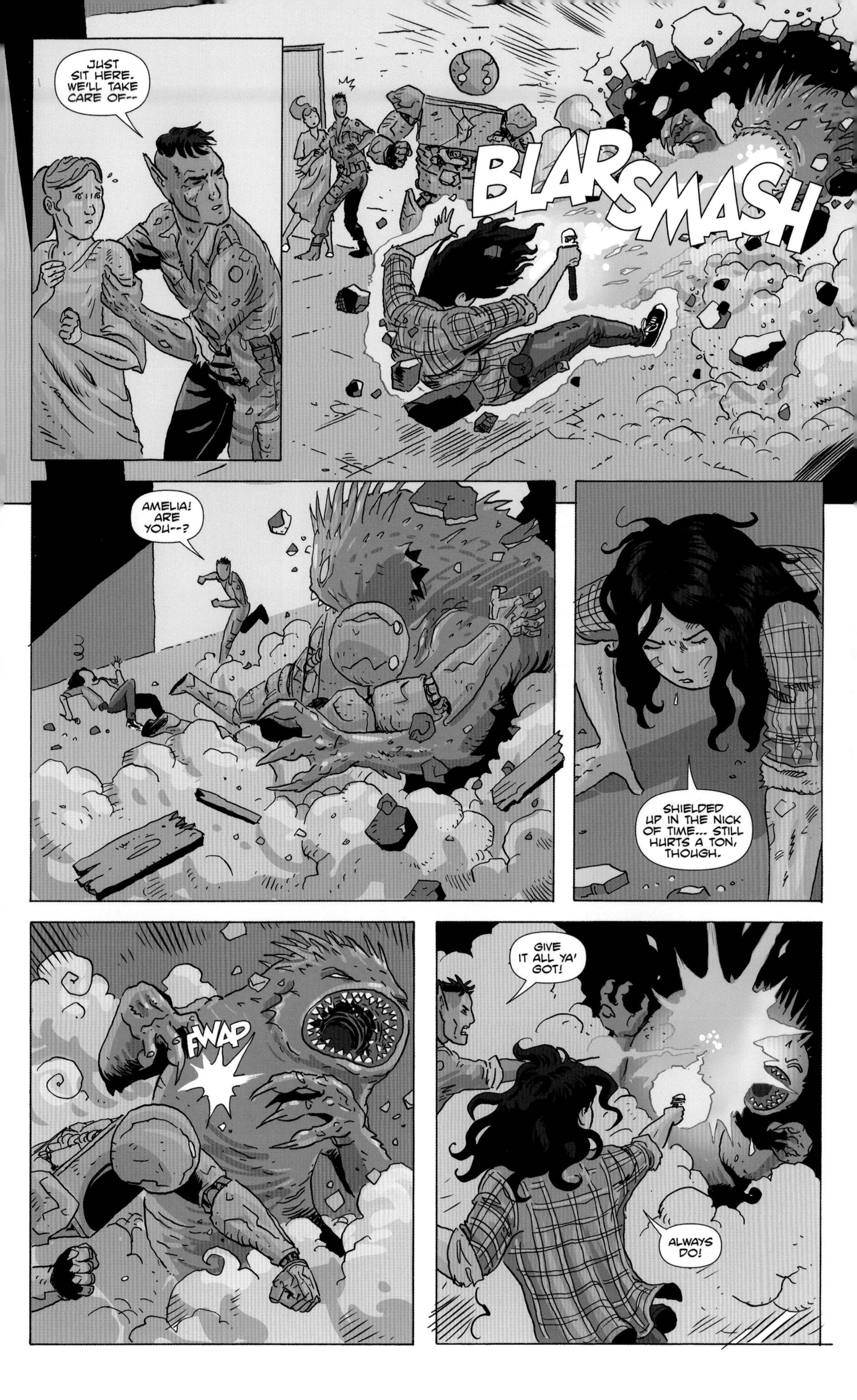
JUST SIT HERE. WE'LL TAKE CARE OF--
BLARSMASH
AMELIA! ARE YOU--?
SHIELDED UP IN THE NICK OF TIME... STILL HURTS A TON, THOUGH.
FWAP
GIVE IT ALL YA' GOT!
ALWAYS DO!

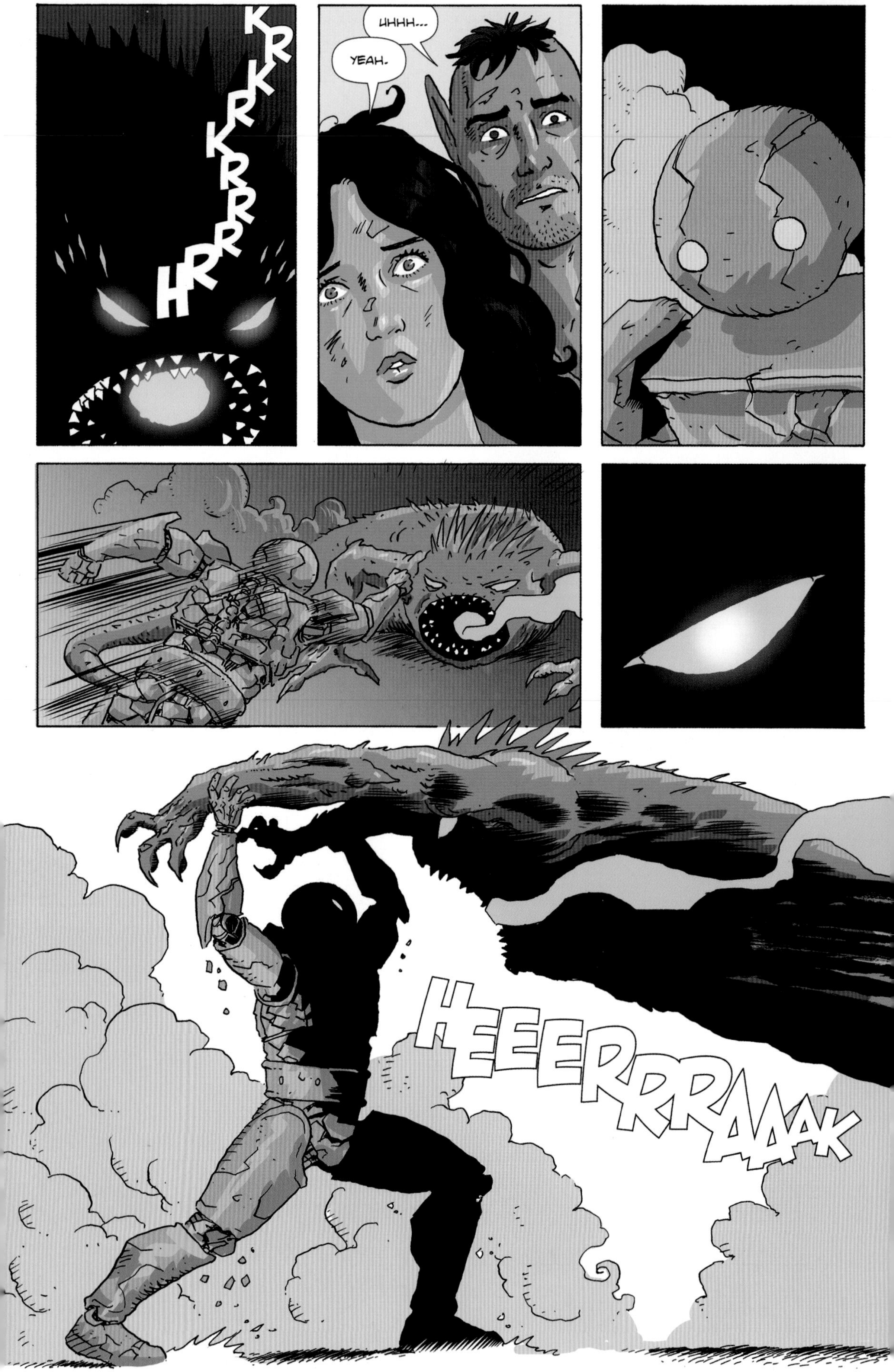
KRKRKRRRRHRRR
UHHH...
YEAH.
HEEERRRRAAAK

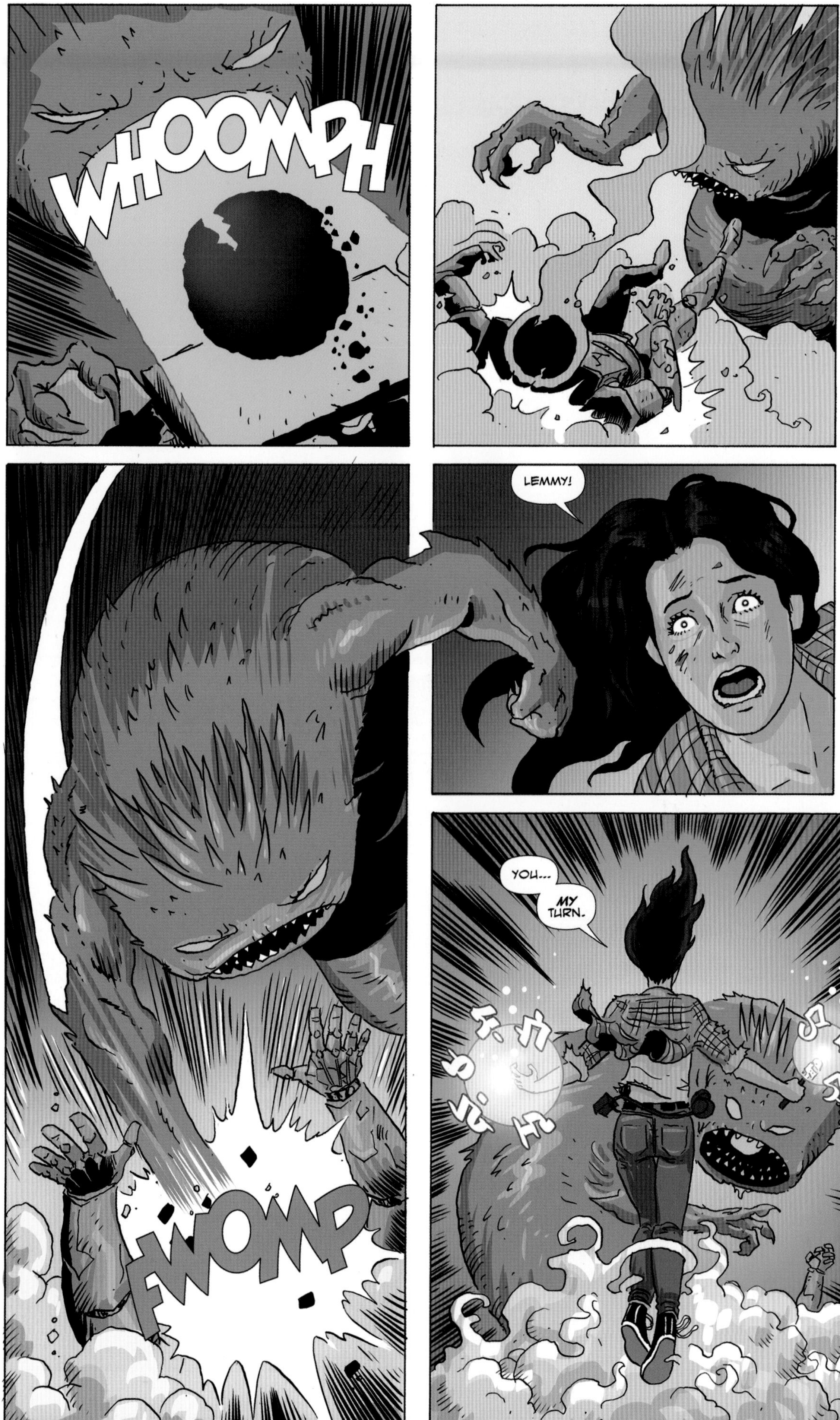
WHOOMPH
LEMMY!
FWOMP
YOU...
MY TURN.

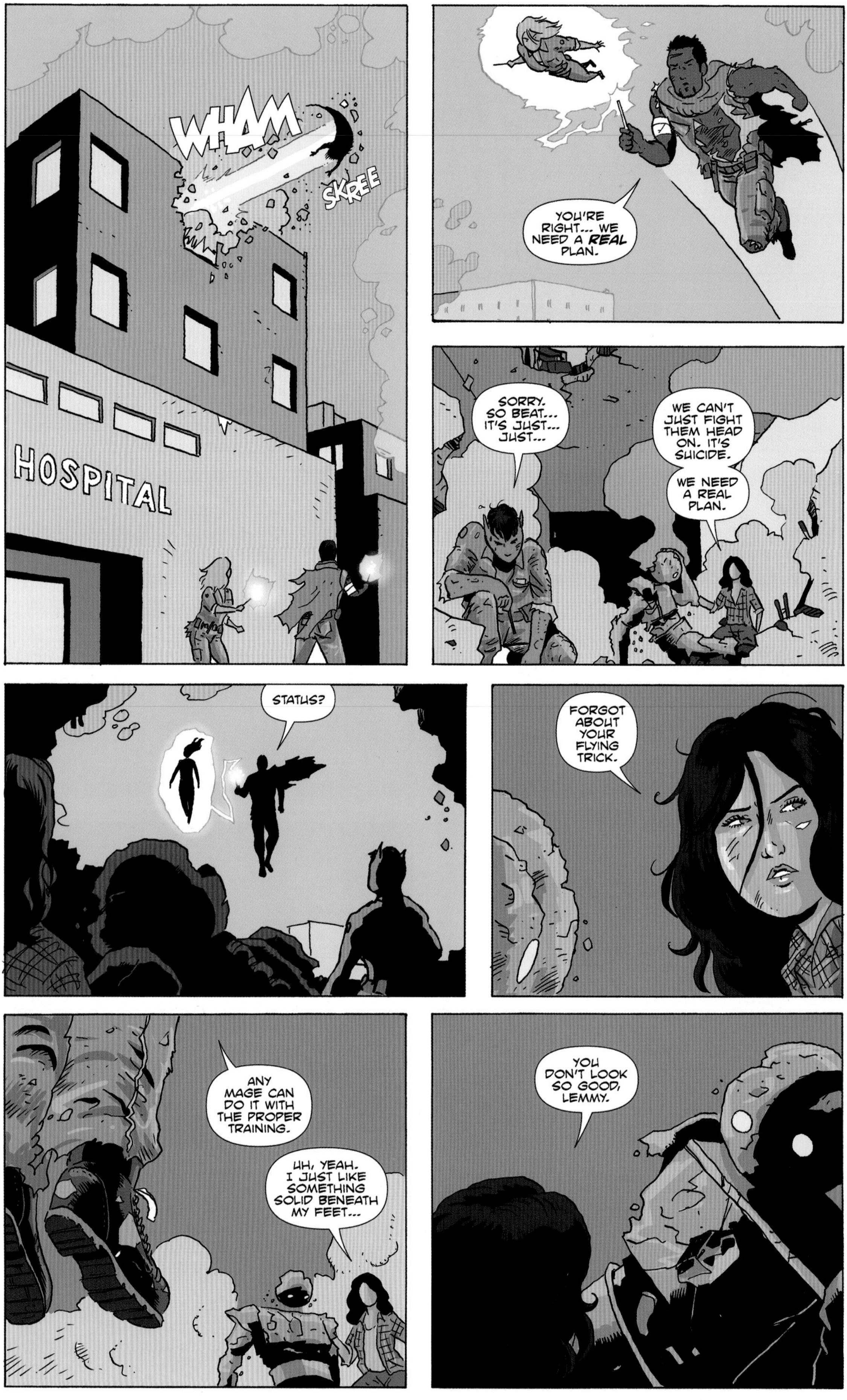
WHAM
SKREE
HOSPITAL
YOU'RE RIGHT... WE NEED A REAL PLAN.
SORRY. SO BEAT... IT'S JUST... JUST...
WE CAN'T JUST FIGHT THEM HEAD ON. IT'S SUICIDE.
WE NEED A REAL PLAN.
STATUS?
FORGOT ABOUT YOUR FLYING TRICK.
ANY MAGE CAN DO IT WITH THE PROPER TRAINING.
UH, YEAH. I JUST LIKE SOMETHING SOLID BENEATH MY FEET...
YOU DON'T LOOK SO GOOD, LEMMY.

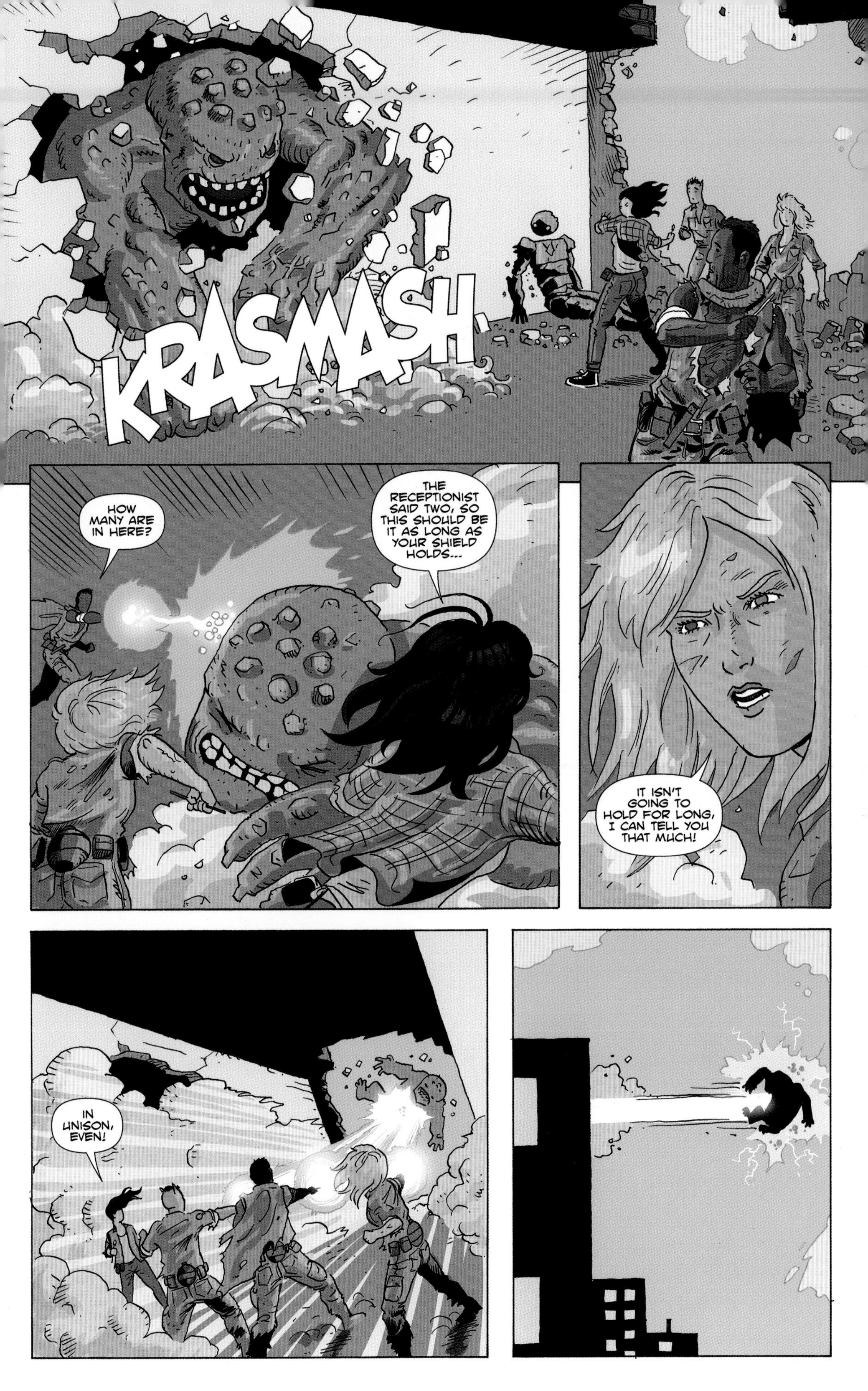
KRASMASH
HOW MANY ARE IN HERE?
THE RECEPTIONIST SAID TWO, SO THIS SHOULD BE IT AS LONG AS YOUR SHIELD HOLDS...
IT ISN'T GOING TO HOLD FOR LONG, I CAN TELL YOU THAT MUCH!
IN UNISON, EVEN!

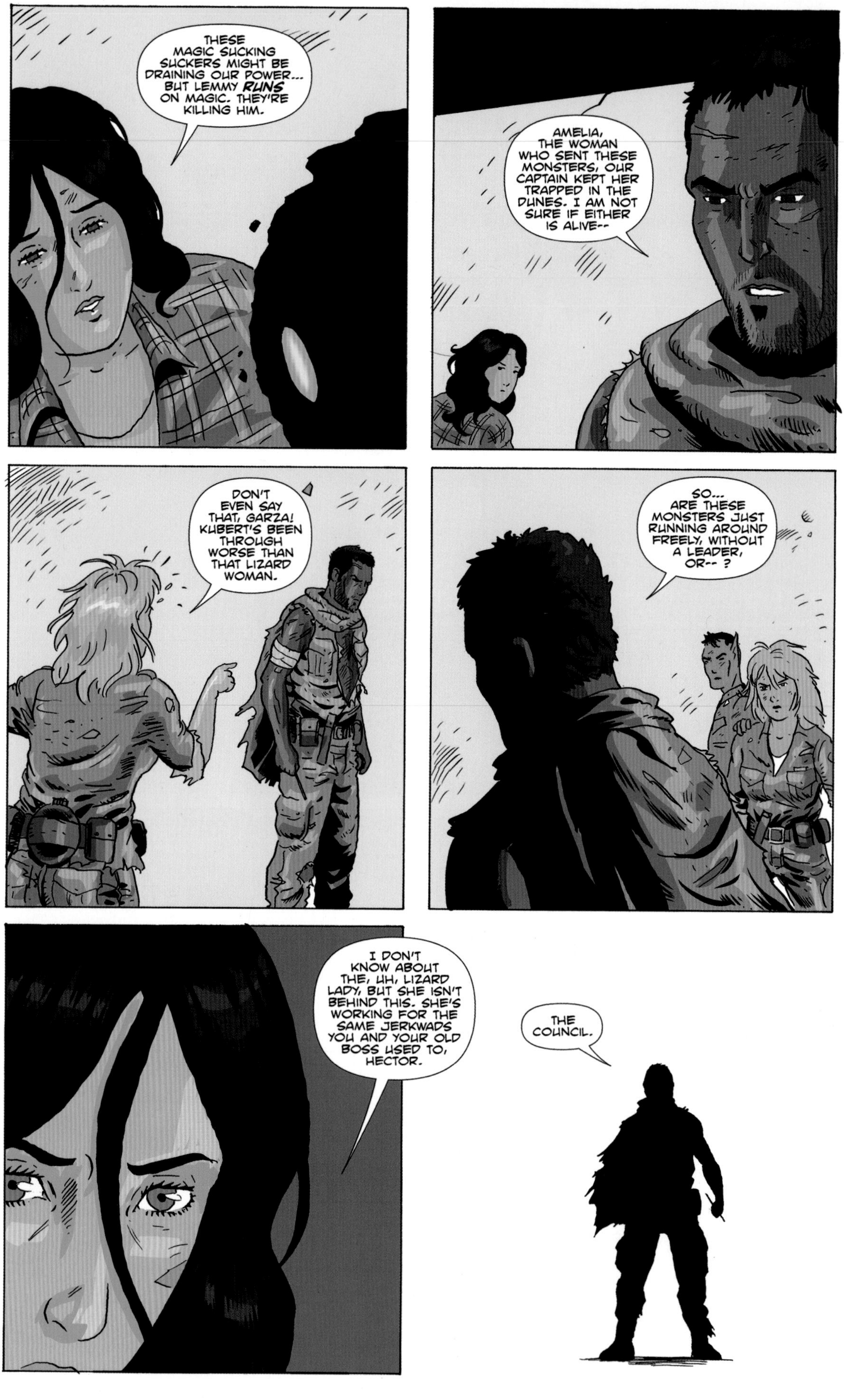
THESE MAGIC SUCKING SUCKERS MIGHT BE DRAINING OUR POWER... BUT LEMMY *RUNS* ON MAGIC. THEY'RE KILLING HIM.
AMELIA, THE WOMAN WHO SENT THESE MONSTERS, OUR CAPTAIN KEPT HER TRAPPED IN THE DUNES. I AM NOT SURE IF EITHER IS ALIVE--
DON'T EVEN SAY THAT, GARZA! KUBERT'S BEEN THROUGH WORSE THAN THAT LIZARD WOMAN.
SO... ARE THESE MONSTERS JUST RUNNING AROUND FREELY, WITHOUT A LEADER, OR-- ?
I DON'T KNOW ABOUT THE, UH, LIZARD LADY, BUT SHE ISN'T BEHIND THIS. SHE'S WORKING FOR THE SAME JERKWADS YOU AND YOUR OLD BOSS USED TO, HECTOR.
THE COUNCIL.

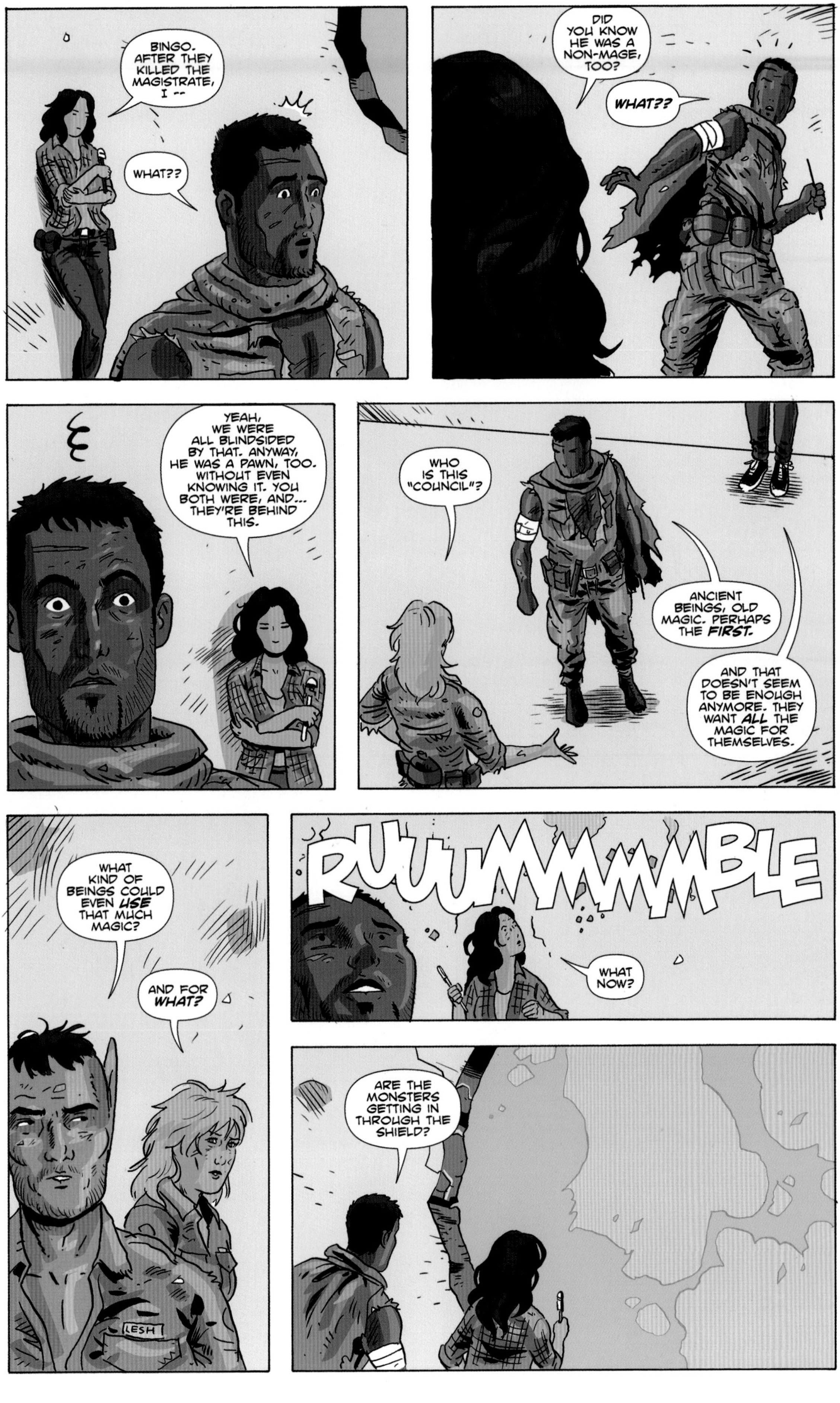
BINGO. AFTER THEY KILLED THE MAGISTRATE, I --
WHAT??
DID YOU KNOW HE WAS A NON-MAGE, TOO?
WHAT??
YEAH, WE WERE ALL BLINDSIDED BY THAT. ANYWAY, HE WAS A PAWN, TOO. WITHOUT EVEN KNOWING IT. YOU BOTH WERE, AND... THEY'RE BEHIND THIS.
WHO IS THIS "COUNCIL"?
ANCIENT BEINGS, OLD MAGIC. PERHAPS THE FIRST.
AND THAT DOESN'T SEEM TO BE ENOUGH ANYMORE. THEY WANT ALL THE MAGIC FOR THEMSELVES.
WHAT KIND OF BEINGS COULD EVEN USE THAT MUCH MAGIC?
AND FOR WHAT?
LESH
RUUUMMMMBLE
WHAT NOW?
ARE THE MONSTERS GETTING IN THROUGH THE SHIELD?

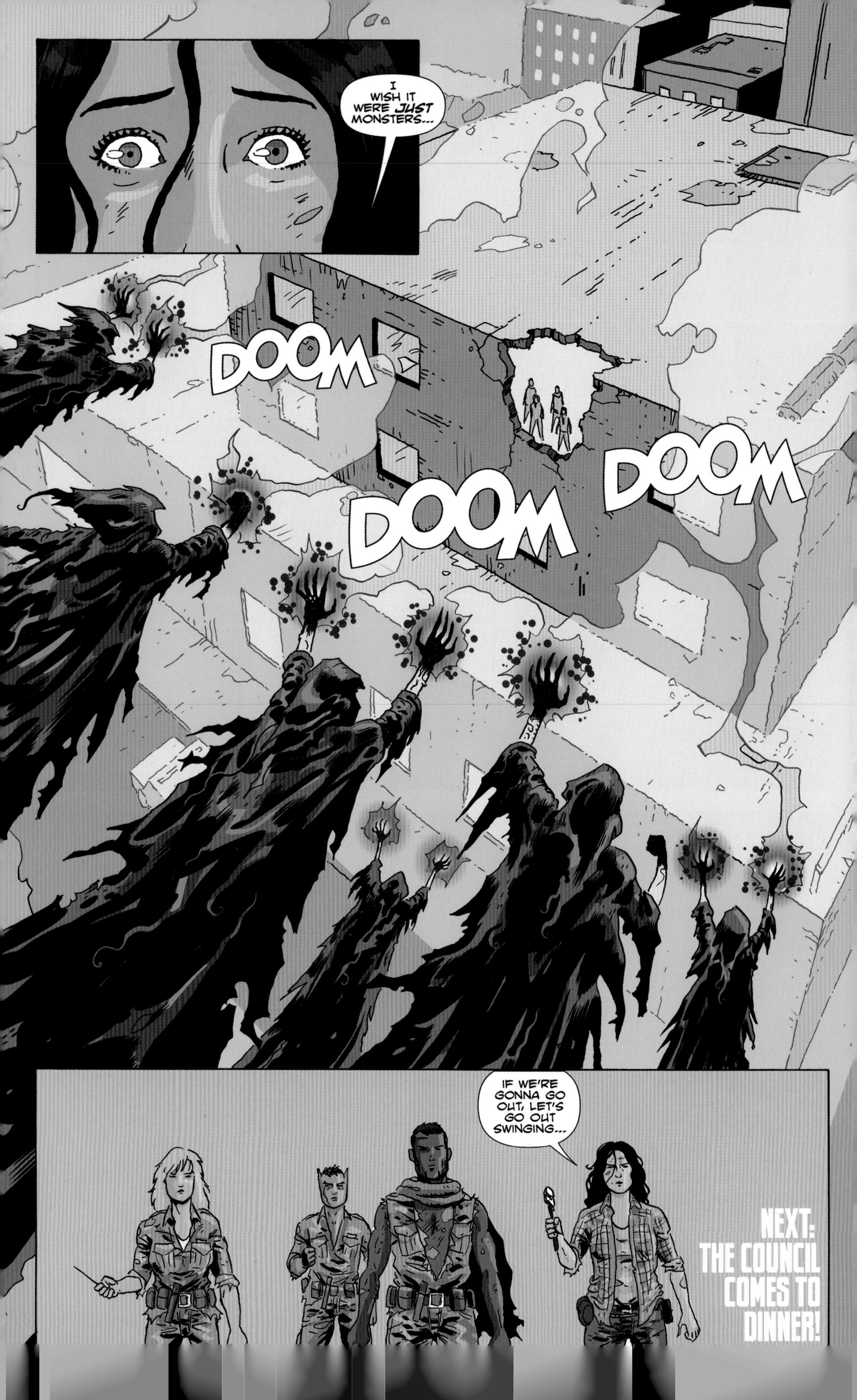
I WISH IT WERE JUST MONSTERS...
DOOM
DOOM
DOOM
IF WE'RE GONNA GO OUT, LET'S GO OUT SWINGING...
NEXT: THE COUNCIL COMES TO DINNER!

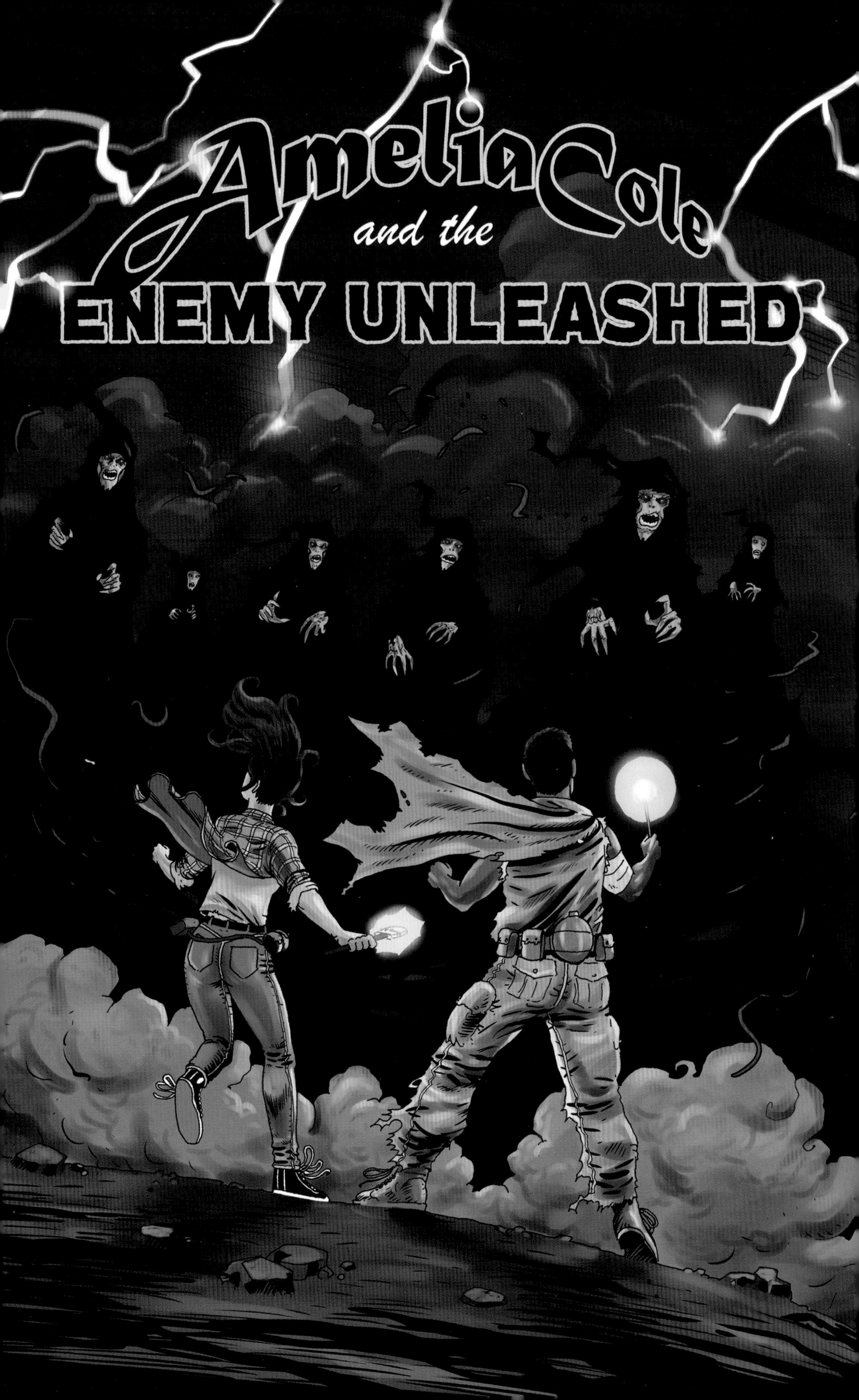
Amelia Cole
and the
ENEMY UNLEASHED

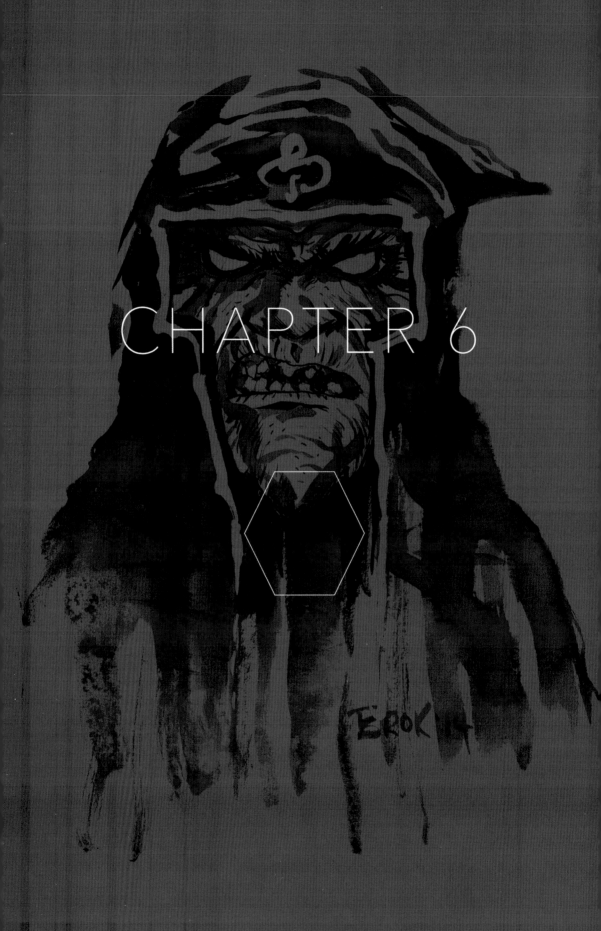

CHAPTER 6

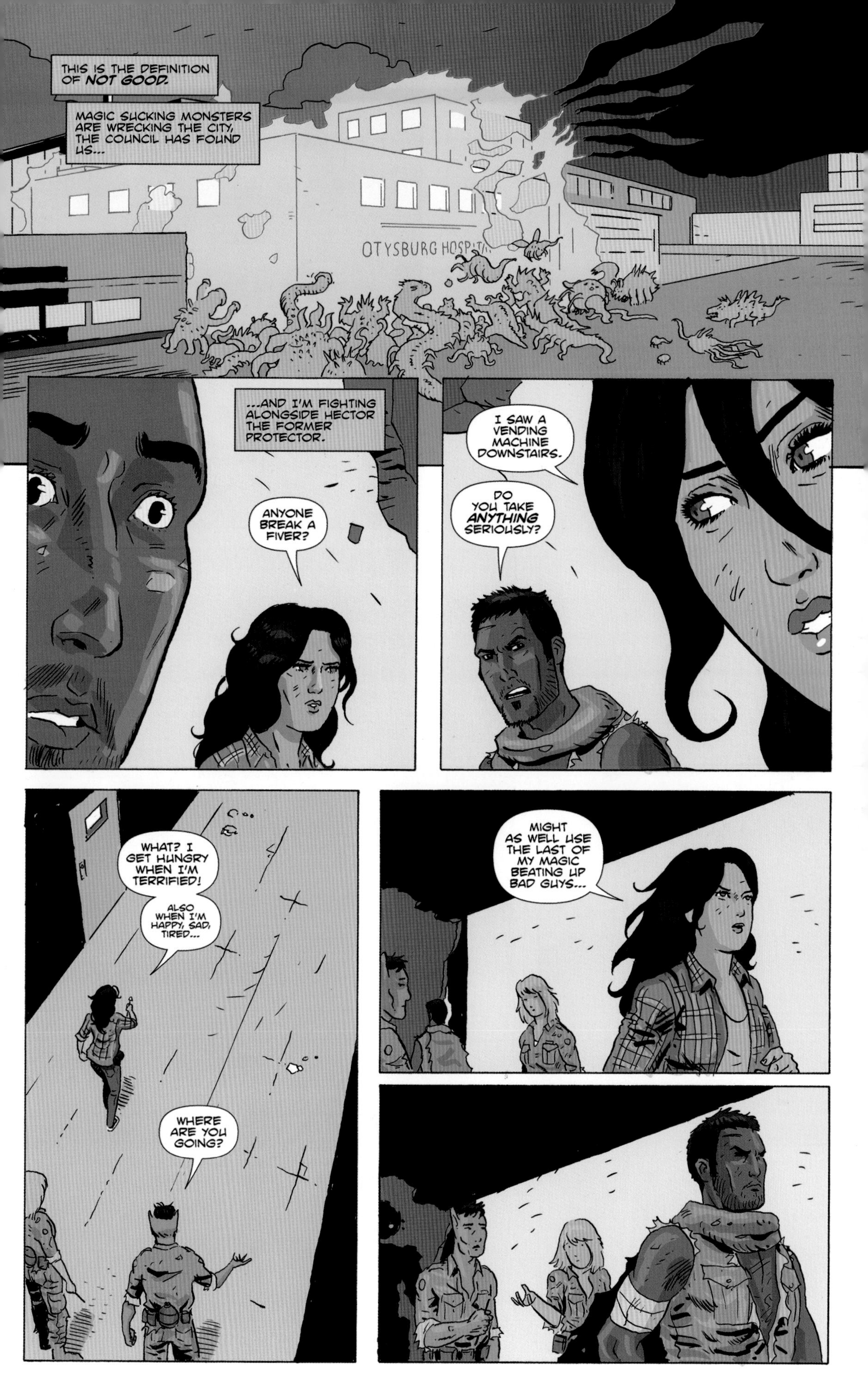
THIS IS THE DEFINITION OF NOT GOOD.
MAGIC SUCKING MONSTERS ARE WRECKING THE CITY, THE COUNCIL HAS FOUND US...
OTYSBURG HOSPITAL
...AND I'M FIGHTING ALONGSIDE HECTOR THE FORMER PROTECTOR.
ANYONE BREAK A FIVER?
I SAW A VENDING MACHINE DOWNSTAIRS.
DO YOU TAKE ANYTHING SERIOUSLY?
WHAT? I GET HUNGRY WHEN I'M TERRIFIED!
ALSO WHEN I'M HAPPY, SAD, TIRED...
WHERE ARE YOU GOING?
MIGHT AS WELL USE THE LAST OF MY MAGIC BEATING UP BAD GUYS...

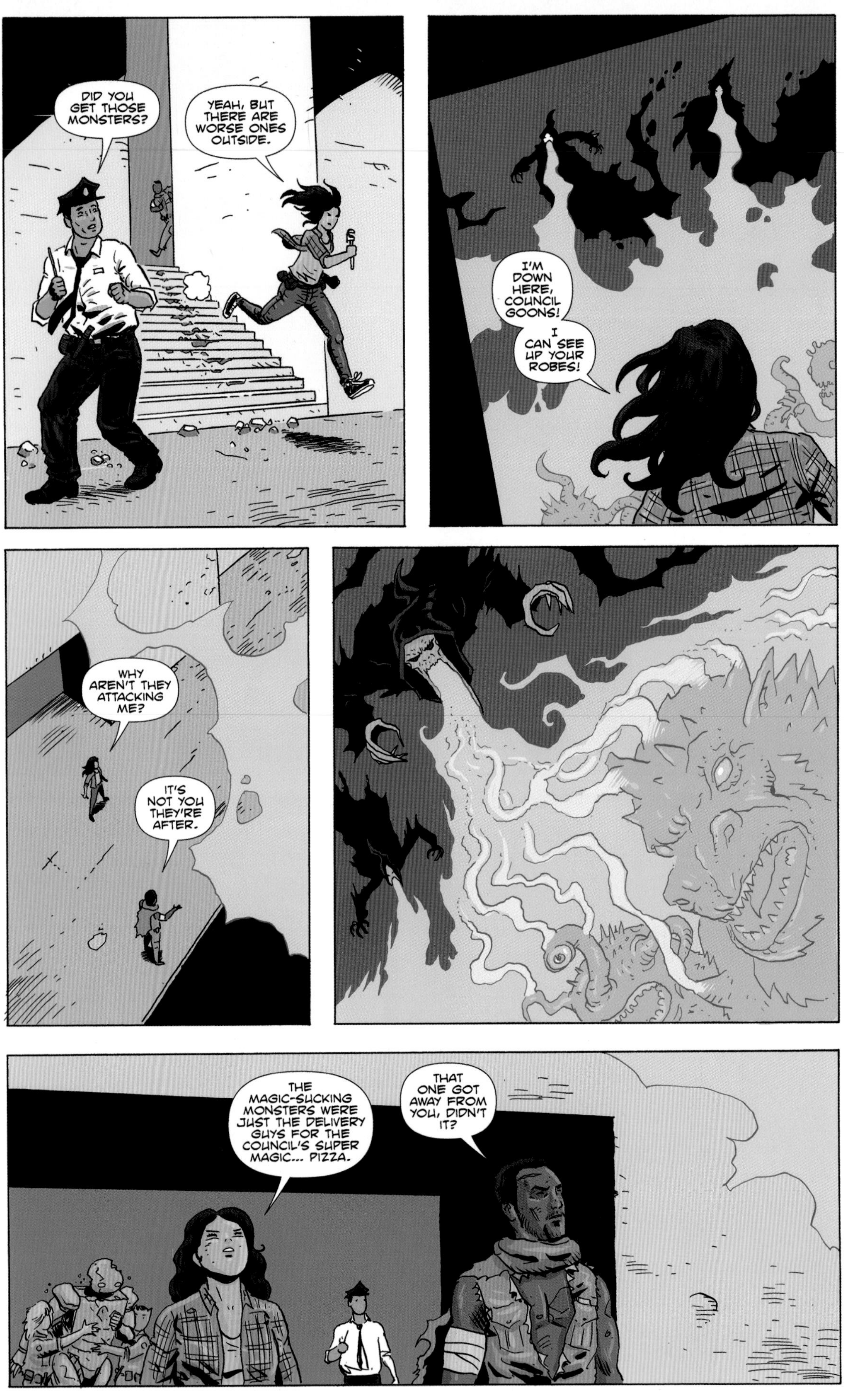
DID YOU GET THOSE MONSTERS?
YEAH, BUT THERE ARE WORSE ONES OUTSIDE.
I'M DOWN HERE, COUNCIL GOONS!
I CAN SEE UP YOUR ROBES!
WHY AREN'T THEY ATTACKING ME?
IT'S NOT YOU THEY'RE AFTER.
THE MAGIC-SUCKING MONSTERS WERE JUST THE DELIVERY GUYS FOR THE COUNCIL'S SUPER MAGIC... PIZZA.
THAT ONE GOT AWAY FROM YOU, DIDN'T IT?

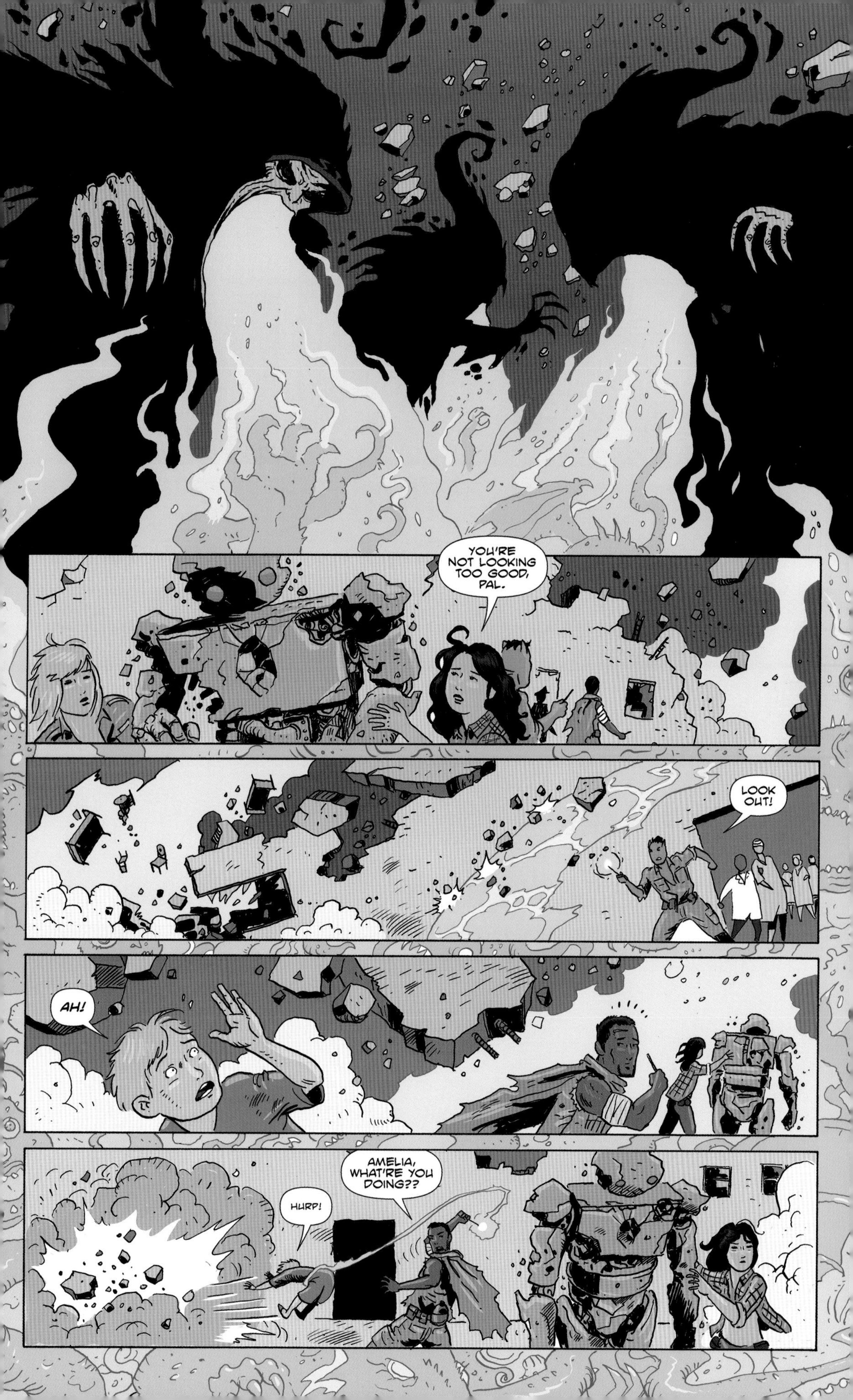
YOU'RE NOT LOOKING TOO GOOD, PAL.
LOOK OUT!
AH!
AMELIA, WHAT'RE YOU DOING??
HURP!

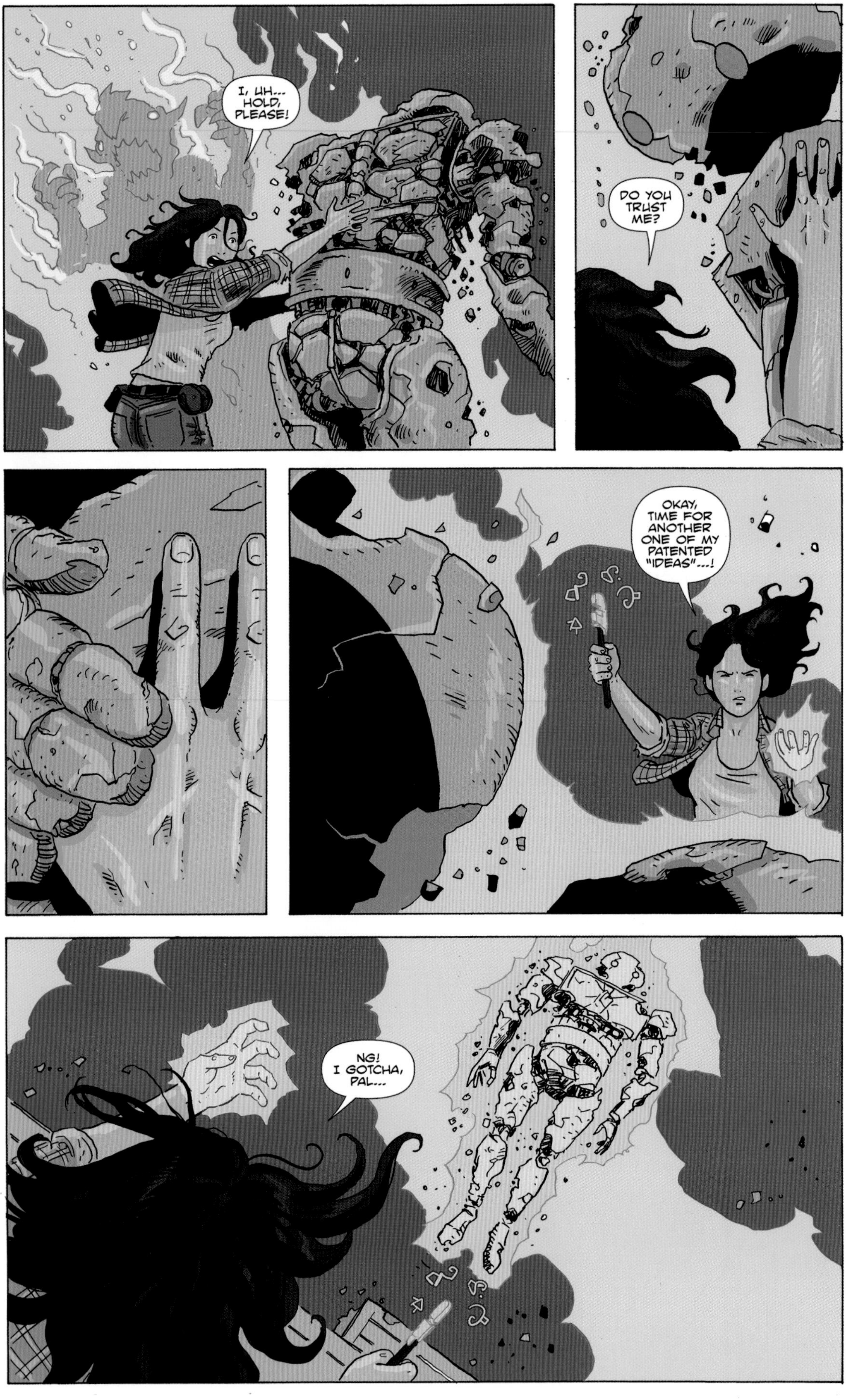
I, UH... HOLD, PLEASE!
DO YOU TRUST ME?
OKAY, TIME FOR ANOTHER ONE OF MY PATENTED "IDEAS"...!
NG! I GOTCHA, PAL...

PLEASE WORK...

?

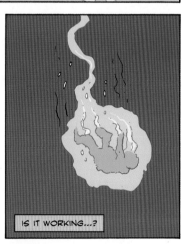

IS IT WORKING...?

PLEASE...

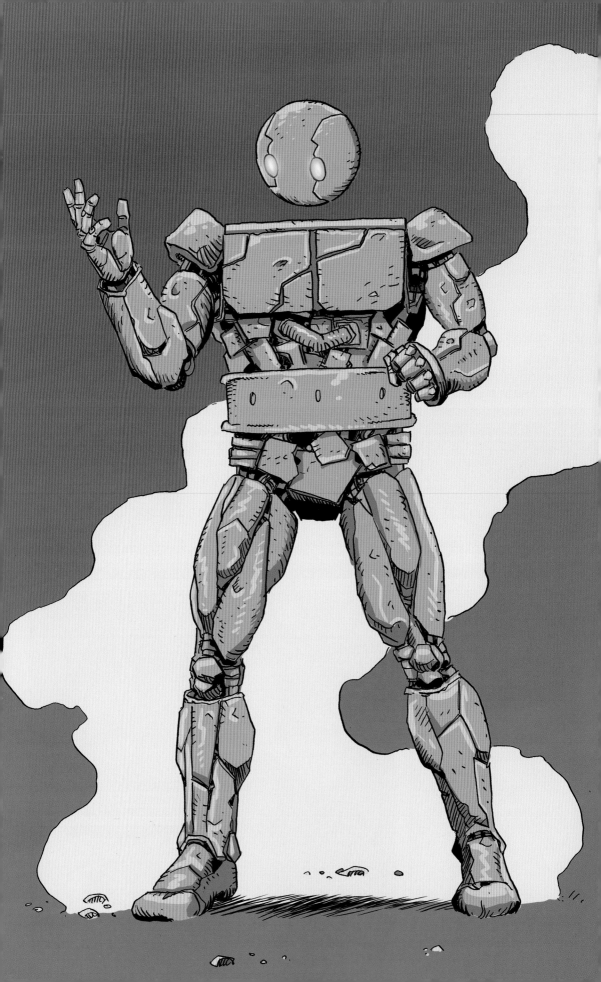

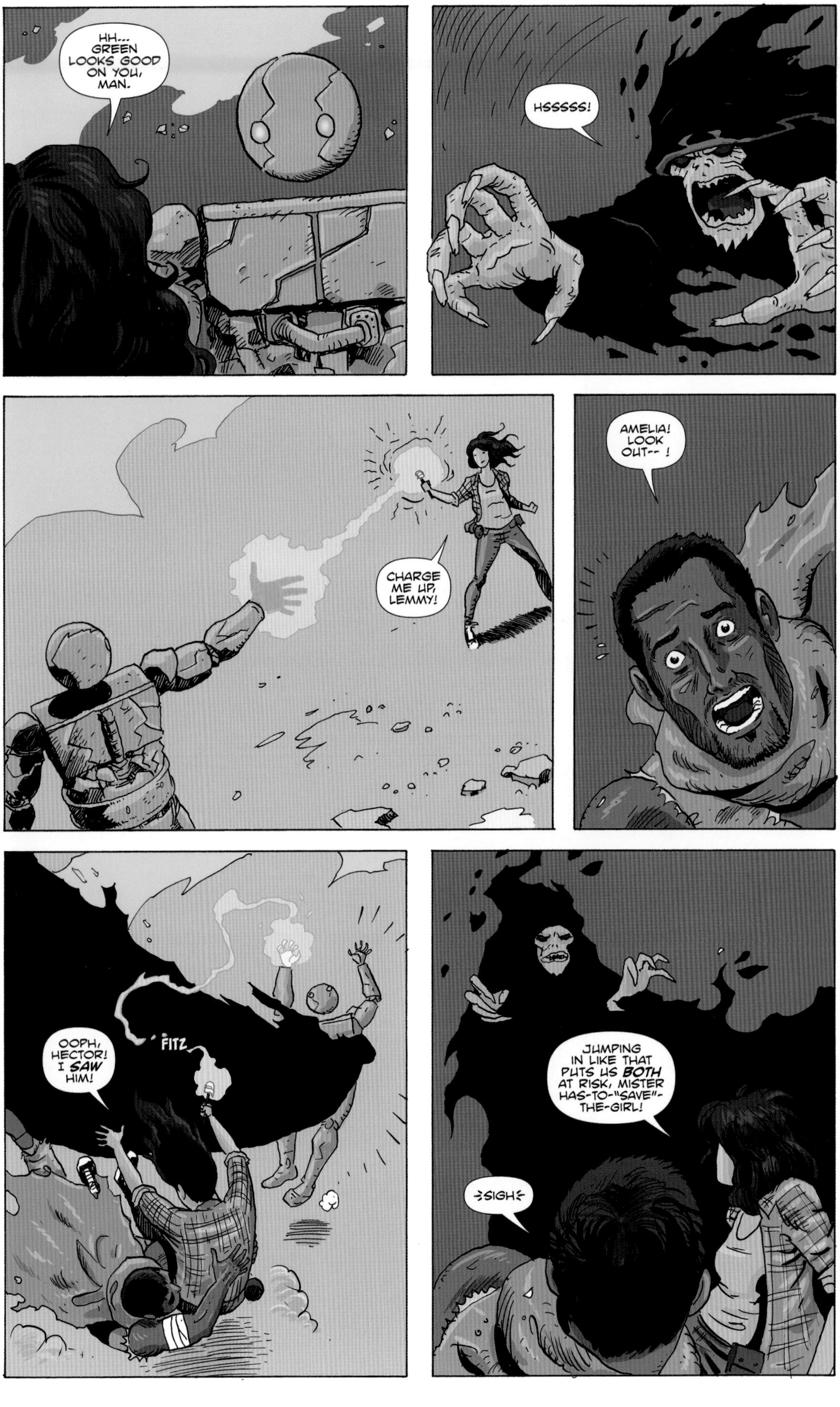
HH... GREEN LOOKS GOOD ON YOU, MAN.
HSSSSS!
CHARGE ME UP, LEMMY!
AMELIA! LOOK OUT-- !
FITZ
OOPH, HECTOR! I SAW HIM!
JUMPING IN LIKE THAT PUTS US BOTH AT RISK, MISTER HAS-TO-"SAVE"-THE-GIRL!
SIGH

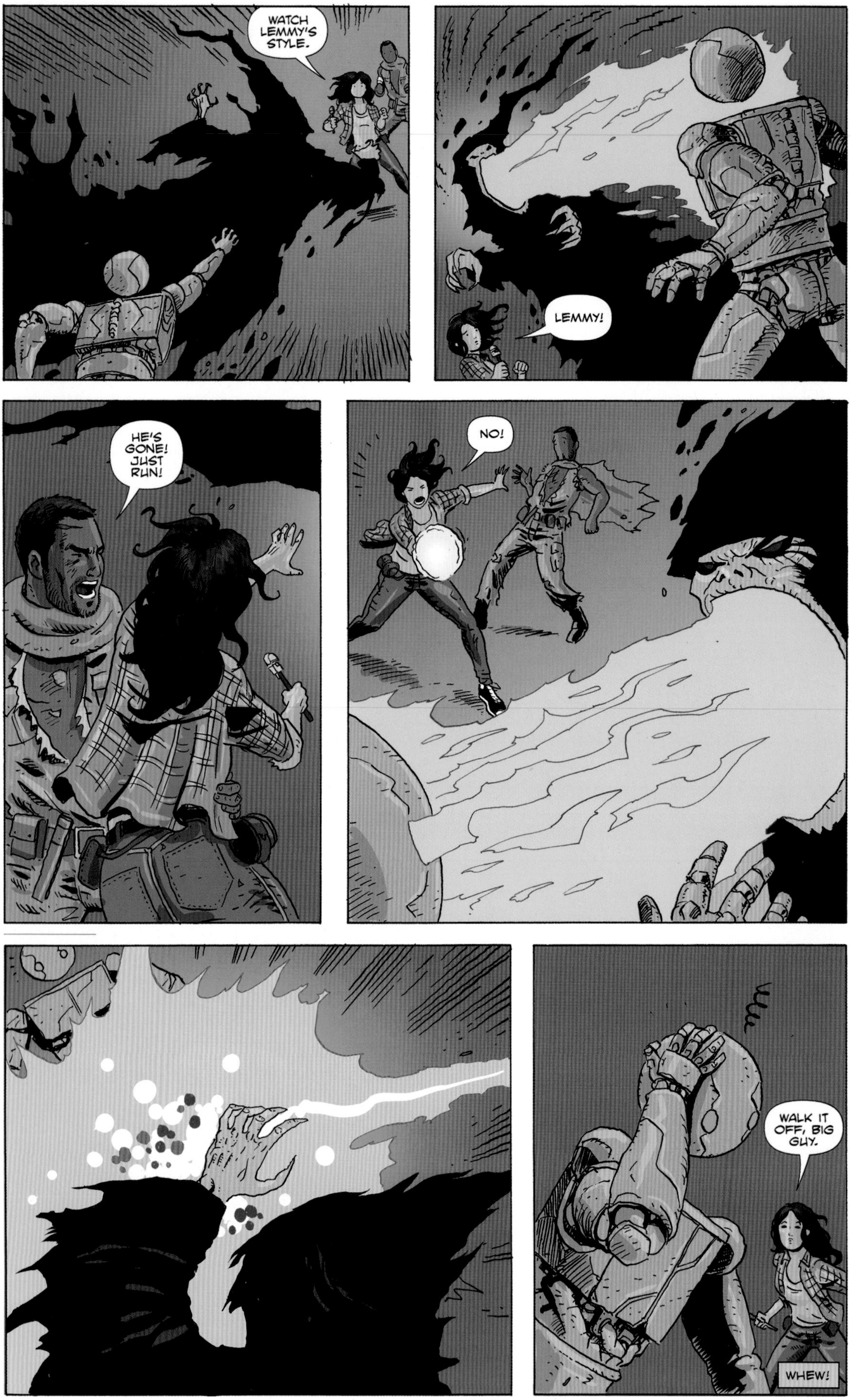
WATCH LEMMY'S STYLE.
LEMMY!
HE'S GONE! JUST RUN!
NO!
WALK IT OFF, BIG GUY.
WHEW!

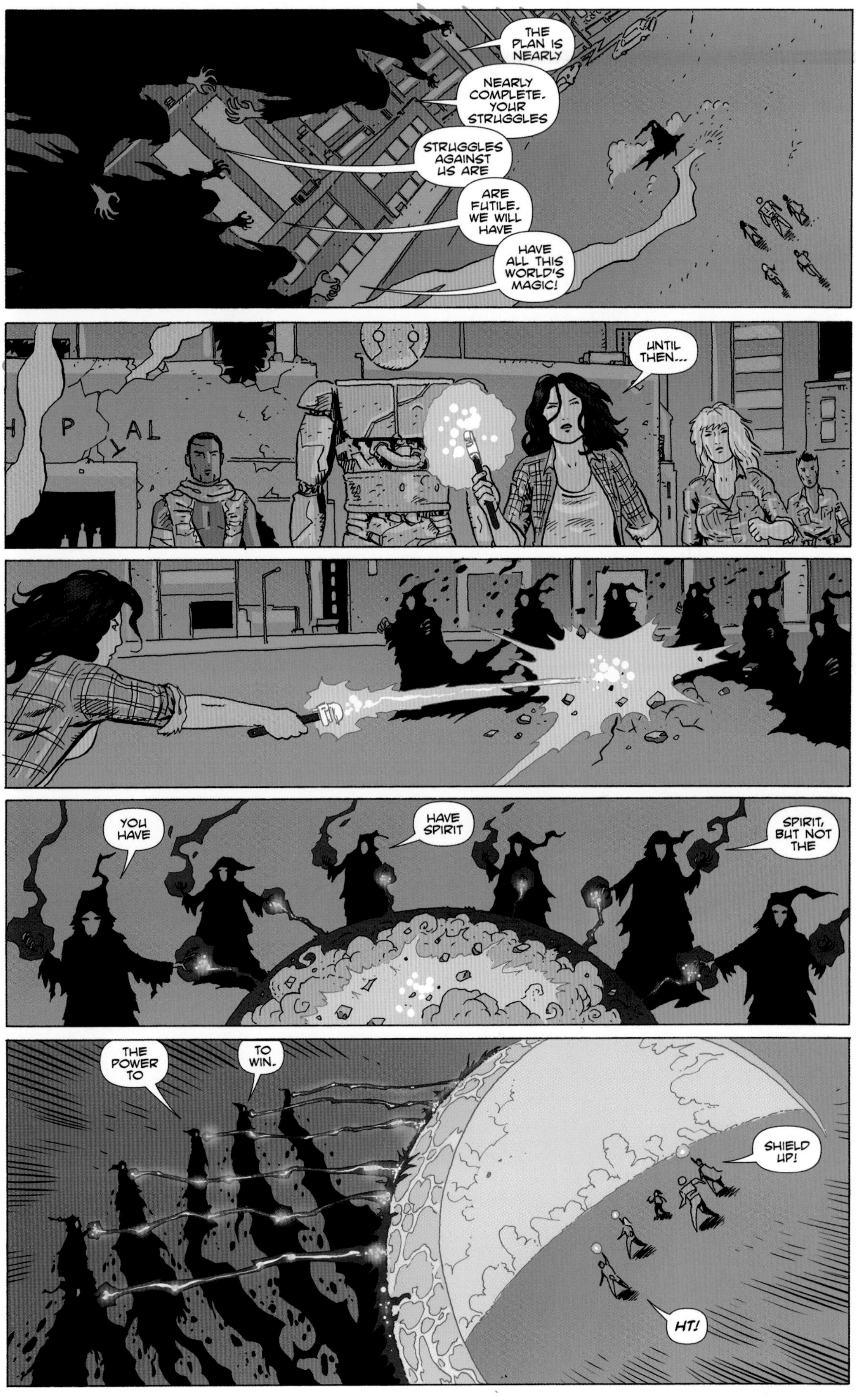
THE PLAN IS NEARLY
NEARLY COMPLETE. YOUR STRUGGLES
STRUGGLES AGAINST US ARE
ARE FUTILE. WE WILL HAVE
HAVE ALL THIS WORLD'S MAGIC!
UNTIL THEN...
YOU HAVE
HAVE SPIRIT
SPIRIT, BUT NOT THE
THE POWER TO
TO WIN.
SHIELD UP!
HT!

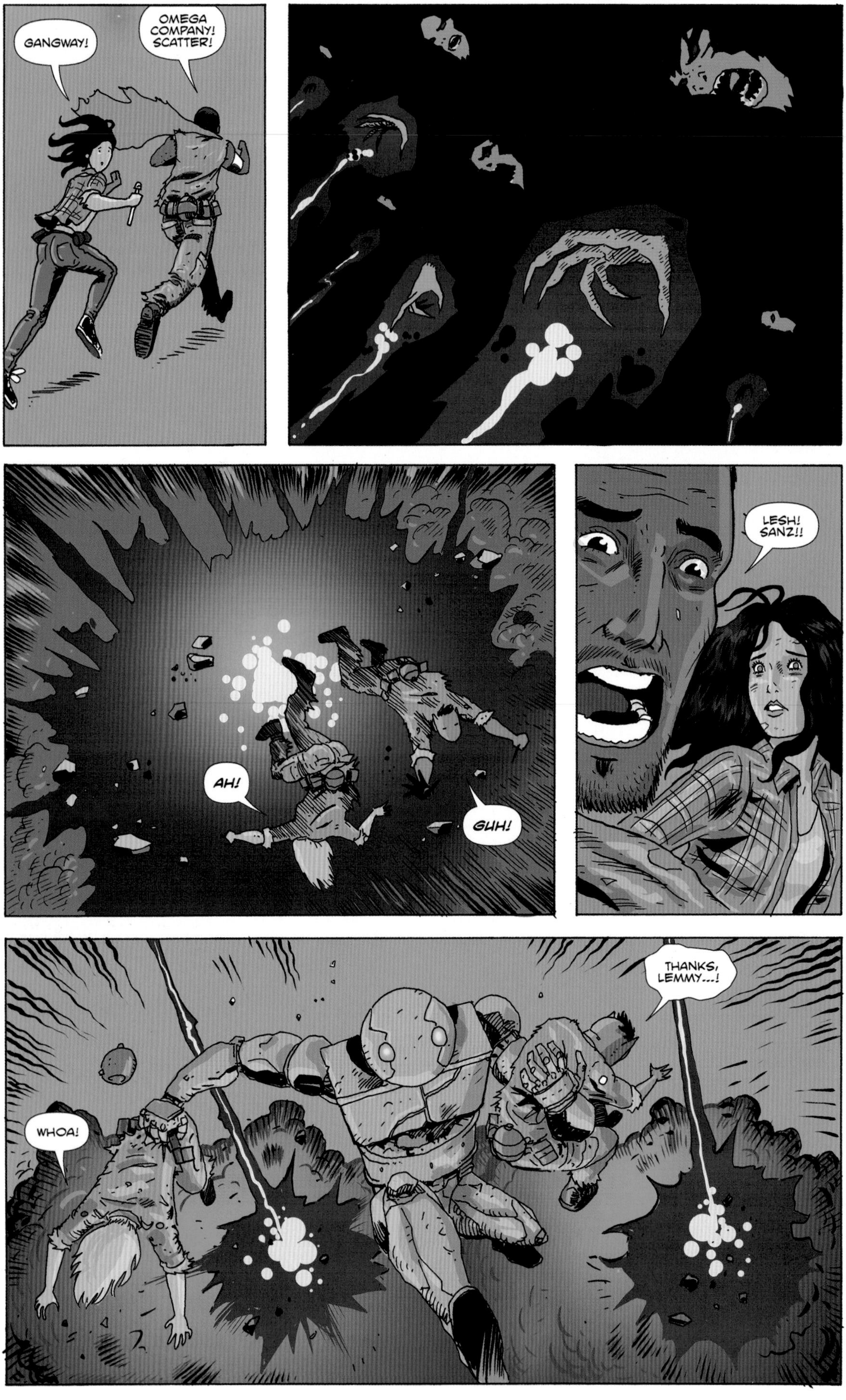
GANGWAY!
OMEGA COMPANY! SCATTER!
AH!
GUH!
LESH! SANZ!!
THANKS, LEMMY...!
WHOA!

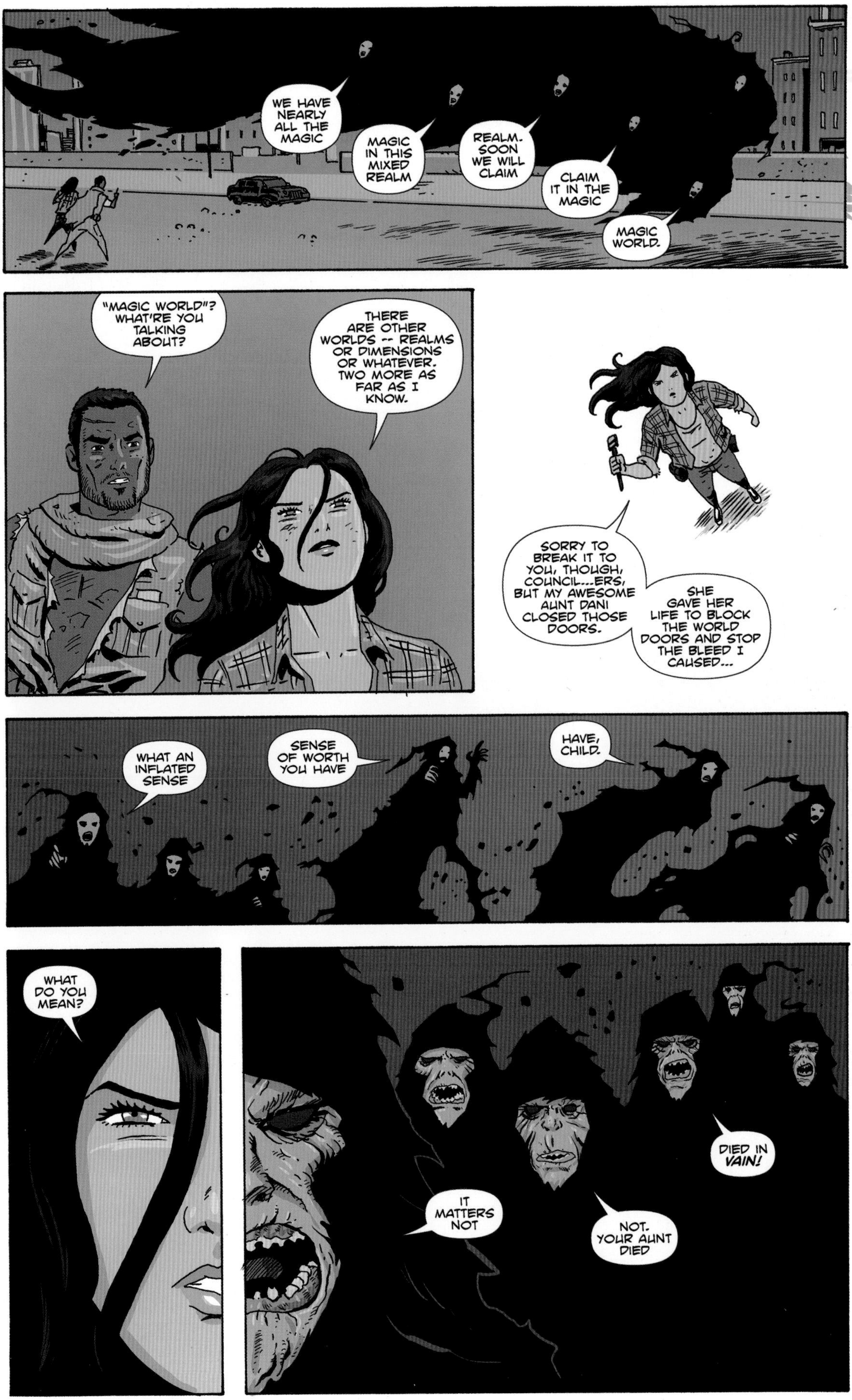
WE HAVE NEARLY ALL THE MAGIC
MAGIC IN THIS MIXED REALM
REALM. SOON WE WILL CLAIM
CLAIM IT IN THE MAGIC
MAGIC WORLD.
"MAGIC WORLD"? WHAT'RE YOU TALKING ABOUT?
THERE ARE OTHER WORLDS -- REALMS OR DIMENSIONS OR WHATEVER. TWO MORE AS FAR AS I KNOW.
SORRY TO BREAK IT TO YOU, THOUGH, COUNCIL...ERS, BUT MY AWESOME AUNT DANI CLOSED THOSE DOORS.
SHE GAVE HER LIFE TO BLOCK THE WORLD DOORS AND STOP THE BLEED I CAUSED...
WHAT AN INFLATED SENSE
SENSE OF WORTH YOU HAVE
HAVE, CHILD.
WHAT DO YOU MEAN?
IT MATTERS NOT
NOT. YOUR AUNT DIED
DIED IN VAIN!

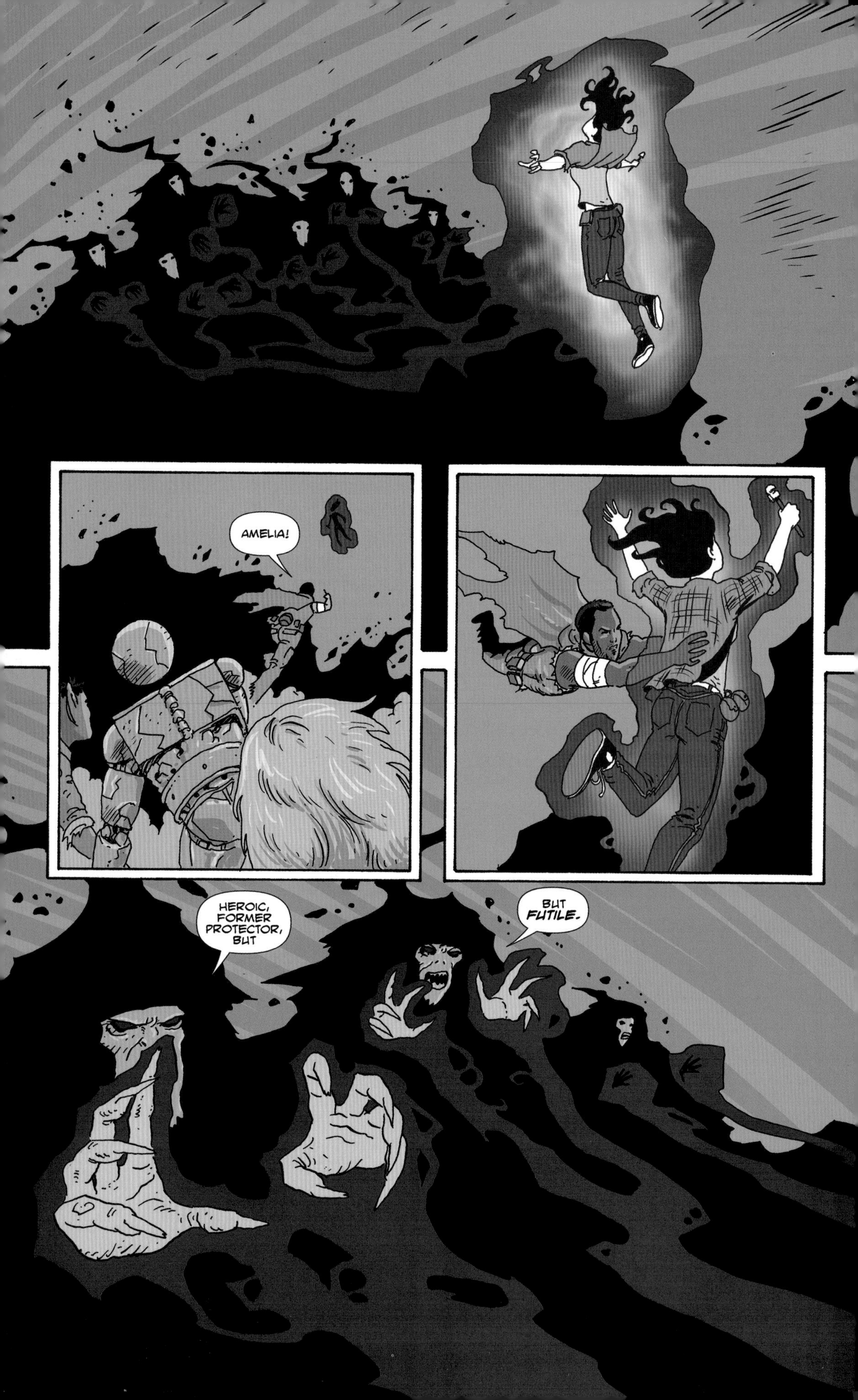
AMELIA!
HEROIC, FORMER PROTECTOR, BUT
BUT FUTILE.

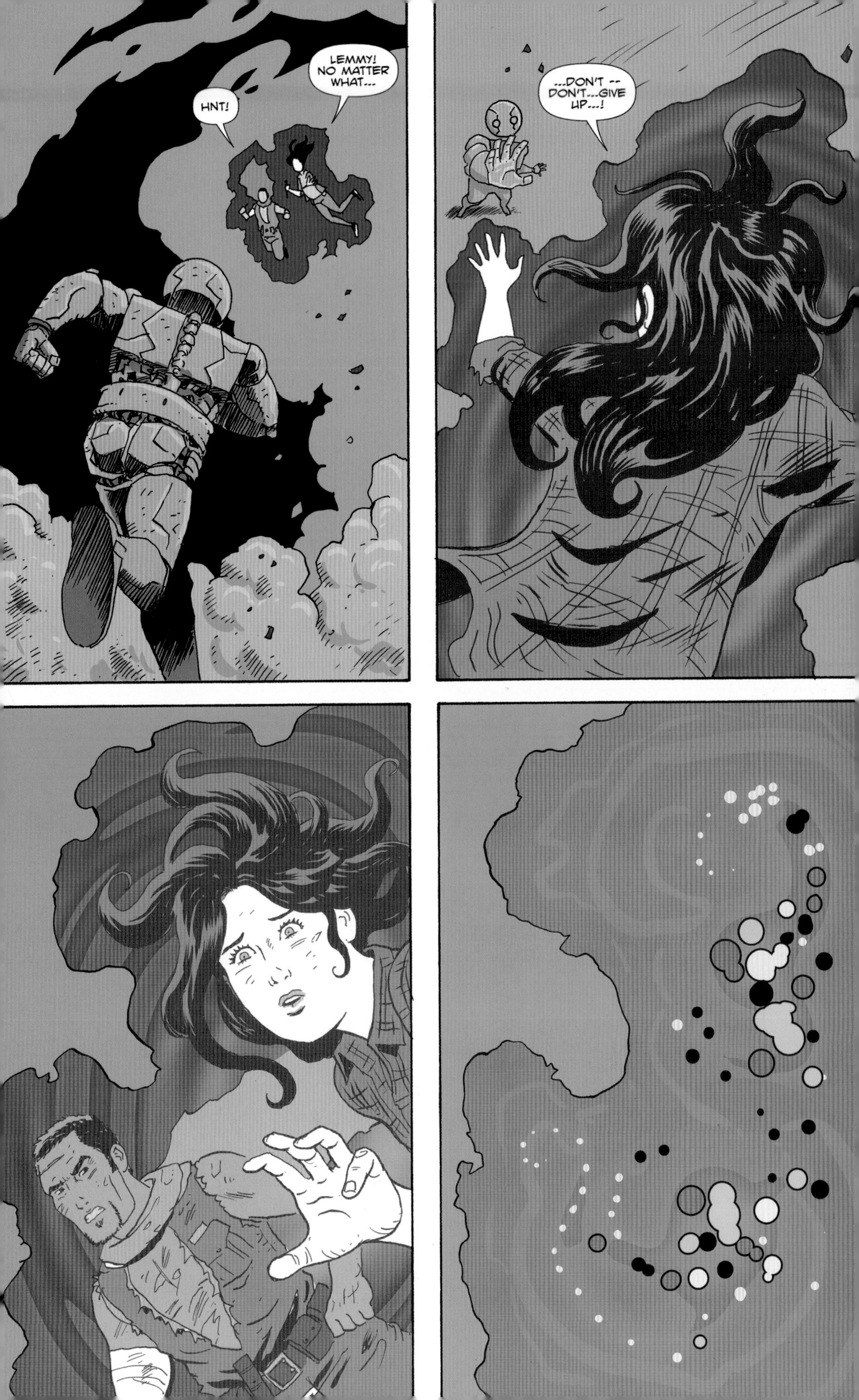
LEMMY! NO MATTER WHAT...
HNT!
...DON'T -- DON'T...GIVE UP...!

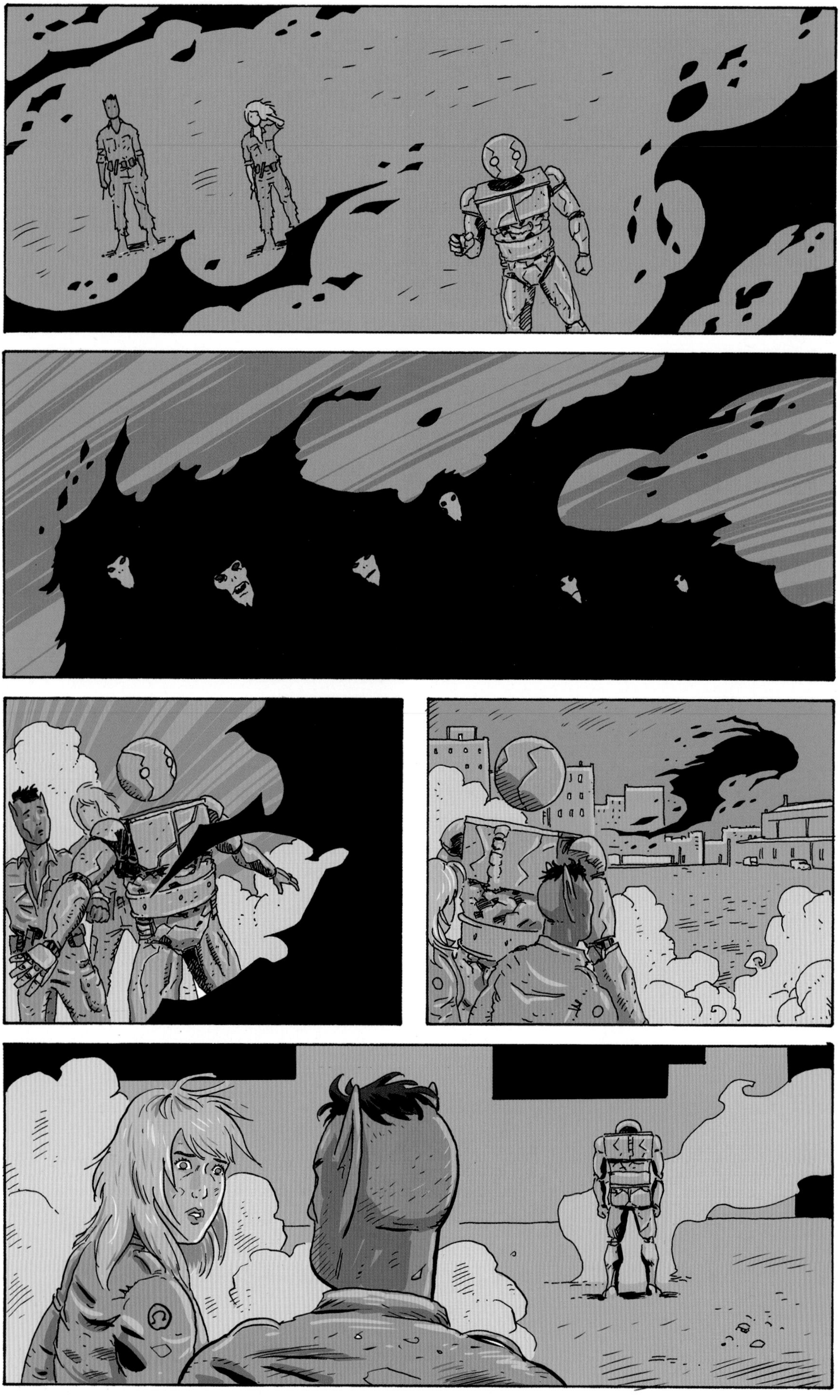

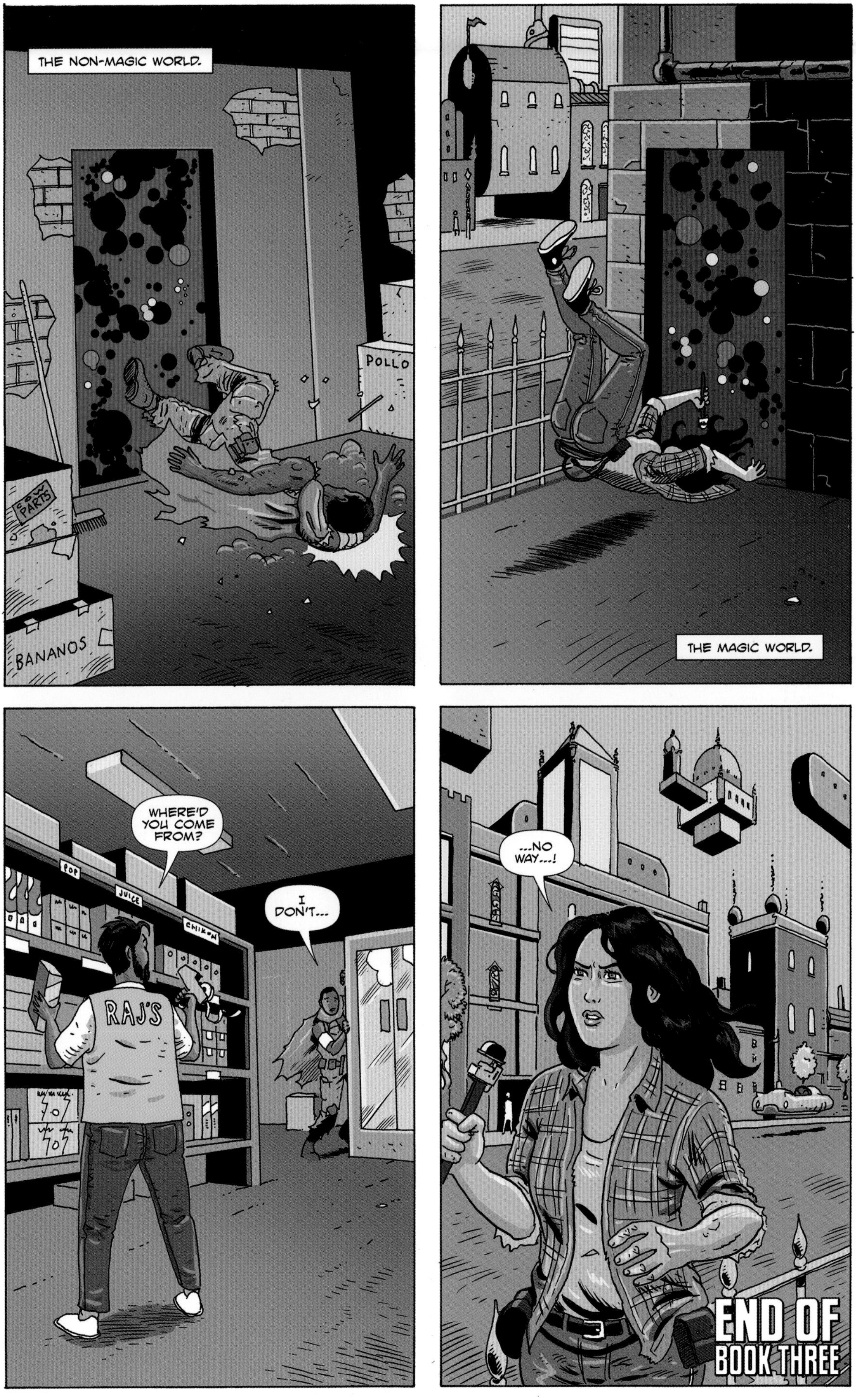
THE NON-MAGIC WORLD.
POLLO
COW PARTS
BANANOS
THE MAGIC WORLD.
POP
JUICE
CHIKEN
RAJ'S
WHERE'D YOU COME FROM?
I DON'T...
...NO WAY...!
END OF BOOK THREE

TALES UNLEASHED

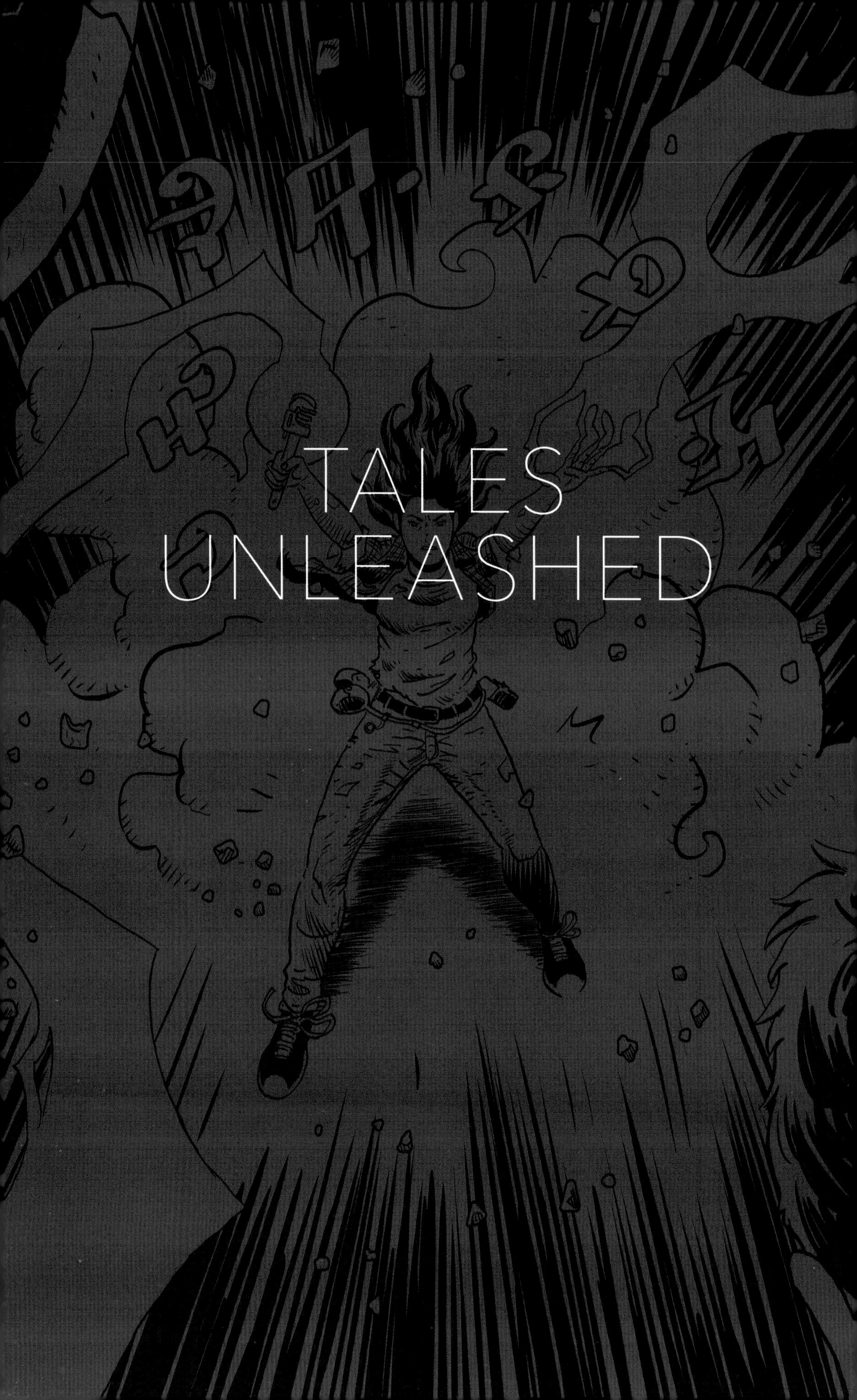

In a storyline as fast paced as *The Enemy Unleashed*, quiet moments and side stories often get pushed aside in favor of the forward action. Still, such moments are nice, and this is where trade extras come in handy.

Nick wrote and fully illustrated two of the tales – "Eye for an Eye" and "Bearfaced Lie" – and worked off of a story by Adam – "Frustration" – and one by D.J. – "Hide and Seek." The fifth is a reprint of the story Team Amelia was honored to do for the *Help The CBLDF Defend Comics* Free Comic Book Day issue called "Amelia Cole and the Freedom of Speech."

ENJOY!

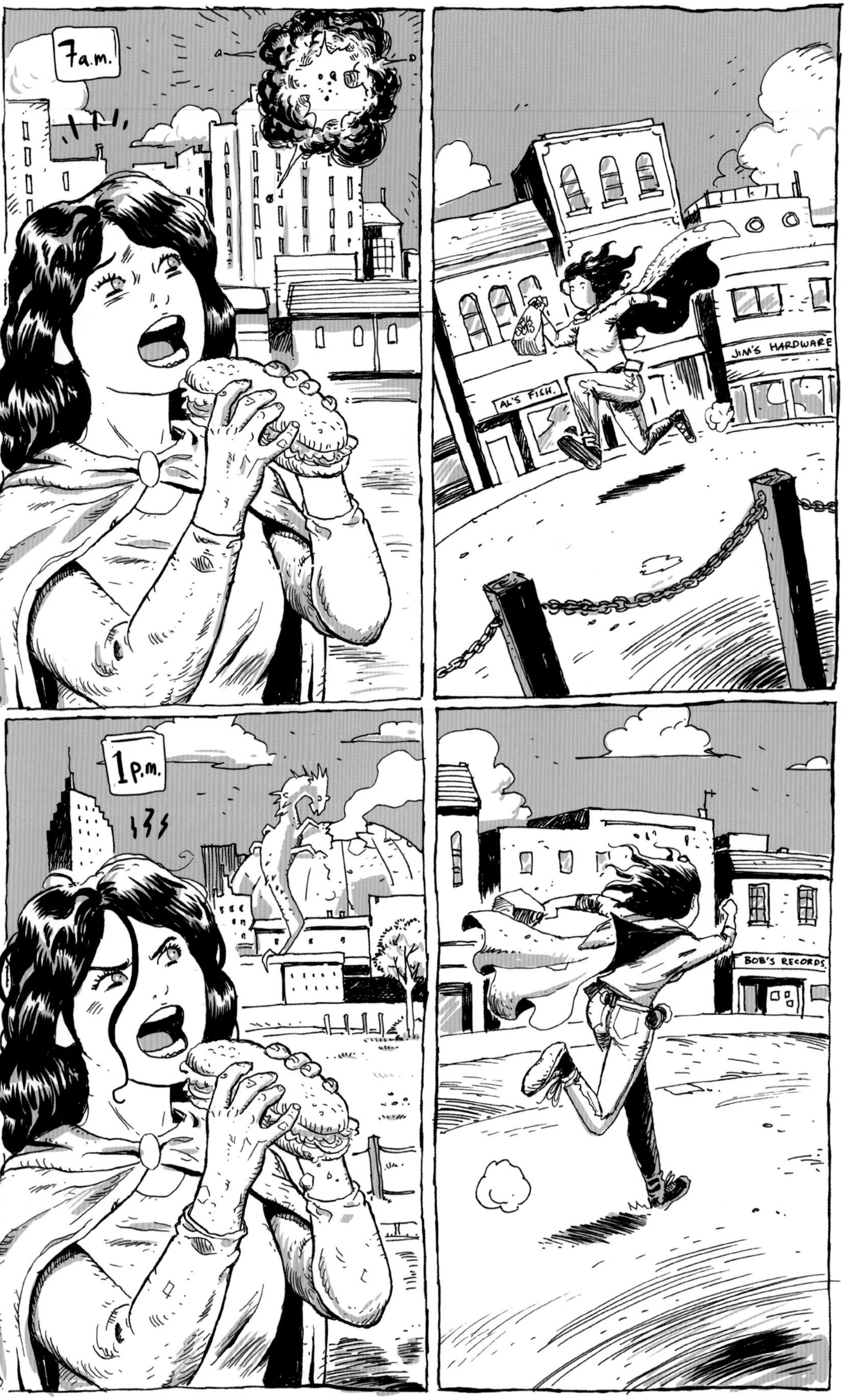
7a.m.
AL'S FISH.
JIM'S HARDWARE
1p.m.
BOB'S RECORDS.

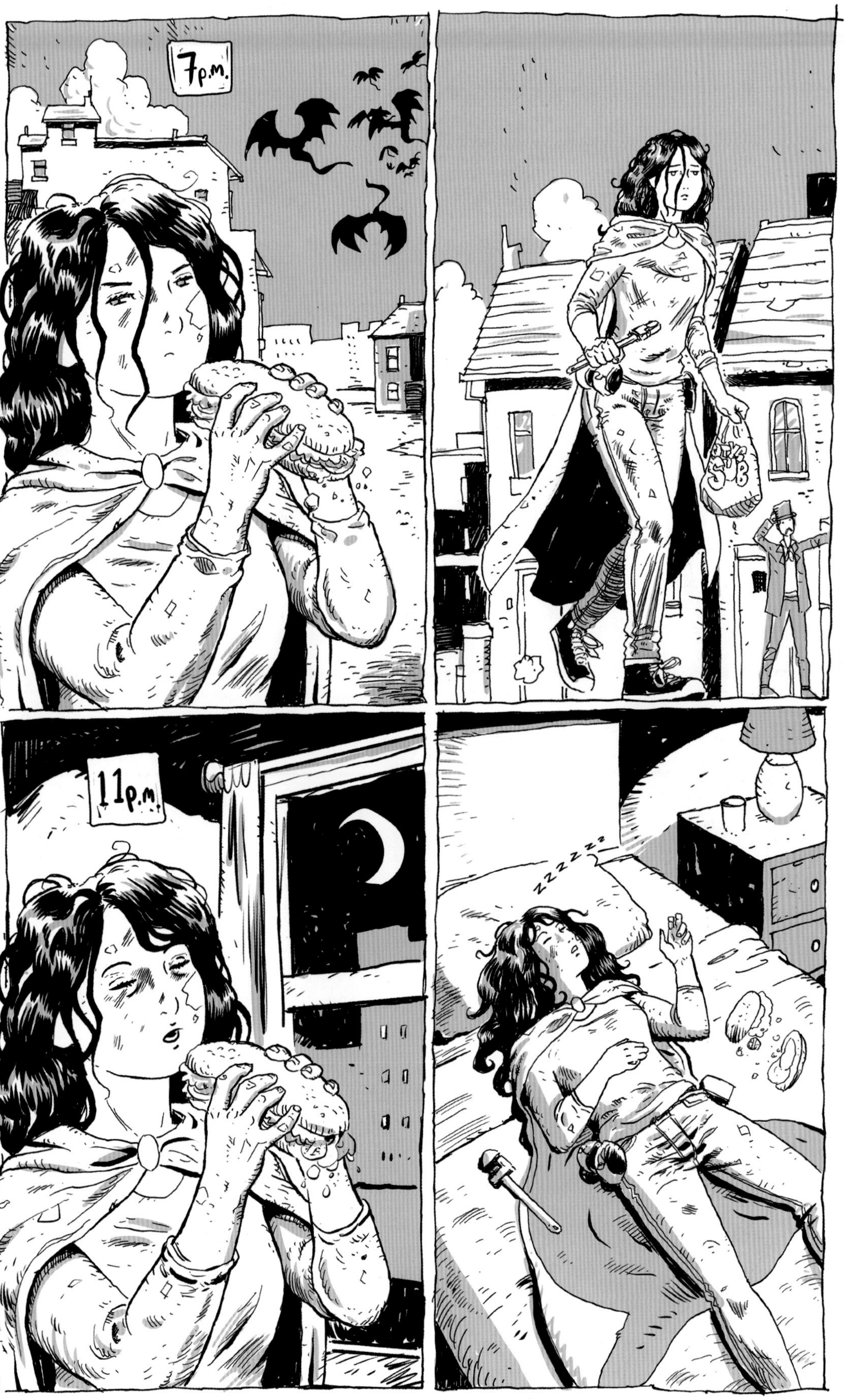
7p.m.
11p.m.
zzzzzz

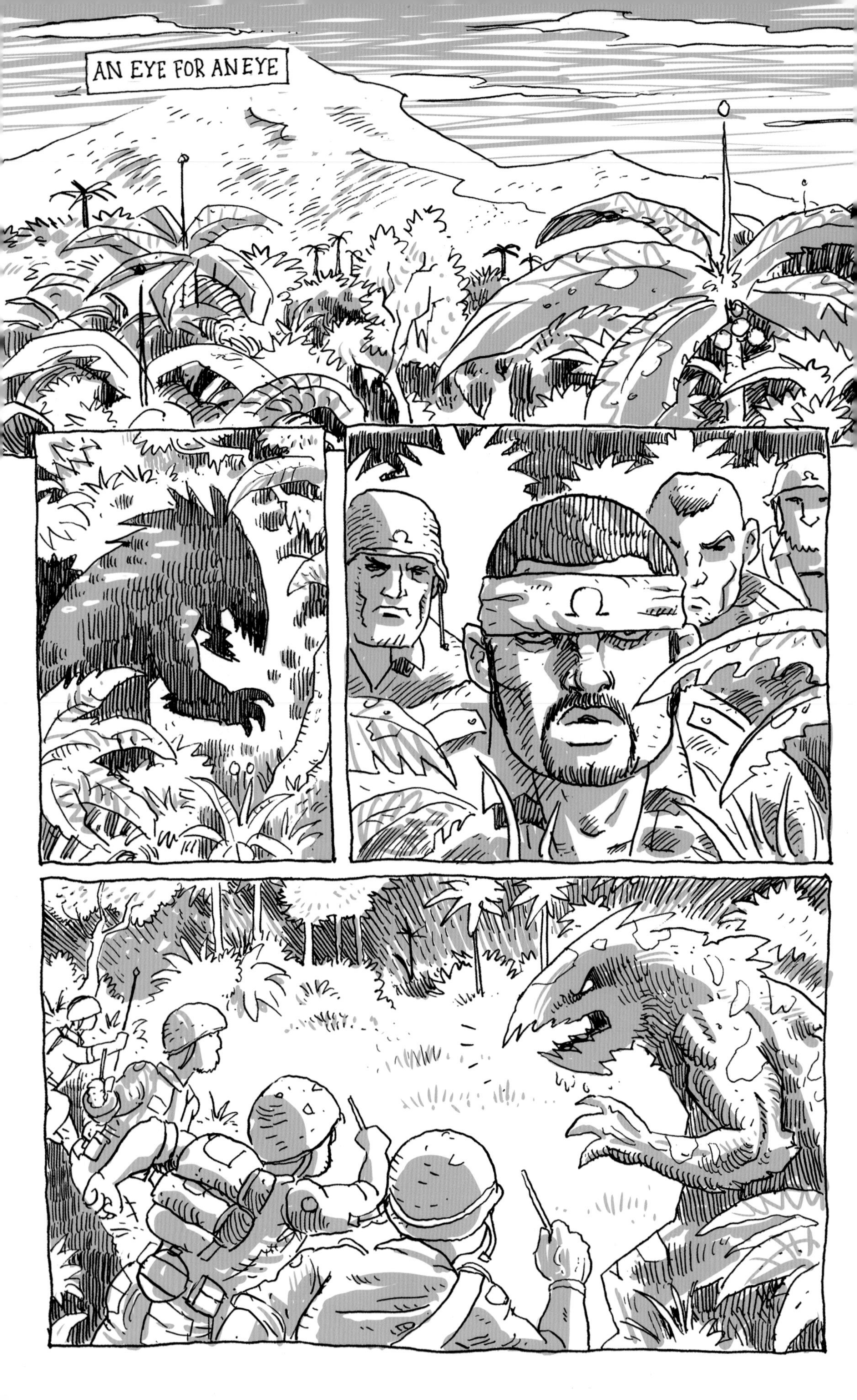
AN EYE FOR AN EYE

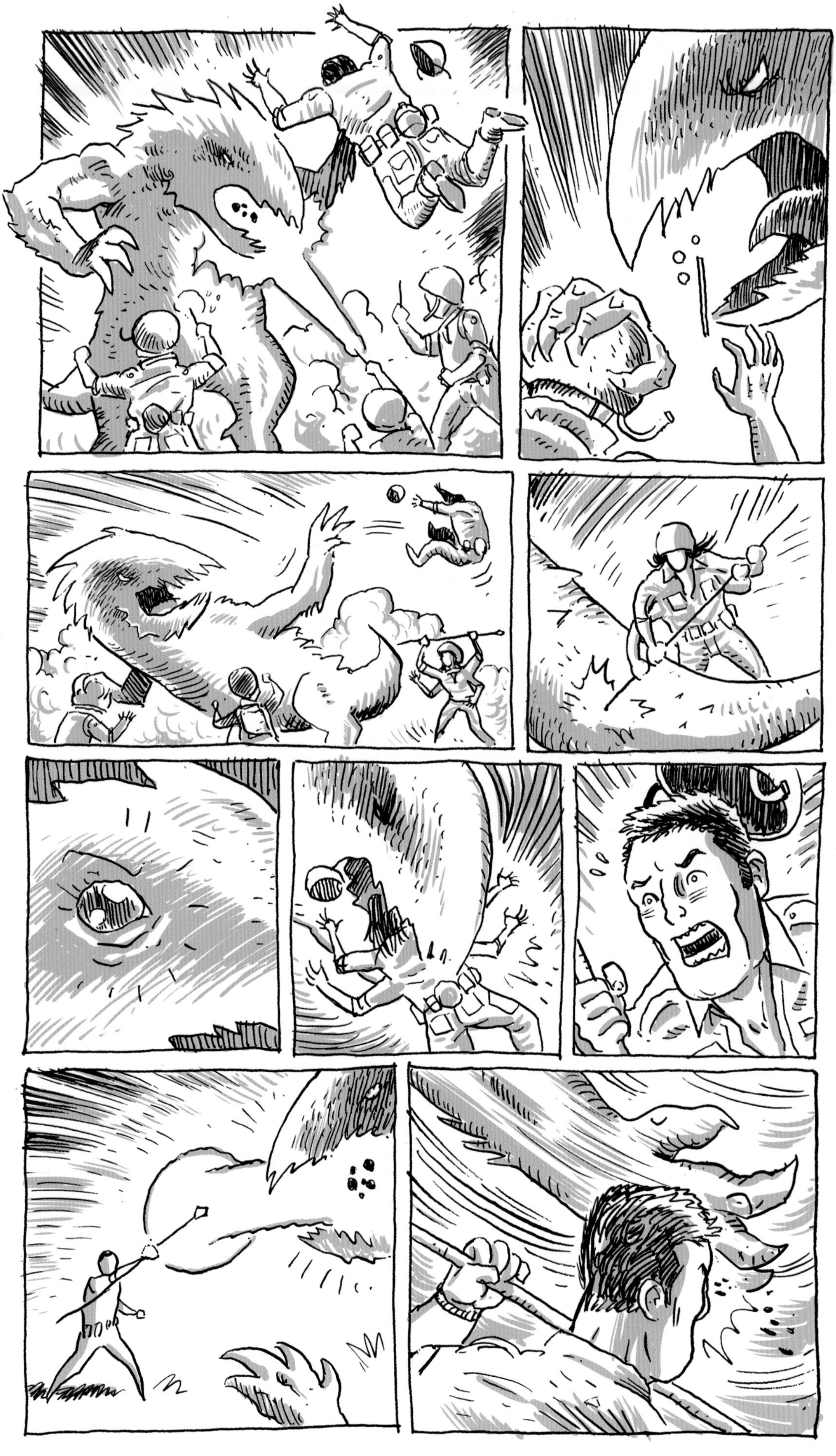

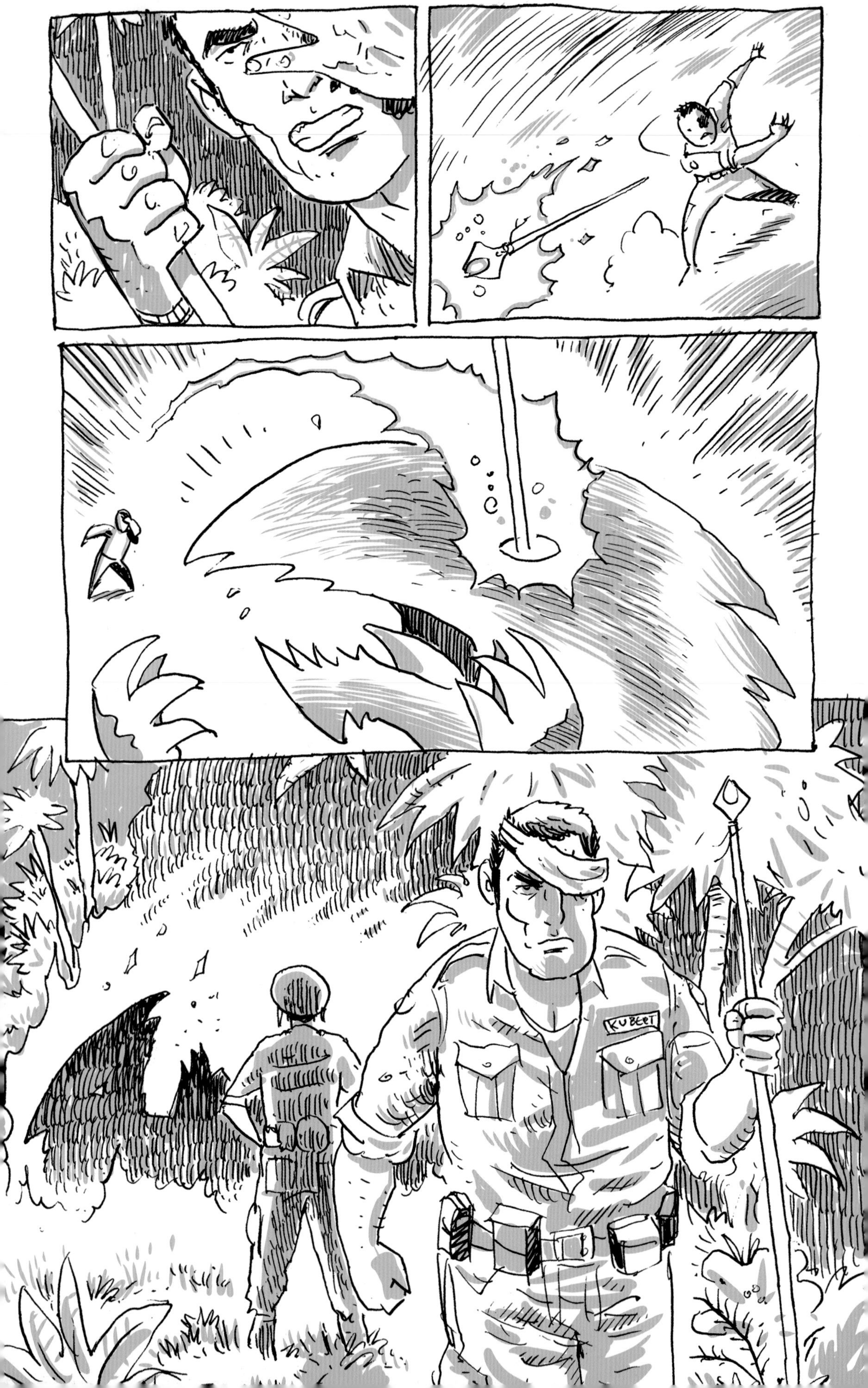
KUBERT

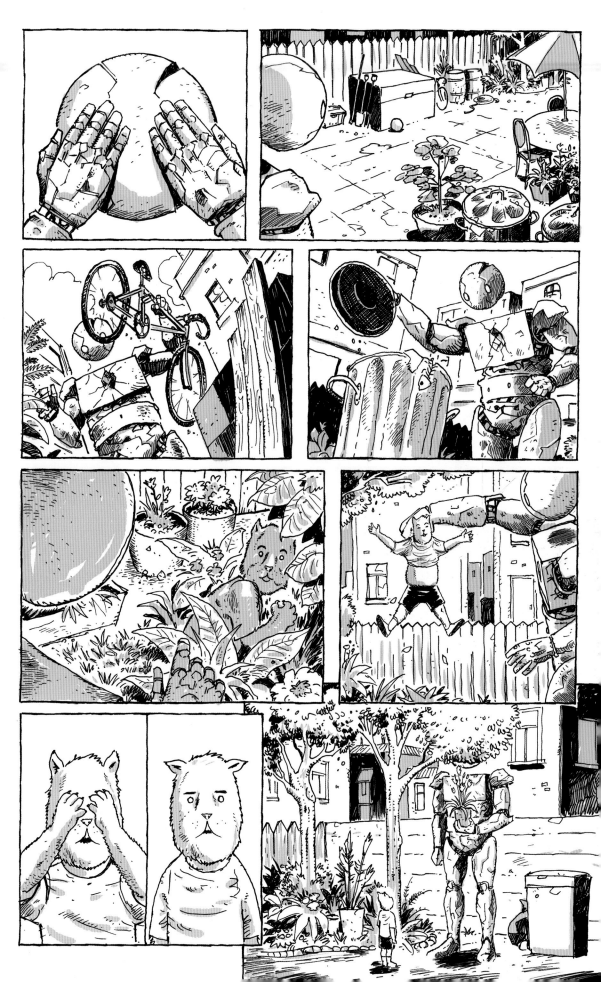

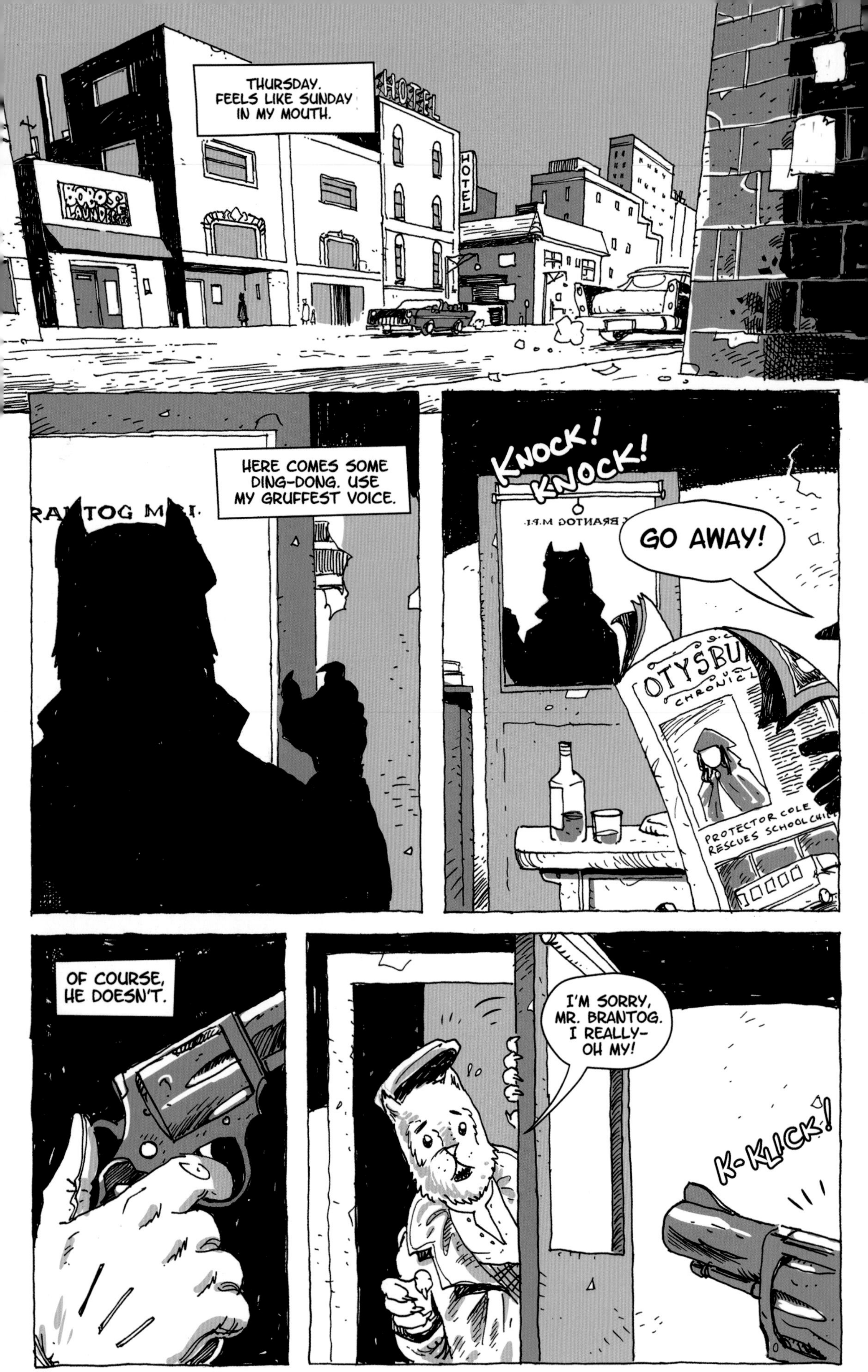
THURSDAY. FEELS LIKE SUNDAY IN MY MOUTH.
HOTEL
HOTEL
HERE COMES SOME DING-DONG. USE MY GRUFFEST VOICE.
KNOCK! KNOCK!
GO AWAY!
PROTECTOR COLE
OF COURSE, HE DOESN'T.
I'M SORRY, MR. BRANTOG. I REALLY- OH MY!
K-KLICK!

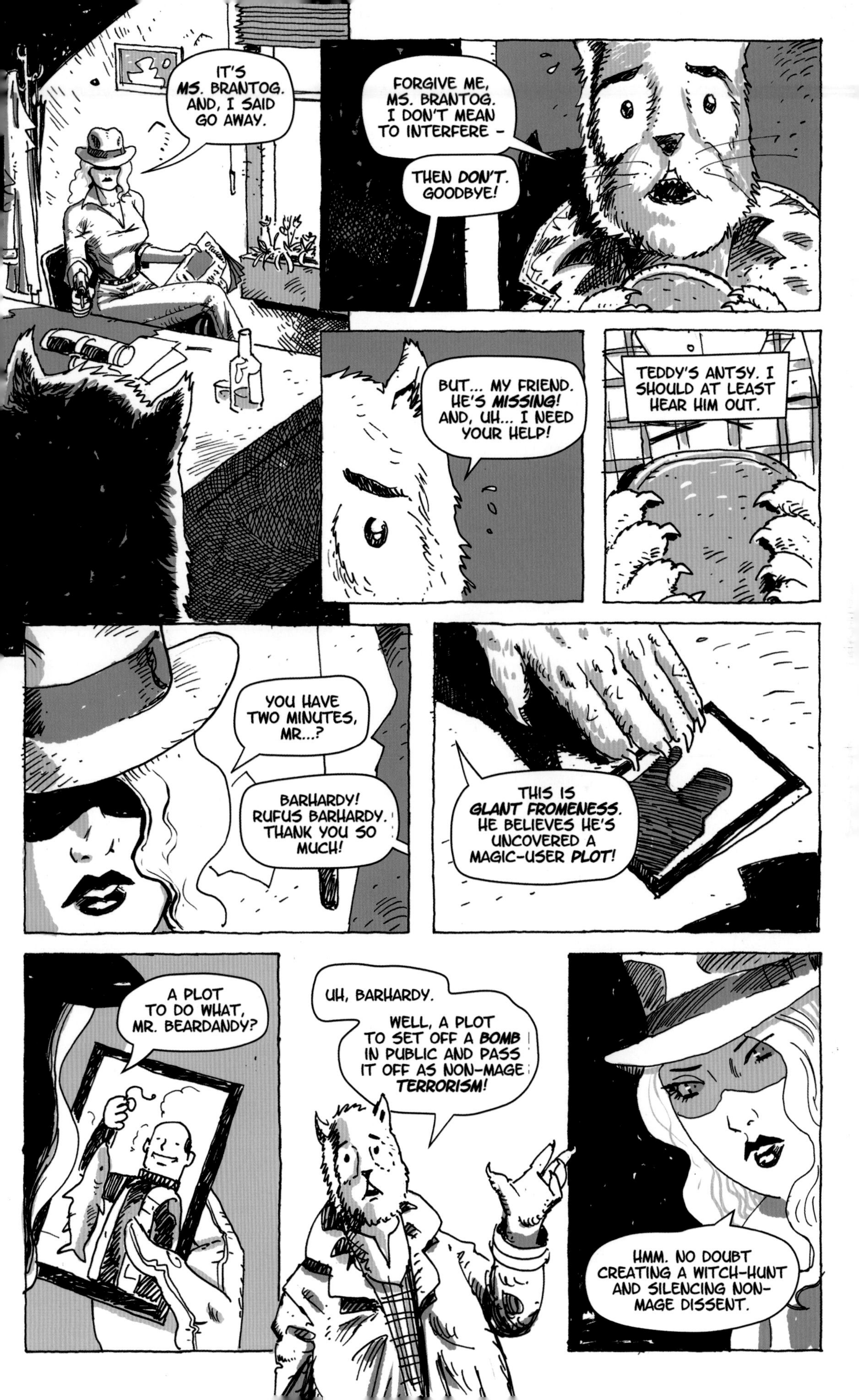
IT'S MS. BRANTOG. AND, I SAID GO AWAY.
FORGIVE ME, MS. BRANTOG. I DON'T MEAN TO INTERFERE –
THEN DON'T. GOODBYE!
BUT... MY FRIEND. HE'S MISSING! AND, UH... I NEED YOUR HELP!
TEDDY'S ANTSY. I SHOULD AT LEAST HEAR HIM OUT.
YOU HAVE TWO MINUTES, MR...?
BARHARDY! RUFUS BARHARDY. THANK YOU SO MUCH!
THIS IS GLANT FROMENESS. HE BELIEVES HE'S UNCOVERED A MAGIC-USER PLOT!
A PLOT TO DO WHAT, MR. BEARDANDY?
UH, BARHARDY.
WELL, A PLOT TO SET OFF A BOMB IN PUBLIC AND PASS IT OFF AS NON-MAGE TERRORISM!
HMM. NO DOUBT CREATING A WITCH-HUNT AND SILENCING NON-MAGE DISSENT.

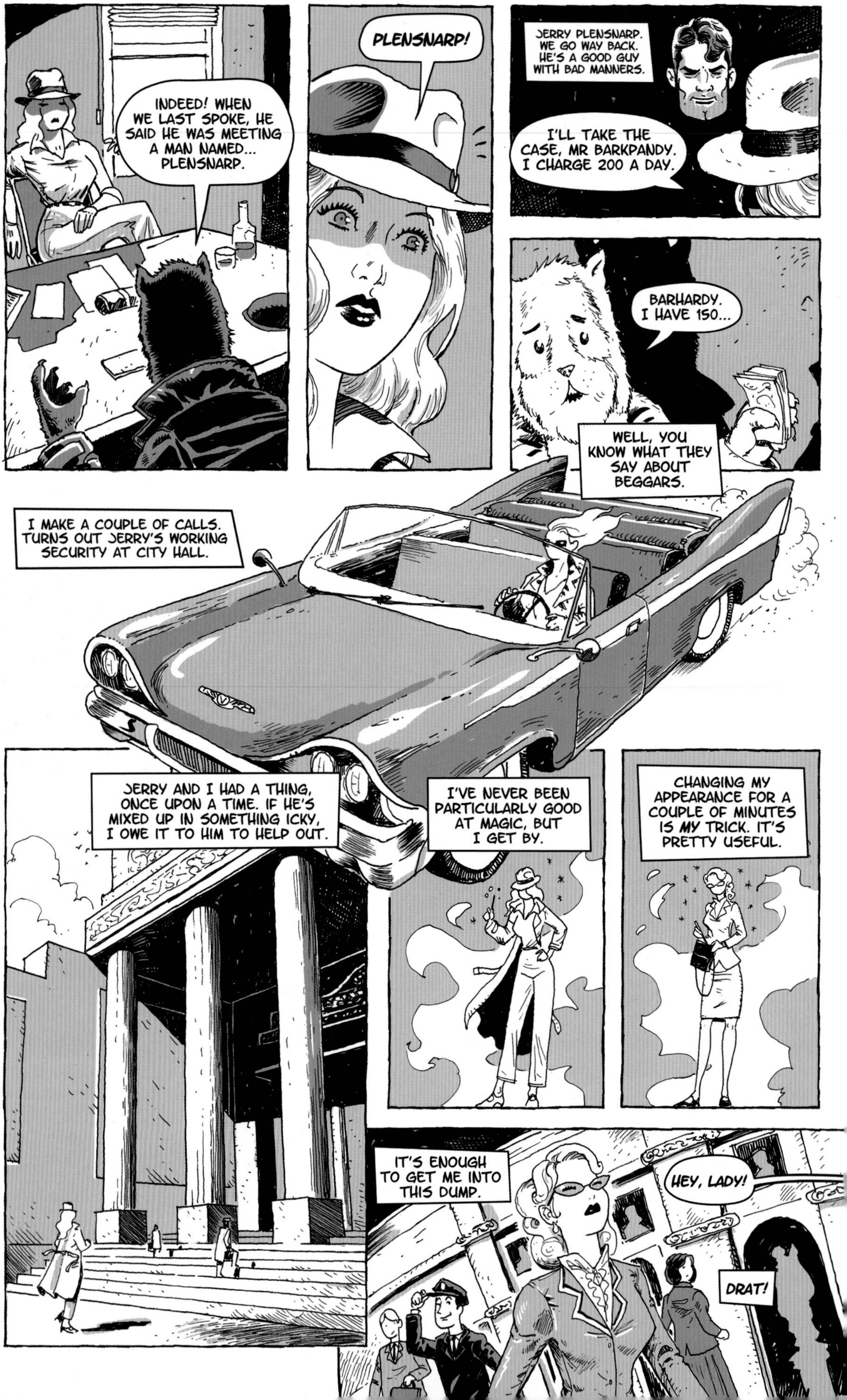
INDEED! WHEN WE LAST SPOKE, HE SAID HE WAS MEETING A MAN NAMED... PLENSNARP.
PLENSNARP!
JERRY PLENSNARP. WE GO WAY BACK. HE'S A GOOD GUY WITH BAD MANNERS.
I'LL TAKE THE CASE, MR BARKPANDY. I CHARGE 200 A DAY.
BARHARDY. I HAVE 150...
WELL, YOU KNOW WHAT THEY SAY ABOUT BEGGARS.
I MAKE A COUPLE OF CALLS. TURNS OUT JERRY'S WORKING SECURITY AT CITY HALL.
JERRY AND I HAD A THING, ONCE UPON A TIME. IF HE'S MIXED UP IN SOMETHING ICKY, I OWE IT TO HIM TO HELP OUT.
I'VE NEVER BEEN PARTICULARLY GOOD AT MAGIC, BUT I GET BY.
CHANGING MY APPEARANCE FOR A COUPLE OF MINUTES IS MY TRICK. IT'S PRETTY USEFUL.
IT'S ENOUGH TO GET ME INTO THIS DUMP.
HEY, LADY!
DRAT!

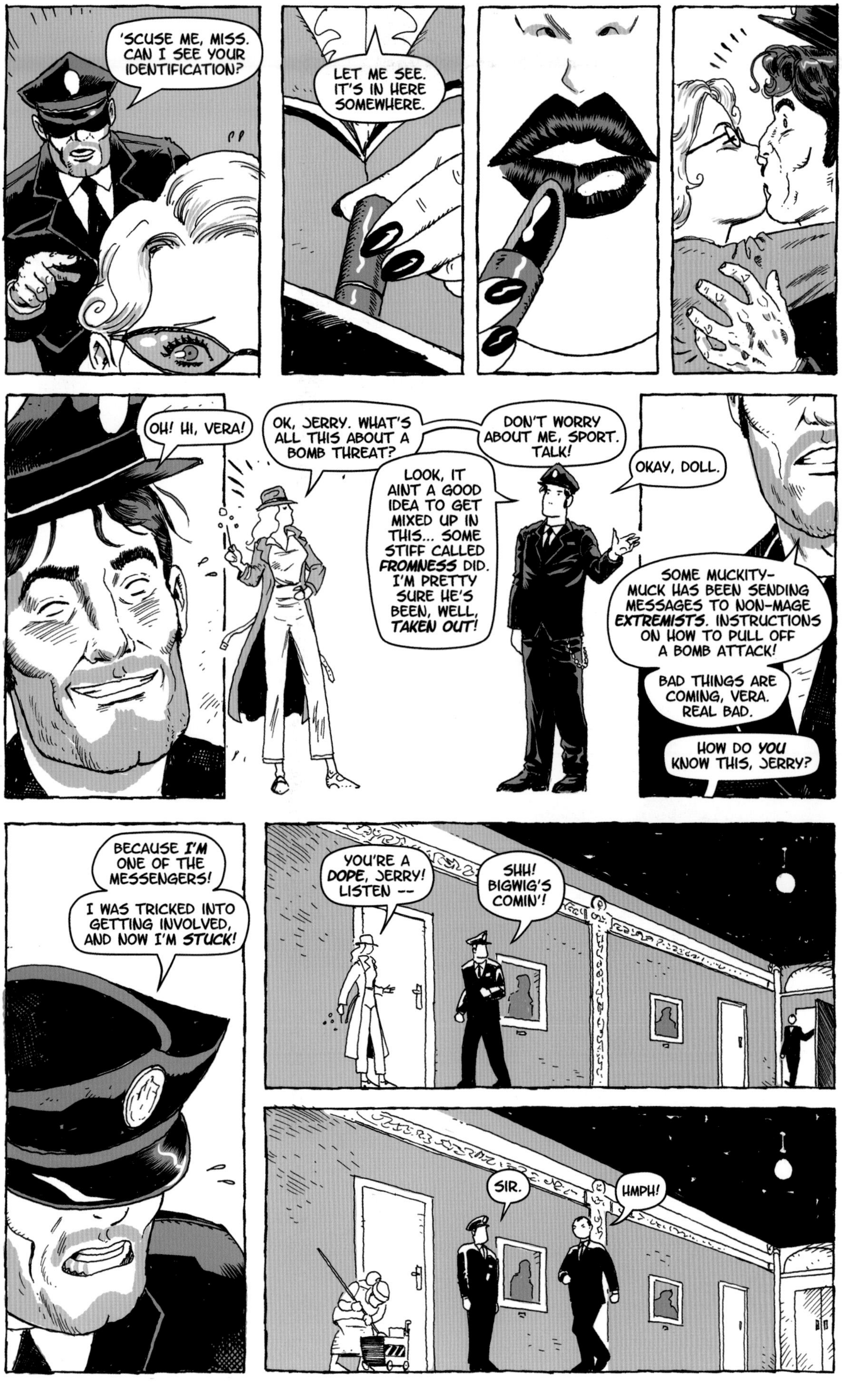
'SCUSE ME, MISS. CAN I SEE YOUR IDENTIFICATION?
LET ME SEE. IT'S IN HERE SOMEWHERE.
OH! HI, VERA!
OK, JERRY. WHAT'S ALL THIS ABOUT A BOMB THREAT?
DON'T WORRY ABOUT ME, SPORT. TALK!
LOOK, IT AINT A GOOD IDEA TO GET MIXED UP IN THIS... SOME STIFF CALLED FROMNESS DID. I'M PRETTY SURE HE'S BEEN, WELL, TAKEN OUT!
OKAY, DOLL.
SOME MUCKITY-MUCK HAS BEEN SENDING MESSAGES TO NON-MAGE EXTREMISTS. INSTRUCTIONS ON HOW TO PULL OFF A BOMB ATTACK!
BAD THINGS ARE COMING, VERA. REAL BAD.
HOW DO YOU KNOW THIS, JERRY?
BECAUSE I'M ONE OF THE MESSENGERS!
I WAS TRICKED INTO GETTING INVOLVED, AND NOW I'M STUCK!
YOU'RE A DOPE, JERRY! LISTEN --
SHH! BIGWIG'S COMIN'!
SIR.
HMPH!

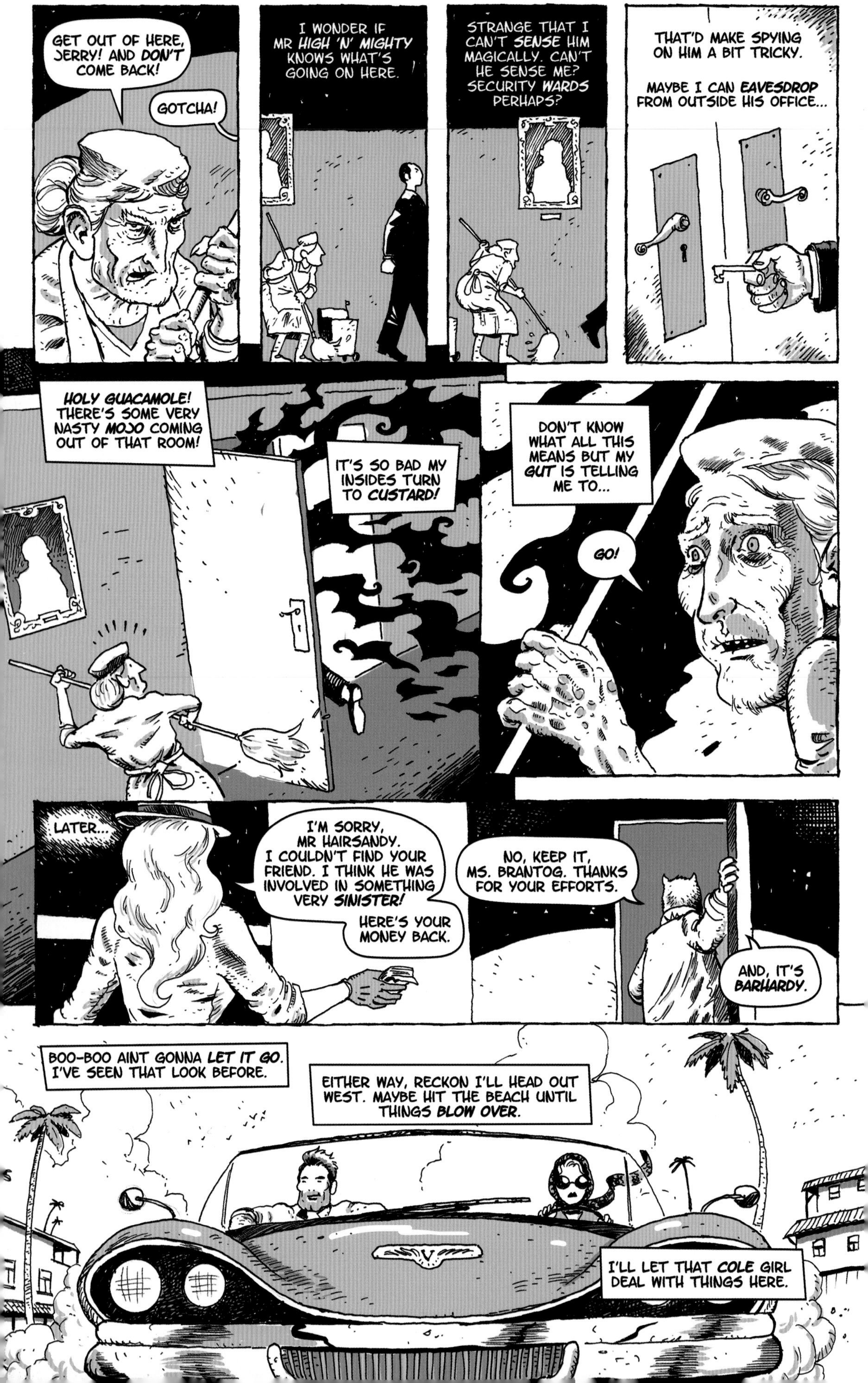
GET OUT OF HERE, JERRY! AND DON'T COME BACK!
GOTCHA!
I WONDER IF MR HIGH 'N' MIGHTY KNOWS WHAT'S GOING ON HERE.
STRANGE THAT I CAN'T SENSE HIM MAGICALLY. CAN'T HE SENSE ME? SECURITY WARDS PERHAPS?
THAT'D MAKE SPYING ON HIM A BIT TRICKY.
MAYBE I CAN EAVESDROP FROM OUTSIDE HIS OFFICE...
HOLY GUACAMOLE! THERE'S SOME VERY NASTY MOJO COMING OUT OF THAT ROOM!
IT'S SO BAD MY INSIDES TURN TO CUSTARD!
DON'T KNOW WHAT ALL THIS MEANS BUT MY GUT IS TELLING ME TO...
GO!
LATER...
I'M SORRY, MR HAIRSANDY. I COULDN'T FIND YOUR FRIEND. I THINK HE WAS INVOLVED IN SOMETHING VERY SINISTER!
HERE'S YOUR MONEY BACK.
NO, KEEP IT, MS. BRANTOG. THANKS FOR YOUR EFFORTS.
AND, IT'S BARHARDY.
BOO-BOO AINT GONNA LET IT GO. I'VE SEEN THAT LOOK BEFORE.
EITHER WAY, RECKON I'LL HEAD OUT WEST. MAYBE HIT THE BEACH UNTIL THINGS BLOW OVER.
I'LL LET THAT COLE GIRL DEAL WITH THINGS HERE.

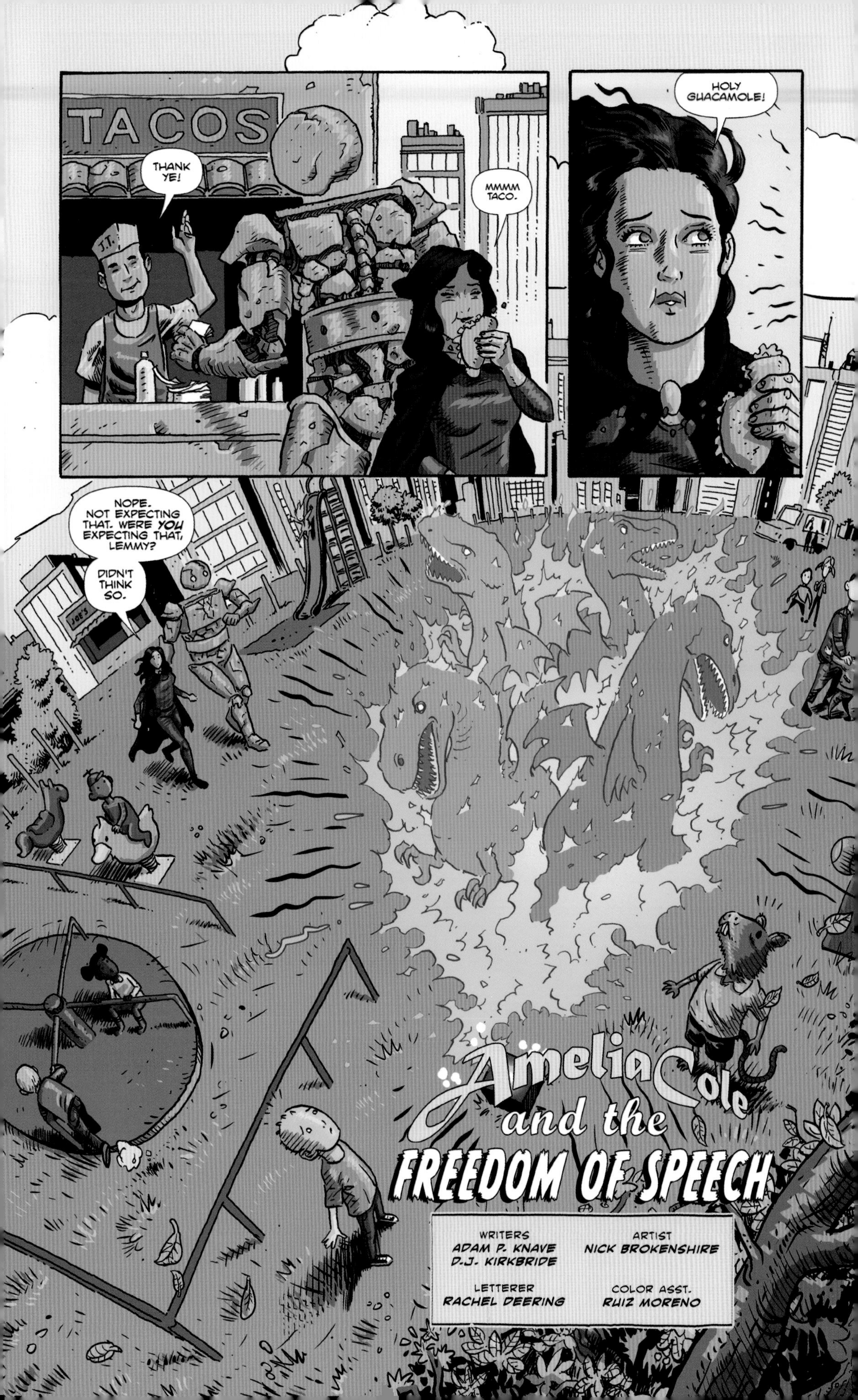
TACOS
THANK YE!
J.T.
MMMM TACO.
HOLY GUACAMOLE!
NOPE. NOT EXPECTING THAT. WERE YOU EXPECTING THAT, LEMMY?
DIDN'T THINK SO.
JOE'S
Amelia Cole and the FREEDOM OF SPEECH
WRITERS
ADAM P. KNAVE
D.J. KIRKBRIDE
ARTIST
NICK BROKENSHIRE
LETTERER
RACHEL DEERING
COLOR ASST.
RUIZ MORENO

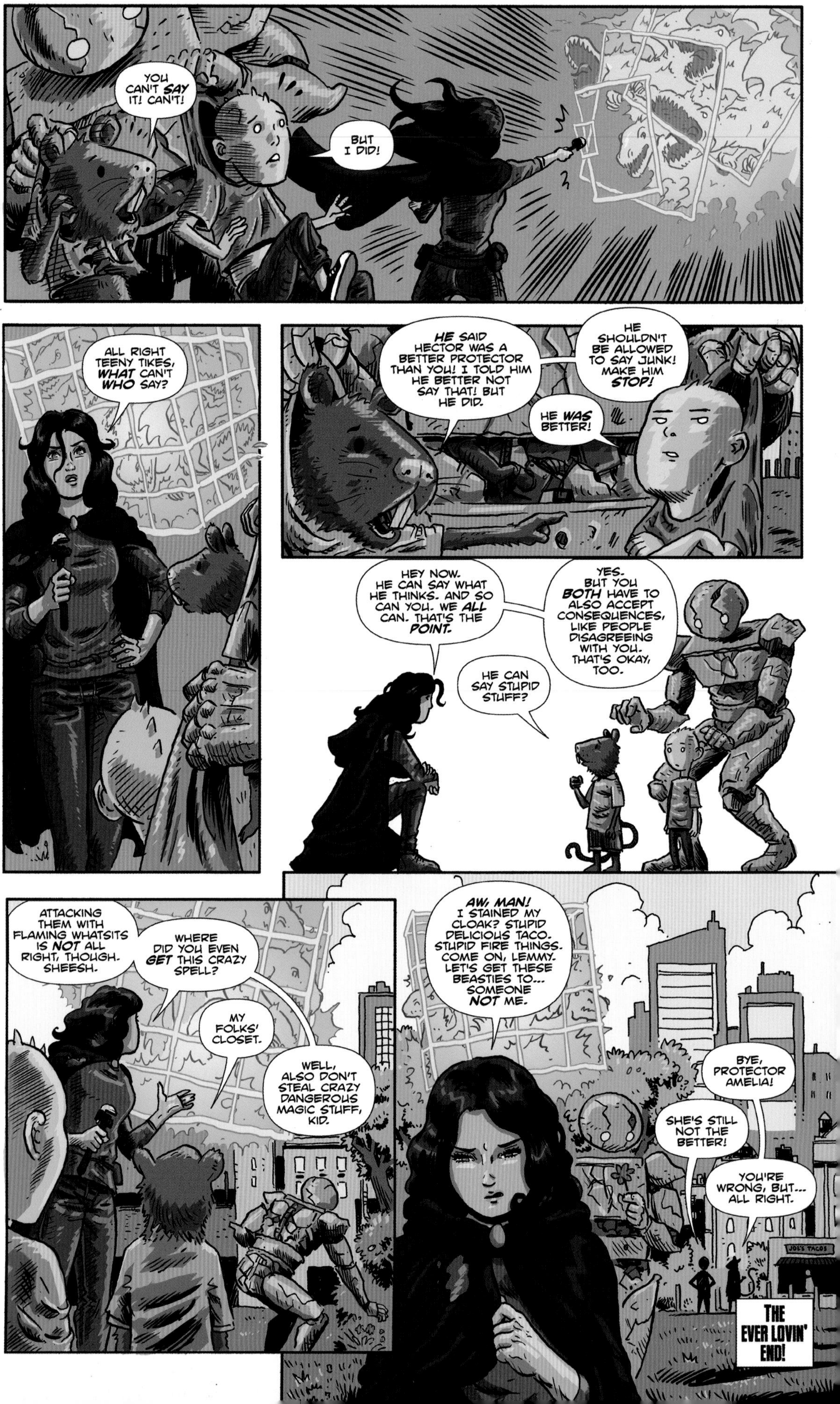
YOU CAN'T SAY IT! CAN'T!
BUT I DID!
ALL RIGHT TEENY TIKES, WHAT CAN'T WHO SAY?
HE SAID HECTOR WAS A BETTER PROTECTOR THAN YOU! I TOLD HIM HE BETTER NOT SAY THAT! BUT HE DID.
HE SHOULDN'T BE ALLOWED TO SAY JUNK! MAKE HIM STOP!
HE WAS BETTER!
HEY NOW. HE CAN SAY WHAT HE THINKS. AND SO CAN YOU. WE ALL CAN. THAT'S THE POINT.
YES. BUT YOU BOTH HAVE TO ALSO ACCEPT CONSEQUENCES, LIKE PEOPLE DISAGREEING WITH YOU. THAT'S OKAY, TOO.
HE CAN SAY STUPID STUFF?
ATTACKING THEM WITH FLAMING WHATSITS IS NOT ALL RIGHT, THOUGH. SHEESH.
WHERE DID YOU EVEN GET THIS CRAZY SPELL?
MY FOLKS' CLOSET.
WELL, ALSO DON'T STEAL CRAZY DANGEROUS MAGIC STUFF, KID.
AW, MAN! I STAINED MY CLOAK? STUPID DELICIOUS TACO. STUPID FIRE THINGS. COME ON, LEMMY. LET'S GET THESE BEASTIES TO... SOMEONE NOT ME.
BYE, PROTECTOR AMELIA!
SHE'S STILL NOT THE BETTER!
YOU'RE WRONG, BUT... ALL RIGHT.
THE EVER LOVIN' END!

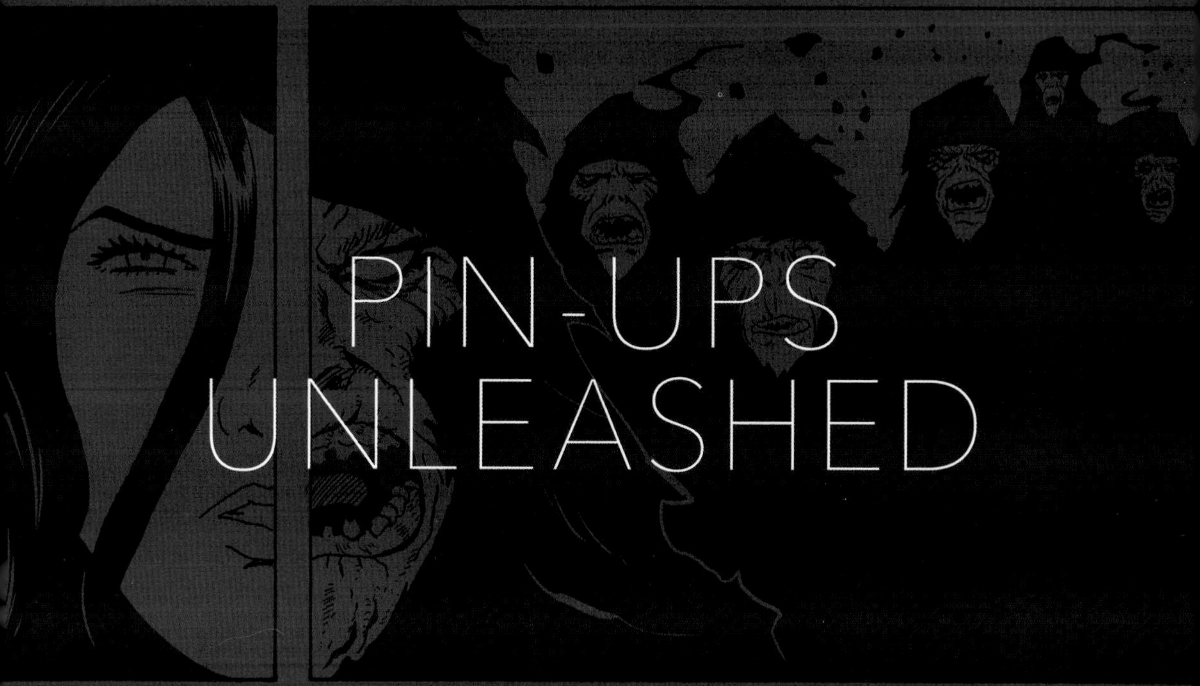

PIN-UPS UNLEASHED

ART BY

ROBERT WILSON IV

KYLE STARKS

ANDREW LOSQ

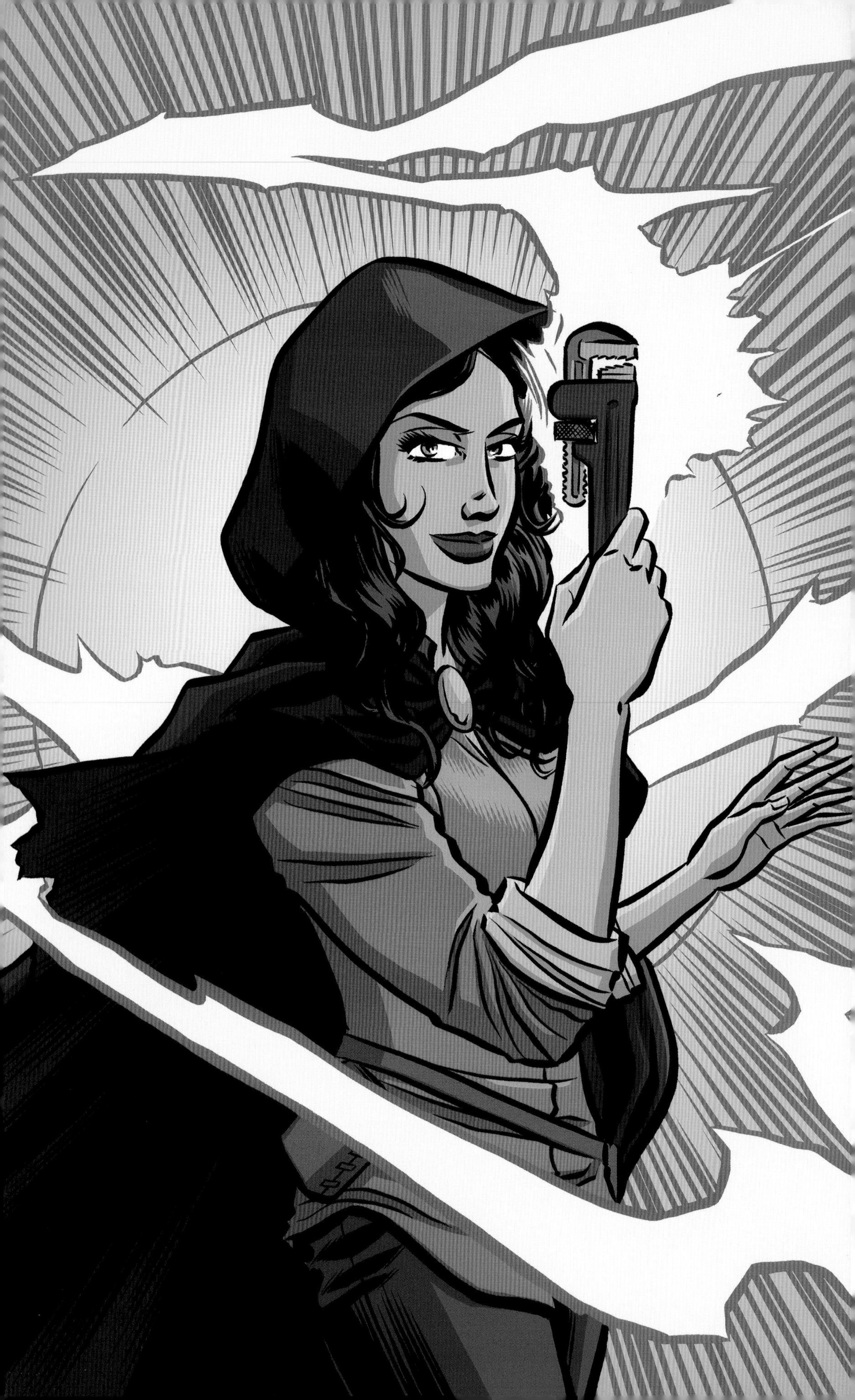

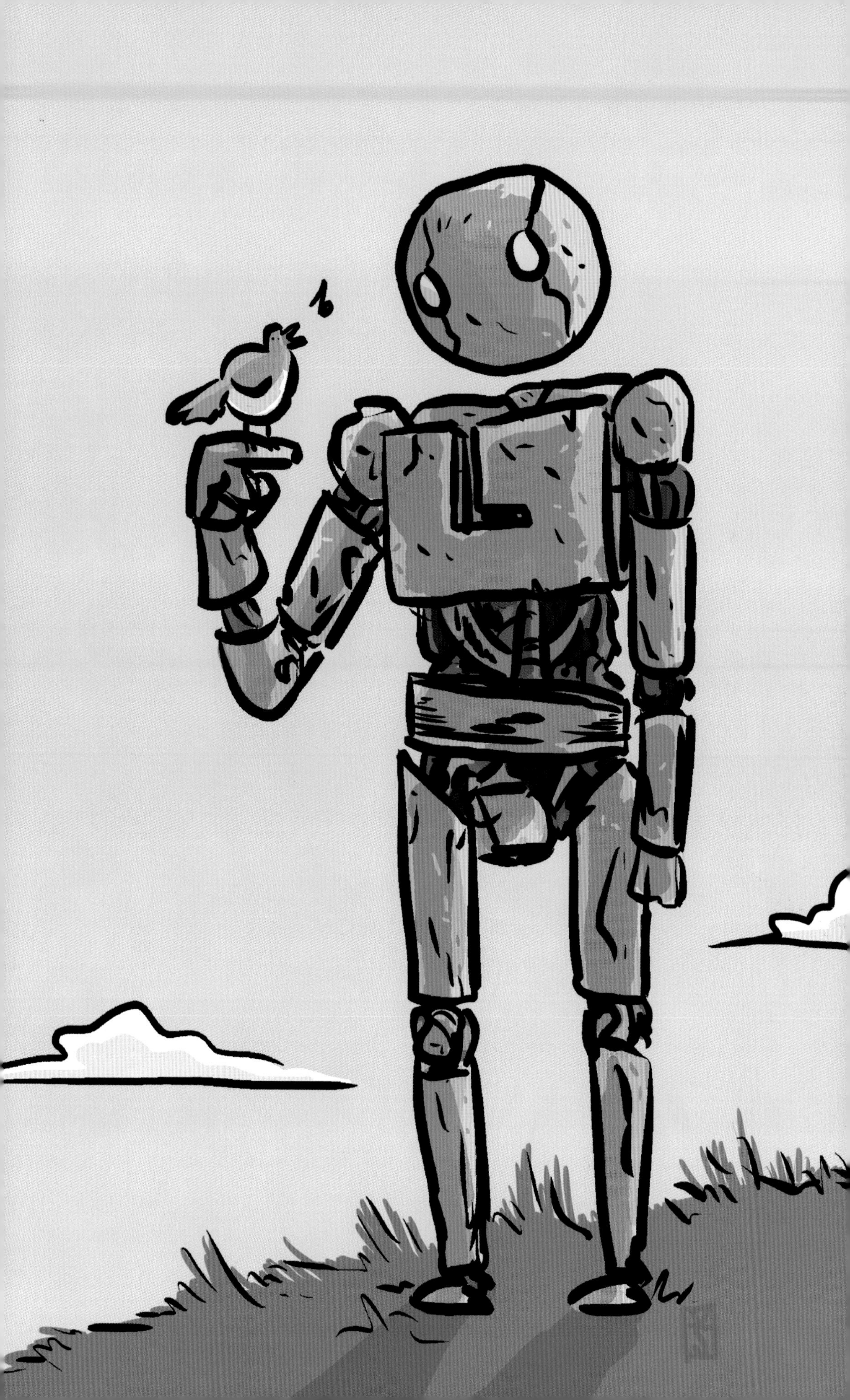

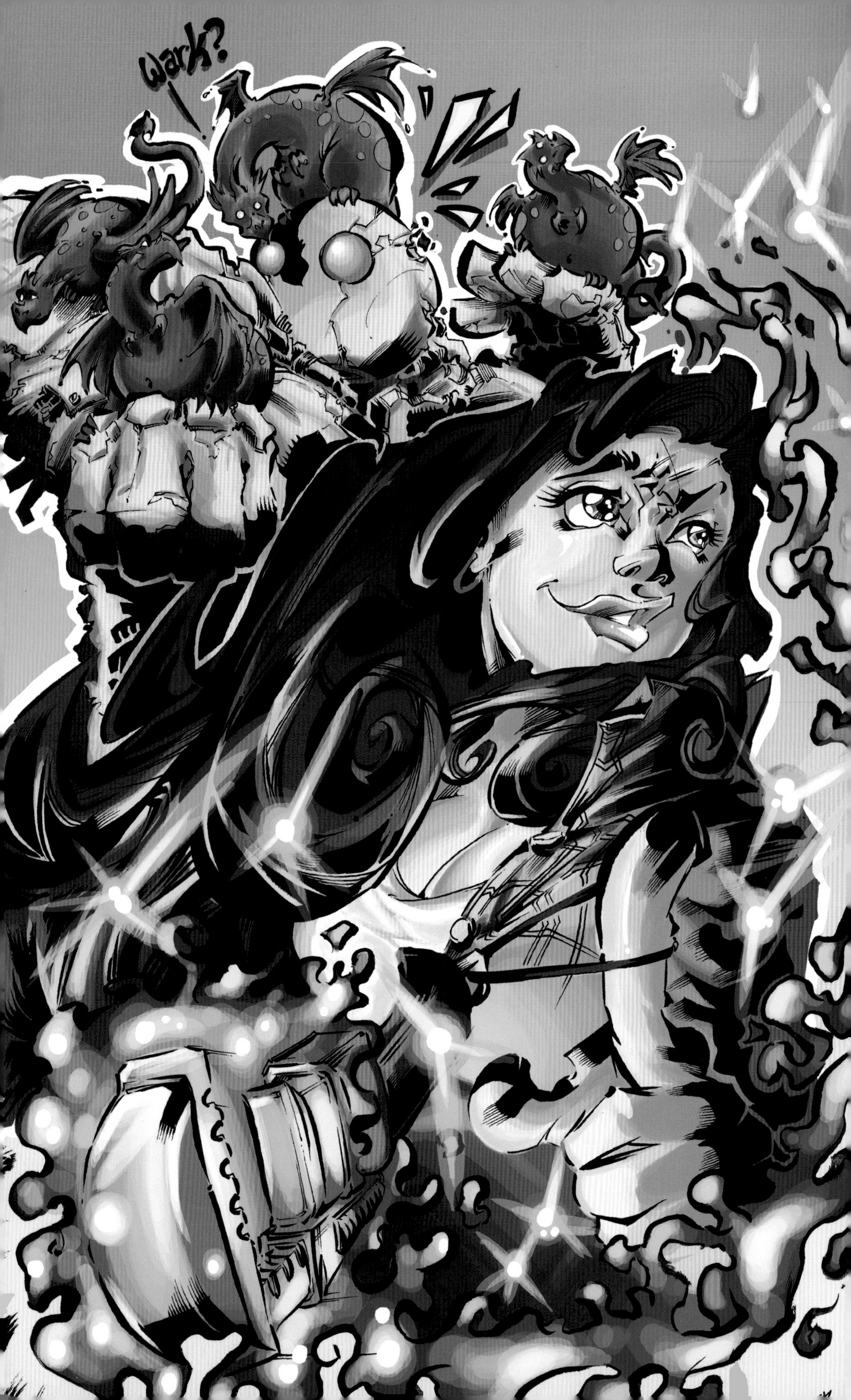
Wark?

CONVERSATION UNLEASHED

Adam, D.J., and Nick talked with ComicBook.com's Russ Burlingame to discuss **THE ENEMY UNLEASHED** arc, where Amelia has been, and where she's going...

RUSS BURLINGAME: *The Enemy Unleashed* has felt like a whirlwind; there wasn't a lot of stopping to breathe. When you're writing an arc like that, do you think, "Okay, here's what to do for new readers starting with this trade?" Or do you just kind of assume that anyone reading a book like this has been on since *Amelia Cole* issue 1?

D.J. KIRKBRIDE: We want each issue to be new reader friendly, in that you'll get a lot of action and fun with cool art, but we also need to move the plot forward. The single issues and the trades have "previously" recaps that we hope get readers up to speed enough to enjoy, but folks with us since the beginning will naturally have a better sense of what's happening as a whole. When I was a kid, I'd get my comics from the spinner rack at the local drug store, and it'd be all about characters and covers and what looked cool. I'd start a comic with issue 242 in the middle of a storyline, and just have fun with it. Maybe I was a weird kid. I mean, my mom once told me I wouldn't leave the house unless I was dressed up like Superman or a cowboy, so – wait, no. I was an awesome kid.

ADAM P. KNAVE: Also I think, personally, that it works like this: your first story needs an end, so people who stayed in just to see can leave and not feel forced to keep buying. It's polite. Your second story needs to work as an intro for new people, but past that

UH, GUYS... CAN WE TALK THIS OUT?

you have to start feeling all right with trusting that people can go back and read older books. Like D.J. says, you want every issue to be accessible – but at the same time this deep in the story we have to be true to the available depth.

RB: We did get quite a bit of character stuff – particularly in the last two issues, as we hashed out just what Hector knew and when. As the cast has become more dynamic, do you ever regret branding the series as *"Amelia Cole and..."*?

APK: Not in the least! This is Amelia's book first and foremost. That isn't going to change. As what we see of the universe gets bigger, other players will be of increased importance as well, but the book is primarily her story. Still, we want all the characters to have depth and be important, so we have to find that balance.

DJK: The world is expanding, but it's still Amelia's world as far as we're concerned. Even with Hector getting his own caption boxes since *The Unknown World* and the parallel narratives we saw playing out in *The Hidden War*, we see it all tying back to Amelia in *The Enemy Unleashed*. We take great care to make sure that, while Hector, the Bahardies, Lesh, Mike, George, Sanz, and the whole gang are all interesting in their own rights – Amelia is our lead character. Even when she's not in a scene or sequence, there's almost always a mention of her.

RB: The art in *Amelia Cole* has evolved quite a bit since the beginning. Do you see the process as continuing that way, or is the hope to find a spot where you're satisfied and stay in that gear?

NICK BROKENSHIRE: As for the art, the reason for stylistic changes is simple. Over the years I've been drawing the story, I've basically been trying out different tools and techniques. The making of this book has been a huge learning curve for me as I'd only done little short pieces before *Amelia Cole*. The aim for me is to find the tools and techniques that best mesh with my natural "hand." I find it best to try new things with every arc and then move on for the next one.

RB: As the series goes on, how will you keep up the tone of the book – so much of it is driven by Amelia's personality and humor – as other characters become more central to the narrative?

DJK: We'll continue to see how Amelia affects other characters as we go on. Even the deathly serious and self-righteous Hector might crack a joke now and again. Plus, her heroism is a huge part of what inspired him to reevaluate his own life. It's also important to note that we started this book with Amelia as a loner, aside from her Aunt Dani – and look at all the trouble that got her into. Part of her journey is realizing she can't do everything alone. Aside from fighting monsters and evil dark magic ghouls, Amelia is also growing up and learning that trust might be the most difficult magic trick of them all. (Did I just come up with a future tagline or totally embarrass myself?)

APK: Her humor is something her friends tend to share, too. I know my friends and I cross-pollinate jokes and ways of speaking slowly.

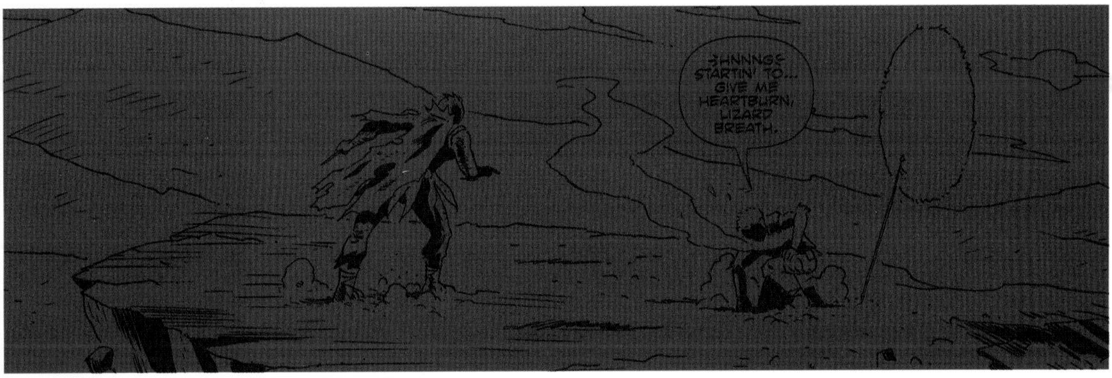
SHNNNGE STARTIN' TO... GIVE ME HEARTBURN, LIZARD BREATH.

So too Amelia and her crew of compadres. The tone and humor spreads as Amelia affects more and more people in the world.

RB: Amelia in particular is an interesting character in that she's not the "typical" comic book woman but obviously is still pretty and, recently, seems a bit thinner. How long did you labor over finding the right balance? Do you think you've got your "definitive" Amelia yet or is she still evolving?

NB: It's these artistic experiments along with general drawing improvement that have led to the evolution of character's portrayal. Amelia, Lemmy, and Hector particularly have changed the most as I discover new ways of doing things. There is no end point, really. Learning never stops. I assume that the more I learn and the more skill I pick up, the more stable the look of things will get. A lot of us grew up with different artists drawing their versions of the same comic book characters. One artists take on Batman could be quite different from the next so I figure it's okay to let changes happen as long as it doesn't affect the story.

RB: Speaking of other characters, we did see the "death" of one key character during this arc. Given the ending of *The Enemy Unleashed,* I have to ask: what REALLY happened to The Magistrate?

APK: Oh, he's dead. Now, given that, why Amelia and Hector didn't die is a question we know is there. It was set up that way on purpose. The reasons behind The Council's actions are still unfolding. Then again, maybe they just messed up. They like to come off as perfect, but who is, really?

DJK: Yeah, even super powerful beings can make mistakes sometimes. Also, we purposely built up The Magistrate to be Amelia's ultimate nemesis, the bad guy behind the bad guys – and then The Council ghoulishly float out of the shadows to blast him into dust! You thought The Magistrate and his machinations and schemes were tough? Well, here are baddies way badder than he could have ever been.

RB: On that note, are there any more plans for Kubert and Sophia?

DJK: I feel like Kubert went out like a hero. That final silent shot of his staff was a good send off. Having said that, we're not so stringent in our planning that we won't let a great idea take us off course a bit, so... look, he's dead right now. I'm totally fine with him dying a hero's death. He did have a lot of adventures before we met him, though. As for Sophia, good riddance. Right?

APK: I don't want to say we will never sneak undo a death in our time writing this book but so far we haven't made plans to, certainly. As much fun as the book is it is tempered by the reality of the stakes, and I think that's important for readers to feel.

RB: Do you have an endgame in mind for *Amelia Cole*? At first it seemed like the big status quo shifts at the end of each volume were just to bring you to your comfort zone so you could start telling a certain kind of stories, but now it seems like it's all been building in a specific direction.

ASIDE FROM FIGHTING MONSTERS AND EVIL DARK MAGIC GHOULS, AMELIA IS ALSO GROWING UP AND LEARNING THAT TRUST MIGHT BE THE MOST DIFFICULT MAGIC TRICK OF THEM ALL.

APK: We are 100% building toward something and always have been. What that is and when it happens is something we don't want to ruin for readers. We can say that we have plans and intend to finish the story. We are committed to that. After that, will we even tell another big story? Who knows! Well, we do, but why spoil the fun and tell you now?

DJK: We have not only the final scene of this first big grand story, but the final shot written in our minds. It's been around for a long time now, and I get chills thinking about it. Seriously, I'm getting chills right now. And then if we continue after that? It'll be a whole new ballgame! The future is very exciting, and we'd love to continue creating this book as long as the stars align and allow us to do so.

RB: Where does *The Impossible Fate* arc fall in terms of your plans? Are we at the midpoint? Almost done?

DJK: *The Impossible Fate* is the penultimate story arc in our first big overreaching narrative. Whoa, that was just a simple, straightforward answer. Should I have hemmed and hawed a bit more, Adam?

APK: Nope. We stand firm on this. We have a plan. And it is glorious.

• **Adam P. Knave** is an Eisner and Harvey award-winning editor and writer who co-writes *Amelia Cole, Artful Daggers* (with Sean E. Williams) and *Never Ending* (with D.J. again, those two, man, inseparable). He edits Jamal Igle's *Molly Danger*, Sam Read's *Exit Generation*, and was one of the editors on Image's *Popgun* anthology series. He also writes prose, short comics, and edits all sorts of things. He recently moved to Portland, OR after spending his first 38 years in NYC.

Follow him on Twitter **@AdamPKnave**

• **D.J. Kirkbride** co-created the Dark Horse Comics mini-series *Never Ending* with his writing partner Adam P. Knave and artist Robert Love. He's currently writing *The Bigger Bang*, co-created with artist Vassilis Gogtzilas, for IDW Publishing. D.J. won an Eisner and a Harvey for Image Comics' *Popgun* anthologies, and his work has appeared in *Titmouse Mook* volume 2 and *Outlaw Territory* volume 3. He lives in Los Angeles with his fiancée and their two gray cats.

Follow him on Twitter **@DJKirkbride**

• **Nick Brokenshire** is a freelance artist who grew up in Scotland and now lives in the North of England with his wife, Victoria. In addition to *Amelia Cole* series, Nick is working on *Power Trio* with writer Alex Paknadel. He can be heard chatting about geek-related nonsense with some pals on the international smash hit podcast Droppings Science, as well as playing in his two bands: Los Vencidos and Blues Harvest.

Follow him on Twitter **@NickBrokenshire** and
Nick Brokenshire Comics & Illustration on Facebook.

• • • • • • • • • • • • • • • **Rachel Deering** is a freelance writer, editor, and letterer for comics. Her past works include IDW's *Womanthology*, and her creator-owned horror series *Anathema*. She lives in Columbus, Ohio with her wife and their tiny Chihuahua, Hazel, and spends way too much time watching old horror movies.

Follow her on Twitter **@RachelDeering**

• • • • • • • • • • • • • • • **Ruiz Moreno** lives somewhere in Texas. He has three loves in his life: his wife, Brittany, and their daughter, Emma, are his first two. They are his everything. They are awesome. His third love is comics. He has consumed comics since day one. He loves the comics. He wants to keep making the comics. Give me cookie you got cookie.

Follow him on Twitter **@Ruiz_Moreno**

• • • • • • • • • • • • • • • **Dylan Todd** was raised in the neon wasteland of Las Vegas and its mixture of glitz and kitsch, class and crass has tainted him forever. When he's not designing or thinking about designing, he can be found rocking, rolling, reading, or relaxing with his family. If he likes you, he'll make you a mix tape. You can find him at *bigredrobot.net*.

Follow him on Twitter **@BigRedRobot**

Department of Oral Medicine and Pathology, UMDS, Guy's Hospital, London.

Department of Pharmacology, School of Pharmacy, Addis University Ethiopia.

Department of Preventive Medicine, University of Southern California.

Department of Psychiatry and Behavioral Sciences, and Preventative Medicine, University of California School of Medicine, Los Angeles, California.

International Journal of Food Microbiology.

Japan Food Research Laboratories.

Japanese Journal of Pharmacology.

Journal of ET Nursing.

Journal of the American Dietetic Association.

Maruboshi Vinegar Company, Kyushu, Japan.

Massachusetts College of Pharmacy and Allied Health Sciences. Boston.

Medical Journal of Australia.

Nutrition Department, Mount Auburn Hospital, Cambridge, Massachusetts

Ohio State University Colleges of Pharmacy and Medicine

Research Dept. US Industrial Chemicals Co, Cincinnati.

Scandinavian Journal of Dental Research.

University of California.

University of Medicine and Dentistry of New Jersey-Robert Wood Johnson Medical School.

Western Michigan University, Kalamazoo.

A special thank you to:

The Vinegar Institute, Atlanta, Georgia and its members, the manufacturers, bottlers, and suppliers of quality vinegars.

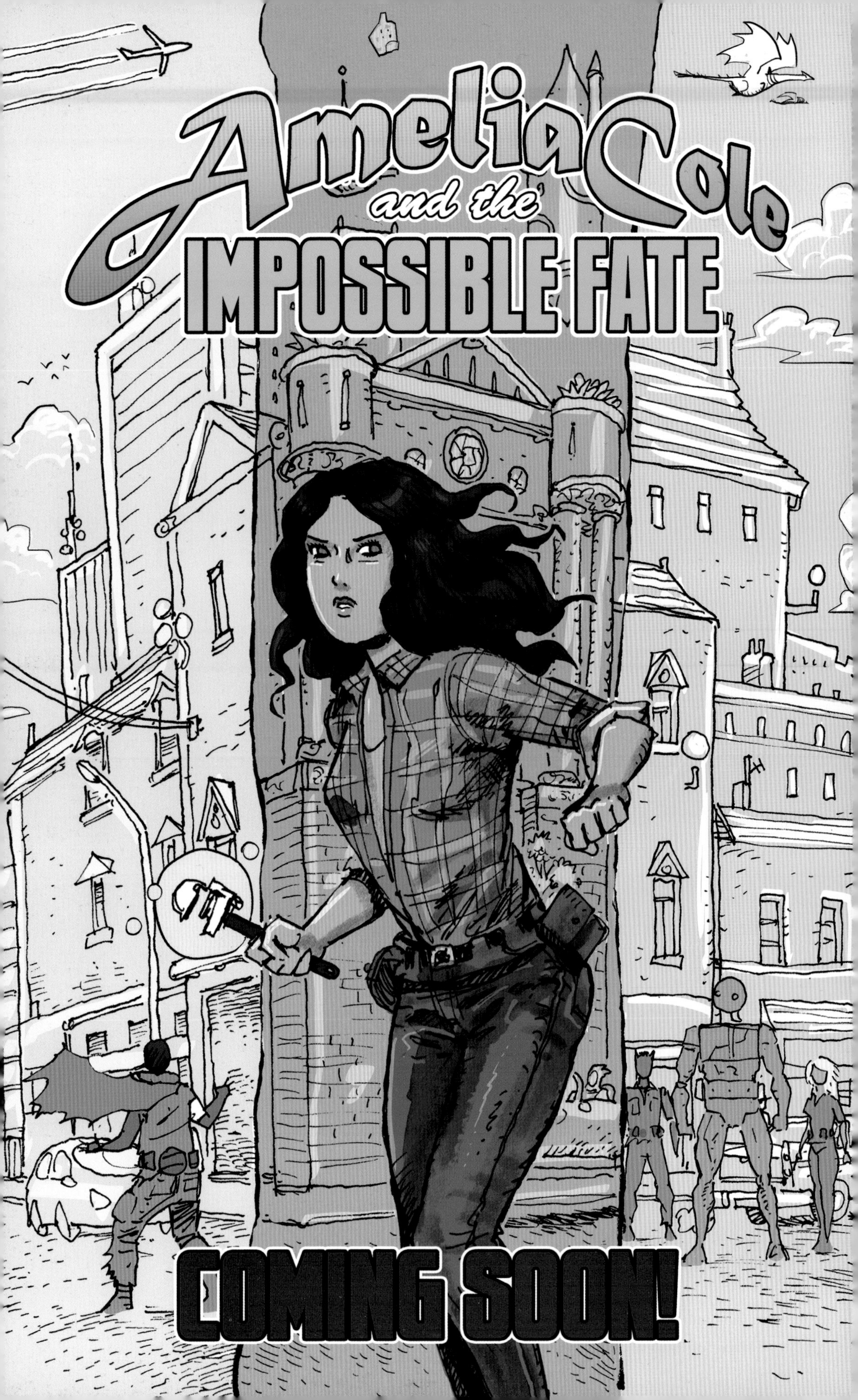
Amelia Cole
and the
IMPOSSIBLE FATE
COMING SOON!